Dickens's Favourite Blacking Factory

The story of Regency entrepreneur Charles Day, his clandestine affair and why Charles Dickens became interested in him

Neil Price

Dickens's Favourite Blacking Factory:
The story of Regency entrepreneur Charles Day, his clandestine affair and why Charles Dickens became interested in him

Published by The Conrad Press Ltd. in the United Kingdom 2023

Tel: +44(0)1227 472 874

www.theconradpress.com

info@theconradpress.com

ISBN 978-1-915494-68-9

Copyright © Neil Price, 2023

All rights reserved.

Typesetting and Cover Design by: Charlotte Mouncey, www.bookstyle.co.uk

Cover image: Portrait of Charles Day (c1820) which hangs in Clothworkers' Hall, London. 58cm x 48cm. Oil on canvas. Artist unknown.
(© The Worshipful Company of Clothworkers)

The Conrad Press logo was designed by Maria Priestley.

Printed and bound in Great Britain by Clays Ltd, Elcograf S.p.A.

Dickens's Favourite Blacking Factory

Previous page shows illustration of Day and Martin's purpose-built
blacking factory at 97 High Holborn, opened in 1808
although this image dates from c1850.
(© The Trustees of the British Museum)

*... a polish which would have struck envy
to the soul of the amiable Mr Warren
(for they used Day and Martin at the White Hart)*

Charles Dickens, *The Pickwick Papers*: Chapter X (1836)

Dedicated to my late father
Hugh John Wallace Price (1921-1986)
who strove all his life, without any success,
to discover the true identity of his great-grandfather
John Price, and fired my obsession since childhood
with our family history
– how I wish he could be reading this now.

Contents

Illustrations   11
Family Trees   13
Maps   17
Preface   23

I. Prologue   29

II. Life   39
    1. Small beginnings to big success   40
    2. Introductions in Regency times   55
    3. Competition and intellectual property   71
    4. Edgware and the Peake sisters   84
    5. The Peakes of Stafford, a likeness and lavish living   95
    6. Births, deaths and almshouses   111
    7. The troublesome daughter and making provisions   132
    8. Towards the end   147

III. Death   167
    The diary of William Foote   168
    Preface   169
    Dramatis Personae   171
    Introduction   173
    The Diary   187

IV. Aftermath	285
1. The beginnings of legal proceedings	286
2. Dufaur	300
3. The Price boys and a census	306
4. The Court of Chancery	316
5. Caterham	331
6. The destination of Charles Day's fortune	339
7. The Dickens connection	354
V. Epilogue	371
The Unmasking of John (or Charles) Price	372

Appendix One
The responses of Susannah Peake in PC53 — 402

Appendix Two
The Will and Codicils of Charles Day — 414

Sources, notes and references — 440

Bibliography — 453

Acknowledgements — 455

Illustrations

1. St Sepulchre Gate, Doncaster, showing in the middle distance on the right The King's Arms pub where the blacking recipe was exchanged in about 1800 (this photo dates from c1900). p. 48

2. Illustrations from 'A Day at Day and Martin's', *The Penny Magazine*, December 1842:
   A. Filling p.61
   B. Sealing p.61
   C. Labelling p.61
   D. Packing Paste-Blacking p.61
   E. Packing Warehouse p.62

3. A Day and Martin blacking bottle (c1815) showing the label that became intellectual property. p.75

4. Blacking Bottle Lodge, built about 1830 by Charles Day at the entrance to Edgware Place (this picture taken c1900) Barnet Libraries' Archives and Local Studies Centre. p.88

5. Sarah Peake "Price", a photograph taken in her brother's home town of Lichfield, probably in 1868 on her journey north to her new home in Scotland. p.102

6. Harley House, Regent's Park, built by Charles Day in 1824 as his London residence. This etching appeared in the Illustrated London News on 11 October 1856 when it was the leased residence of the Queen of Oude (part of modern India) during her visit at that time. p.110

7. The Day Tomb, St Margaret's Church, Edgware, in its current state. The vault was opened by Day following the death of his mother-in-law Mrs Susannah Peake on 4 October 1822. p.115

8. The likely appearance of 29 Earl Street (now Broadley Street), Marylebone, the first residence from 1823 of Sarah Peake "Price" with her infant sons Henry and Alfred. p.117

9. Day's Almshouses, Stonegrove, Edgware, built in 1828 by Charles Day for the poor of the parish, as they appear today. p.128

10. A BRIGHT IDEA – one of a series of humorous advertising cards for Day and Martin, dating from about 1835. p.162

11. The Will of Charles Day – an original copy now kept in the archives of The Clothworkers' Company. p.289

12. The signatures of Charles Day's three executors. p.297

13. The three Price boys:

    A. Henry Price aged 25 from an ambrotype made c1848.*

    B. Alfred Price aged 26 from a photograph taken c1851.*

    C. Edmund Price aged 5 from a silhouette made in 1832. p.311

14. Watercolour of Amsterdam painted in 1841 by Alfred Price when he was just 16 years old.* p.314

15. Caterham Court, a photograph taken c1910, showing the original Georgian house (the residence of Pinder Simpson c1825) with the Victorian west wing on the left. p.333

16. On 13 March 1852, Charles Dickens thanks Challinor for lending him his pamphlet 'The Court of Chancery; Its Inherent Defects' (1849). p.359

17. The headstone of the Price Grave in the Dean Cemetery, Edinburgh, the first named being "Sarah Price, Born 26 June 1795, Died 7 December 1877". p.373

18. The 1877 Scottish death certificate of Sarah Price, stating she was the "Widow of John Price, Fundholder" and that her father was " – Peake, Architect", the informant being "Alfred Price, son". p.374

19. The bound 972-page document kept in The National Archives, Kew, entitled *Dufaur v. Croft and Others – Process. Bro.t in 25th Feb 1839. P.C.53'.* p.391

20. Part of the evidence given by Susannah Peake in PC53, describing the baptism of the three Price boys. p.403

    * Photographs by John Glynn Photography

Family Trees

The Ancestors of Charles Day

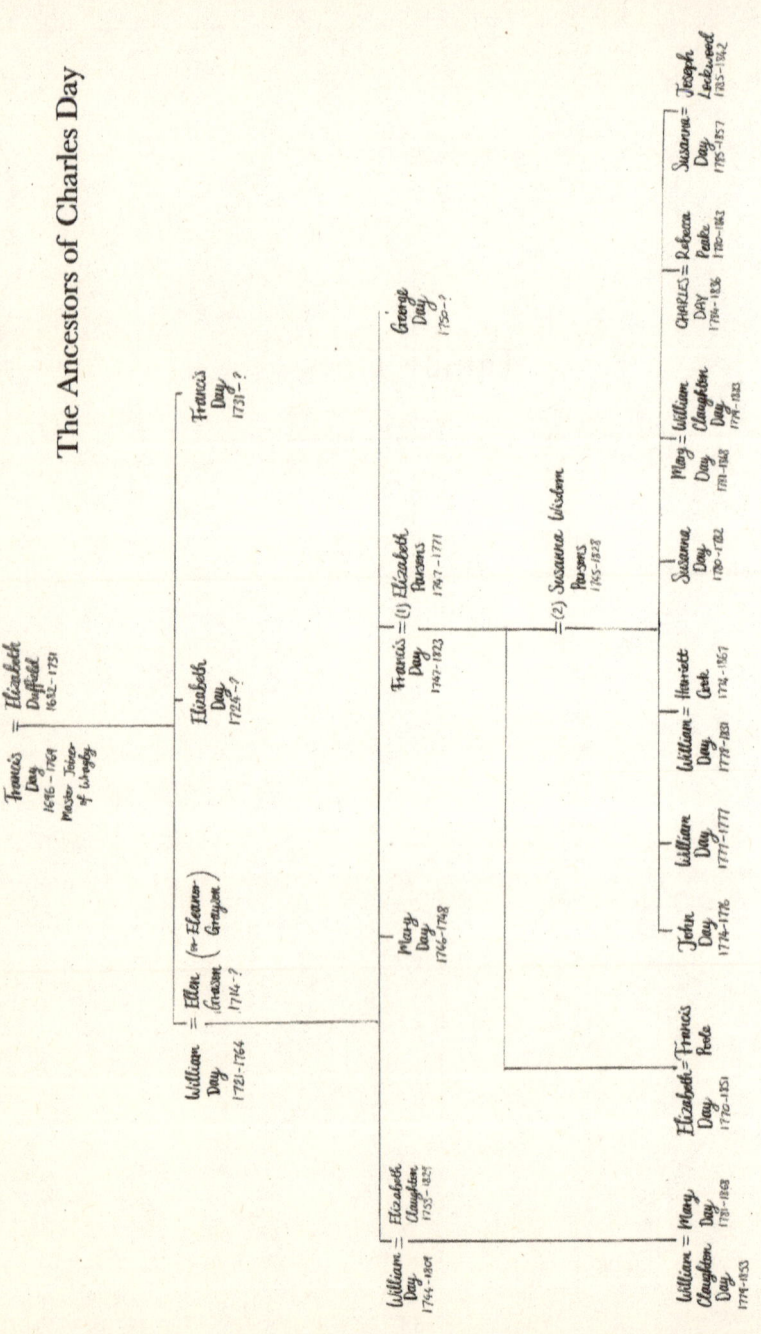

The Descendants of Charles Day

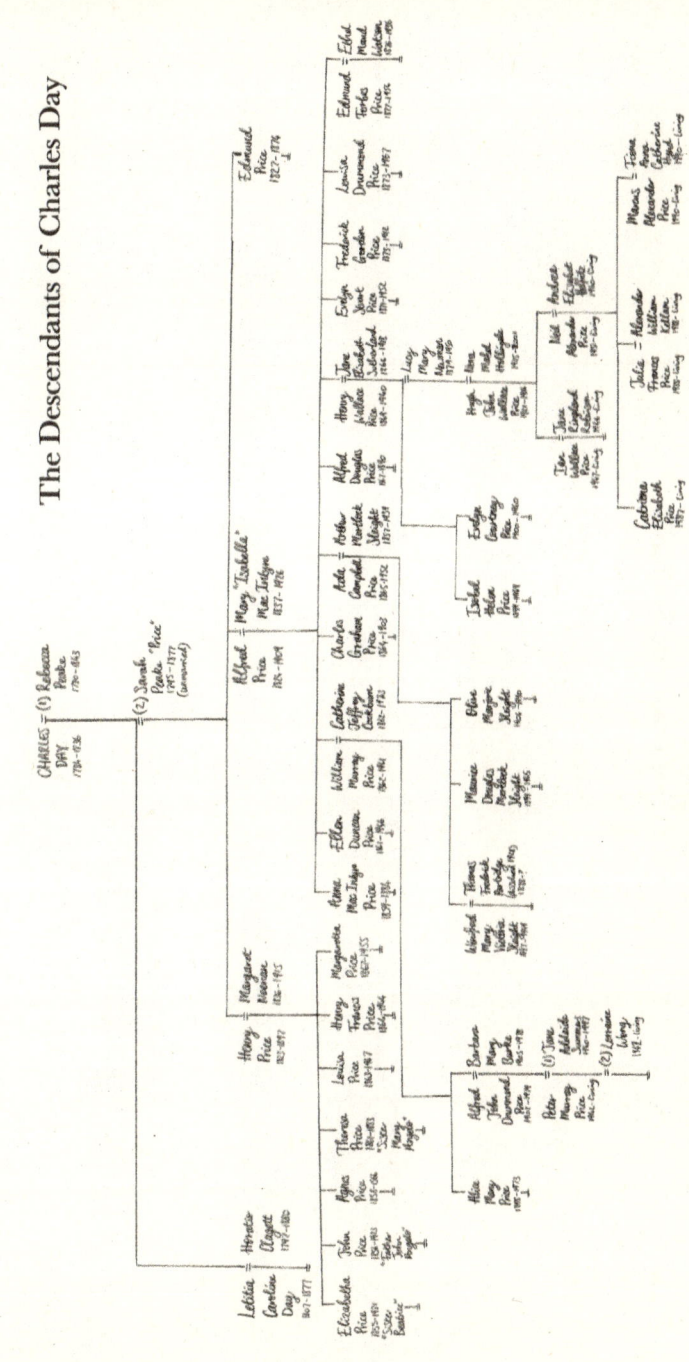

The Peakes of Stafford

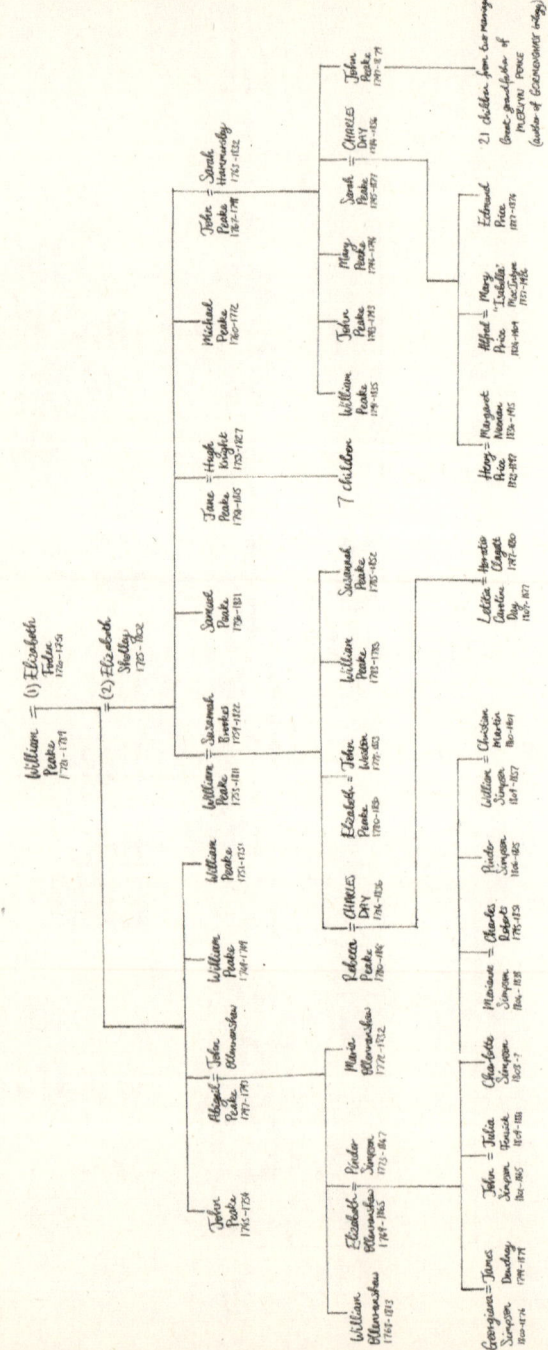

Maps

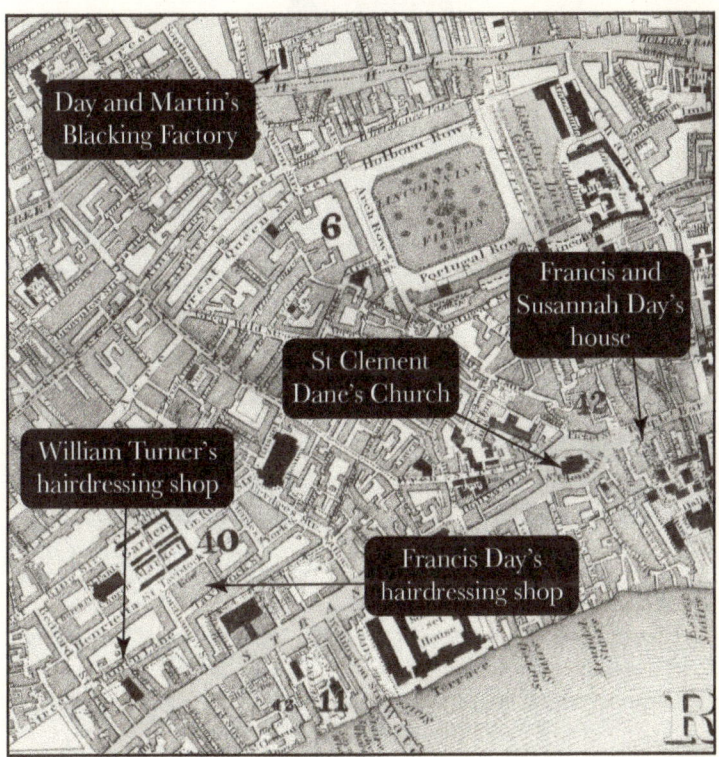

1. Extract from the *Map of London from an Actual Survey made in the years 1824, 1825 and 1826 by C and J Greenwood*, Harvard University, Harvard Map Collection, G5754_L7_1830_G7_Stitched, being the district around Covent Garden showing important sites in the early life of Charles Day.

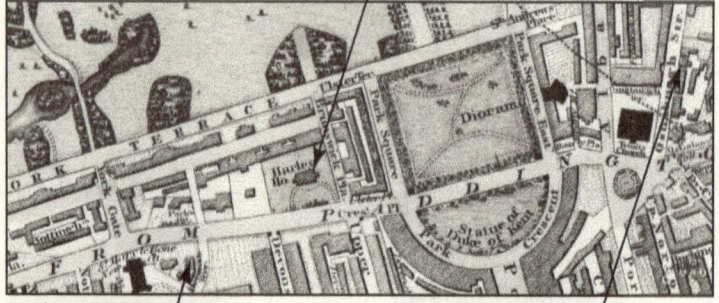

2. Extract from the *Map of London from an Actual Survey made in the years 1824, 1825 and 1826 by C and J Greenwood* Harvard University, Harvard Map Collection, G5754_L7_1830_G7_Stitched, being the district near Regent's Park showing the proximity of Charles Dickens's and Charles Day's residences and the residence of Susannah and Sarah Peake and the Price boys.

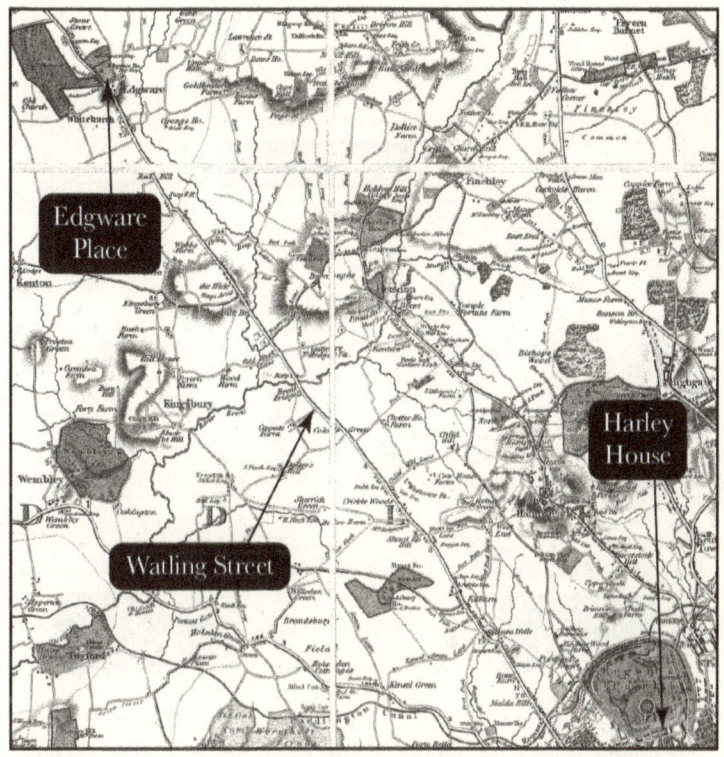

3. Extract from the *Map of Country Twelve Miles round London*, September 1822, by Charles Smith (Lloyd Reeds Map Collection, McMaster University Library), showing the route between Charles Day's two residences of Harley House and Edgware Place. The old Roman road of Watling Street can be clearly seen connecting the two. In modern times, this has become known as Edgware Road and eventually the A5 trunk road.

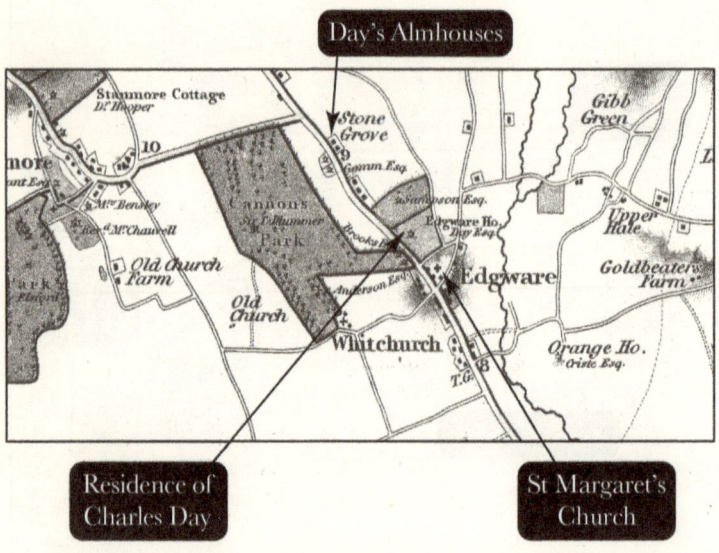

4. Extract from the *Map of Country Twelve Miles round London*, September 1822, by Charles Smith (Lloyd Reeds Map Collection, McMaster University Library), showing the village of Edgware, Charles Day's residence, St Margaret's Church and the future site of Day's Almshouses built in 1828.

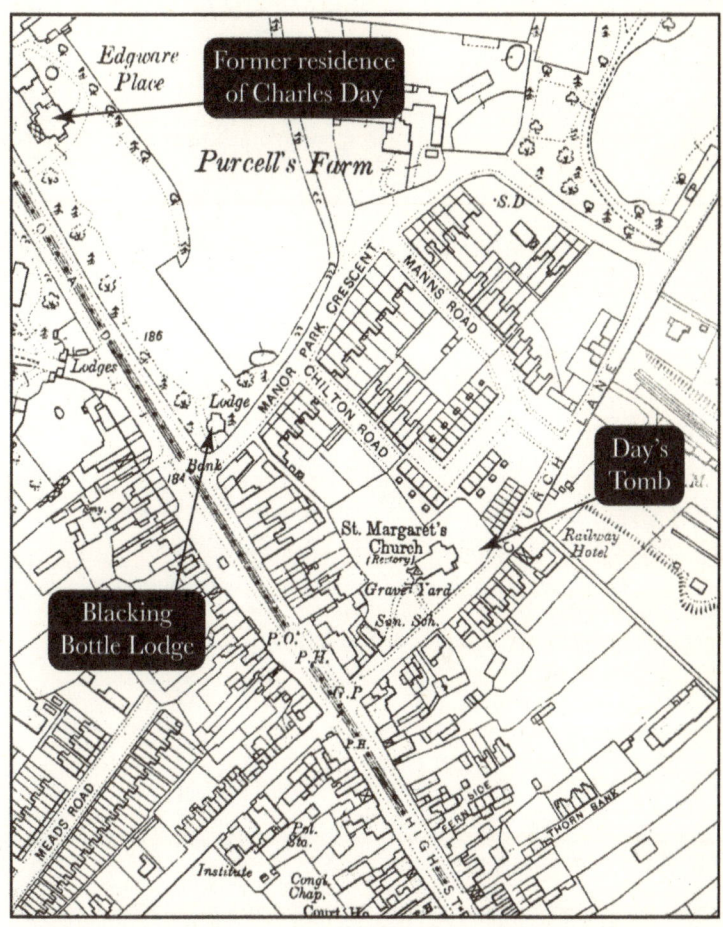

5. A late-nineteenth century map of Edgware drafted before the demolition of Edgware Place and the Blacking Bottle Lodge and showing the site of Day's Tomb.

Preface

Methodology

This is the methodology I followed in writing *Dickens's Favourite Blacking Factory*:

Following careful research into the life of my great-great-grandfather Charles Day (1784-1836), I wrote the book's central section, 'Death', as a fictitious diary composed by Charles Day's real-life doctor, friend and neighbour, William Foote. The diary covers the two-month period leading up to Charles Day's death.

On either side of this are two sections, 'Life' and 'Aftermath'. The 'Life' section is a largely factual account of Charles Day's life and times, up to the two-month period covered by the diary. The 'Aftermath' section is factual, describing the events that occurred in the years after Day's death, mainly in connection with the administration of his Will in the Court of Chancery.

Finally, the outermost sections ('Prologue' and 'Epilogue') are my own personal reflections on how a major mystery in my family's history, the mystery of who was John Price, presented itself and how it was solved following the fluke discovery by my distant cousin Jenny Turnbull of the real-life Will of Charles Day.

Overall, in writing *Dickens's Favourite Blacking Factory*, my aim has been to take the reader into the deepest recesses of Day's confused and syphilitic mind and then to reverse the process back to the contemporary starting-point.

Why did I want to write the fictional diary? The answer is that on a remarkable day in April 2015, when I was researching in the National Archives at Kew, London, I discovered an extraordinary document entitled *Dufaur v Croft and Others – Process brought on 25 Feb 1839 – P.C. 53* (PC53).

The document contains all the earlier and the final versions of Charles Day's Will, together with the evidence of thirty witnesses when the case was heard before the Prerogative Court of Canterbury (PCC) in the eighteen months after Charles Day's death.

The document is extremely helpful and precious, but not exactly an easy read. I decided to turn it on its side, so to speak, and create from it a timeline for each day of the two months it covered. Clearly, it should be presented as a diary, but whose? The obvious candidate was Charles Day's real-life doctor, friend and neighbour, William Foote, who was visiting Day's house several times a day during the period in question. He also turned out to be an interesting character in himself. There were several days in which nothing of note happened and I have omitted these in the editing process. However, all the facts presented in the diary are true, as described clearly in PC53. So, the fictitious diary I have written is, yes, fundamentally fiction but it is based closely around real events and I felt it was the only way that I could make best use of this remarkable material.

The 'Life' section is based on my research into Charles Day's biography. The business side was clearly documented but I have had to indulge in a certain amount of speculation on his personal life.

Nowhere is it actually stated that Day suffered from syphilis. However, the evidence seems to be overwhelming, bearing in mind the symptoms and when they occurred. Also, I have checked that fertility can be maintained after the initial primary and secondary phases of the disease, which cannot be passed on after these phases.

The surname 'Day' quite often appears in its old form of 'Dey'. These are the same and interchangeable. In particular William Claughton Dey (or Day) always used this old form and so when he married his cousin Mary Day, she usually referred to herself subsequently as Mary Dey, ie Mary Day and Mary Dey are the same person.

There are several gaps in the story. I have done my best to fill these in by using reasonable and informed guesswork. For example, the discovery that Susannah Peake was the central person in Day's life after he became blind led me to assume that it was Susannah who introduced him to her cousin Sarah. But there is nothing to prove that this was definitely the case. The section of the story where she goes to Stafford on holiday and returns to London with Sarah, who then enters Day's employment as his 'eyes' about the house, is purely an informed guess.

Likewise, the part of the story where Sarah disappears to Brighton to give birth to her first child, Henry, has enjoyed a certain amount of imaginative embellishment by me. Henry was certainly born in Brighton according to subsequent census returns. I feel it is reasonable to assume that, with Charles's mother's family living there, it was arranged that Sarah should stay with them. She had absolutely no other connections with the town. Also, as I have said at the end of the book, nowhere is it actually stated that Sarah was the mother of the three boys. It does say on her Scottish death certificate that the informant, Alfred Price, was her son, but that need not be definitive. From photographs of her and Henry, there is certainly a physical resemblance. Also, I have established DNA links between myself and distant Day and Peake cousins. All this points to a virtual certainty that she was the mother.

Dickens's Favourite Blacking Factory is emphatically not an academic book and I would certainly not want it to be regarded as such. I have therefore not cluttered the book with endless pages of footnotes. Instead, I have included a section after the narrative giving the general sources for each chapter. I trust the reader finds this sufficient.

Overall, I would like *Dickens's Favourite Blacking Factory* to be an interesting addendum to the remarkable and famous life of Charles Dickens.

The transcription of PC53

PC53 is the appeal by Frederick Dufaur to the judgement of the case heard by the PCC and, as such, is the document that was presented to the Privy Council. Consequently, it was known as *Dufaur v. Croft and Others* whereas the original case (in which the executors challenged the beneficiaries, for reasons that are described) was known as *Croft v Day and Others*. It therefore amounts to all the papers of the original PCC case, which were laboriously copied out by numerous copyists, in varying degrees of legibility, and bound into a thick volume which is now kept at Kew.

I found this volume soon after I discovered the true identity of John Price. The volume amounted to a staggering 962 pages of copperplate handwriting. However, there was no index, contents page or page numbers, and any quest for detail amounted to looking for a needle in a haystack. I knew nothing about the formalities and language of legal documents, let alone ones relating to the early Victorian era, and the learning curve was steep.

It was quickly clear to me that, in amongst the vast amounts of mid-nineteenth century legalese (with virtually no punctuation, sentences or paragraphs), there were numerous details of the Day family life relevant to my family history. But with no means of referencing them or knowing that I had found them all, the only foolproof solution was to transcribe the entire document into a readable (by early twenty-first century standards) document. To do this, I had to photograph every page. So began a two-year task resulting in a volume of 170,000 words. I have made two bound copies, but it is basically in digital form.

In itself, it is my hope that this volume will be of interest to legal historians. However, my reasons for undertaking this task were to build up a clear picture of a remarkable episode, not only in my family history but also in the history of the first half of the nineteenth century, which has now formed the basis of *Dickens's Favourite Blacking Factory*.

Links with Charles Dickens

Naturally, I hope *Dickens's Favourite Blacking Factory* does make some contribution towards Dickensian scholarship. In reading *Bleak House*, and benefitting from a detailed knowledge of the Charles Day Will case, I have become fairly convinced that the link between the two is more than Dickens simply using the Charles Day Will case to justify the fictional circumstances of 'Jarndyce and Jarndyce'.

There seem to be considerable resonances between the details of Day's life and the plot of *Bleak House*, not the least of which is the topic of illegitimacy and the disgrace that went with it at the time. This theory is strengthened by Dickens's residence at 1 Devonshire Terrace between 1839 and 1851, being literally over the road from the home of Day's widow, daughter and son-in-law at Harley House on the Marylebone Road. There is no evidence that Dickens ever met them but nor is there any evidence that he didn't. The Charles Day Will case was before the Privy Council from 1838 to 1840 prior to being referred to the Court of Chancery. I have amplified these observations in the final chapter of the 'Aftermath' section, entitled 'The Dickens connection'.

Neil Price
Edinburgh, August 2023

I. Prologue

LONDON. Autumn term 1960 just beginning, and I start my education as an eight-year-old entrant into the First Form of King's College Junior School. My brother Ian was four years ahead of me. My father Hugh had spent all his schooldays there, finishing just before the outbreak of World War II. His father Henry had retired in 1934 as the so-called 'Vice-Master' (effectively the Headmaster's deputy) of the same school, having taught there since its move, from the basement of King's College in The Strand, to Wimbledon in 1897. He had been born and brought up in Scotland, where he had attended Daniel Stewart's College with his four brothers and Edinburgh University. His father Alfred had been born in 1824 in London, the son of John Price. My father always told me that we knew nothing about this John Price except two facts passed down orally, that he was a merchant in London and that his funeral had taken place during the riots that ravaged many parts of the country prior to the passing of the 1832 Reform Act.

My time at King's in the 1960s is now a distant memory, but some childhood experiences will always linger in the mind as though they only happened yesterday. One of these involved my winter homeward journeys, after school finished at 3.50pm. These were the days of the London smogs, the pea-soupers as we called them, that came down after a clear morning and reduced visibility to a matter of feet. Inhaling this filth while walking the mile home was an undoubted health risk. My father was at work, my mother didn't drive. Other mothers with bubble-cars would collect their sons and take pity on us walkers. We piled into their Heinkels or Messerschmitts for distribution around the neighbourhood. No seat belts, but safety was observed by preventing us breathing the vile air. Records for the numbers of humans who could be crammed into these tiny cars must have been broken. From within, visibility was virtually nothing. The benevolent mother of the day crept along the road with fog lights blazing. Nothing was going faster than 0mph+. Any collision could only have been a gentle bump – quite safe, even in our barely tin-foil casing. There was gratitude all round when home was reached.

The school was, and still is, a high academic achiever and so exposure to serious literature from the outset was mandatory. This meant, amongst other things, Dickens. Our deeply committed masters would read what seemed to us vast, bleeding chunks of the stuff and we were at a loss to understand why. It even descended into unfortunate ridicule on one occasion when our form master was so overcome by emotion in one tragic passage from *David Copperfield* that he could not hide the tears that were streaming down his face. We did not reciprocate, having to suppress the schoolboy giggles instead.

But one day, in an attempt to redeem himself, this same master decided to try and convince us that there was much humour in Dickens, a concept that had completely escaped us up to that point. So, with another smog descending on the area outside and, as Dickens would say, 'Fog everywhere', he was inspired to read us the famous Chapter 1 of *Bleak House*. With immaculate delivery, he took a deep breath and commenced:

LONDON. Michaelmas term lately over, and the Lord Chancellor sitting in

Lincoln's Inn Hall. Implacable November weather. As much mud in the streets as if the waters had but newly retired from the face of the earth, and it would not be wonderful to meet a Megalosaurus, forty feet long or so, waddling like an elephantine lizard up Holborn Hill.

We had never heard descriptive writing like this and the fog outside helped to transport us immediately into Dickens's London of the 1830s and the symbolism of using it to describe the inert Court of Chancery which Dickens so wanted to satire. We could easily identify with the black specks of soot in the fog being inhaled through our noses and into our lungs. It seemed little had changed in the intervening 130 years. It was still wet and cold out there and our clothes and shoes were splattered every day with the downtrodden mud of busy pedestrians. And to hammer home the general feeling of filth, Dickens took us all around London and the surrounding districts. He identified with the common man in all his activities and different guises. And having brought us to the gutter, he waded in with:

The raw afternoon is rawest, and the dense fog is densest, and the muddy streets are muddiest near that leaden-headed old obstruction, appropriate ornament for the threshold of a leaden-headed old corporation, Temple Bar. And hard by Temple Bar, in Lincoln's Inn Hall, at the very heart of the fog, sits the Lord High Chancellor in his High Court of Chancery.

And on and on our master went… introducing us, as Dickens does, to the case of 'Jarndyce and Jarndyce' and all the ghastly delays and procrastinating meanderings to which that case had been subjected over decades of time, lost in its own fog and confusion. No one understood it any more. It had sunk into the mists of Chancery.

We were genuinely impressed. Our rapt attention had produced an otherwise-unheard-of silence. The master finished with a satisfied smirk on his face. By that time, the smog was as thick as guts, with a dirty yellow colour similar to that of a child suffering from jaundice, a word uncomfortably close to 'Jarndyce' we thought. We packed our bags, donned our coats, caps, gloves and scarves and ventured outside, trying not to draw any breath before arriving at the awaiting Heinkels and Messerschmitts. In only a few preceding minutes, Dickens, who previously had been detached from our fairly comfortable mid-twentieth century lives in its own world of seeming mid-nineteenth century misery, had come to life. Perhaps there was something in this turgid stuff after all.

LONDON. Summer 2014, and I very unexpectedly find myself retiring from Orkney, which had been my home for thirty-five years, to London, the city of my birth and schooling, and living in Fulham, not too far from Wimbledon and my old school. Some friendships that had lapsed for nearly fifty years were rekindled and we found ourselves reminiscing. This led me back to the memories of the smogs, Charles Dickens and *Bleak House* in particular.

Some years earlier, I had bought a bargain basement complete works of Dickens in paperback, merely because it was there and I felt we ought to have it. My opinion of Dickens had changed little since my schooldays but, against my better judgement, nostalgia and curiosity led me to pick this door-stopper of a novel off our bookshelf. Attempting to put off my actual reading of the text (all 887 pages of it), I glanced through the biographical note, the introduction, the editor's note on the text, the list of further reading, an appendix giving the full memoranda for *Bleak House* that are bound up with the original manuscript and even the editor's footnotes at the back of the book. All that remained, before I would have to face the evil hour of actually reading the book, was the author's preface. Startlingly brief for Dickens (it just goes on to a third page), I hoped that even I could cope with it before sleep would be induced. It was written after the book was finished in August 1853 and in it, Dickens successfully justifies his damning satire of the Court of Chancery. One sentence in particular caught my attention in which Dickens refers, although not by name, to an actual case that was stuck at that very time in the mire and fog of that dreaded legal institution.

I was intrigued and my inquisitive mind was diverted still longer from reading the book. What was this actual case? And how did Dickens acquire such detailed knowledge of it? Some initial enquiries led me to the Dickens Museum in London's Doughty Street where there is kept in the library the remarkable piece of scholarship which is the twelve-volume *The Letters of Charles Dickens* edited by Storey, Tillotson and Easson. The year 1853 is covered in Volume 7 and on Sunday 7 August of that year, I found Dickens in Boulogne, France (where he was completing *Bleak House* on one of his many travels abroad), writing to W H Wills, his close friend and secretary, sub-editor and co-proprietor with Dickens of the journal *Household Words*. He was asking Wills for the latest information on the 'Day Chancery Cause' because he wished to refer to it, though not by name, in the preface to his new book.

In footnotes to this letter, the editors describe the 'Day Chancery Cause' as:

Day v. Croft, an administration suit arising out of the estate of Charles Day, of Day & Martin, blacking manufacturers, of High Holborn. Day had died in 1836; the case had begun before the Master of the Rolls in November 1838 and was still being heard in 1854. The estate was of over £100,000. Costs had exceeded £70,000 in May 1851.

Wills obligingly had replied by return and this clearly was the source of Dickens' statement in his preface.

I was also directed towards Clare Tomalin's wonderful

biography of Charles Dickens. I was interested to note his experience of working in Warren's boot-blacking factory, situated off The Strand on what is now Charing Cross station by the River Thames. Interrupting his schooling at the tender age of just twelve and with his father in a debtors' prison, this had left a deep impression on the young Dickens. His dreary task was the endless sticking of labels onto blacking bottles, in solitary and disgusting conditions. It was an episode in his life to which he often referred and, perhaps to have a swipe at his former harsh employers, wrote about boot-blacking in his novels *The Pickwick Papers* and *Oliver Twist*, but mentioning Warren's main competitors, Day and Martin. The picture was becoming clearer.

I discovered that Day and Martin were the boot-blacking market leaders in the early nineteenth century, a household word rather like Hoover became to vacuum cleaners in our own times.

The entire world has heard of Day and Martin. The two names are so associated that we can hardly conceive a Day without a Martin, or a Martin without a Day; and that either Day or Martin should ever die, or be succeeded by others, seems a kind of commercial impossibility – a thing not to be thought of. Day and Martin it has been for forty years, and Day and Martin it will probably be for forty years to come, or perhaps till blacking itself shall be no more.

That quotation was from a verbose but informative article entitled 'A Day at Day and Martin's' which appeared in *The Penny Magazine* in December 1842, published by 'The Office of the Society for the Diffusion of Useful Knowledge'.

The article, which was written six years after Day's death, further revealed that little was given away about the precise ingredients of the great blacking potion. But the factory and the processes that went on there were described in great detail. The business was still being run by John Weston who had been Day's manager since 1816. The article gave an overall impression of great efficiency. The product was made in daily batches and work began at 5am each day. Child labour was frequently mentioned, but I was struck by the fact that the grim working conditions, so often described in such cases by Dickens in his novels, were not referred to – quite the contrary. Although hard work and effort was expected from the workforce, this was rewarded by a fair employer in terms of wages and the factory environment. It seemed that this had been a deliberate ethos adopted by Day and continued after his death. Certainly, in the twenty years since Dickens' own grim experience at Warren's, the process of sticking labels on bottles, which is described in the article in excessive detail, seemed to have become far more humane.

And the firm's fame spread throughout the country. The *Chambers Edinburgh Journal* stated on 28 December 1844:

No one can deny that the names of those very respectable blacking-makers of High Holborn, Messrs Day and Martin, are quite as well known to the public at large as Scott of Abbotsford, and Wellington of Waterloo. Such are amongst the glories of advertising, when that art is vigorously carried out!

Putting *Bleak House* to one side (with a certain amount of relief, which I later realised was completely unjustified), I decided to continue my enquiries into what seemed to be a fascinating case. Who was this Charles Day and what was the story behind his blacking manufacturers' business Day and Martin? How could he amass such a fortune from boot-blacking, only for the money to fall into the hands of the legal profession and court costs after his death?

I was in London, the right place to take this further, and retired, with time on my hands. Here was a project to pursue. The forthcoming pages reveal the extraordinary story that was waiting to be uncovered.

II. Life

1. Small beginnings to big success

The origins of Day and Martin go back to the busy life of Francis Day's hairdresser's shop in Covent Garden, London in the 1790s. Francis had come down to London from his native Yorkshire in the late 1760s when he was in his early twenties.

He came from a family of joiners. His grandfather, also Francis Day, was a Master Joiner whose marriage in 1720 to his first wife had taken him to the village of Wragby, south-east of Wakefield. Soon after this, Sir Rowland Winn and his family started to construct the large, Palladian stately home known as Nostell Priory on the site of the twelfth century Augustinian priory of St Oswald that had been dissolved by Henry VIII. Subsequently, the Winns employed the great furniture maker Thomas Chippendale, who came from nearby Otley, to make over one hundred pieces of furniture for the house. The village of Wragby is on the boundary of the estate.

It is likely that this construction project provided continuous labour for Francis and his family, including his oldest son William, for decades. However, his wife died in 1731 leaving three children under ten. He remarried two years later, had another son, but then his second wife died in 1742. He carried on working and, with his Master status, he was still taking on apprentices in 1759. By this time, William had married and started his own family. His oldest son, also William, followed into the family trade of joinery, so the next son Francis had to find another trade. He chose hair-dressing and wig-making but there is no evidence as to how he obtained his training as an apprentice or whether he rose to be a master. But it was probably after his grandfather died aged seventy-three in 1769 that, with the family dispersing and the figurehead gone, he would try his luck and venture down to London. And the best place to set up as a barber in London would be Covent Garden, the capital's hub for fashion, high-living and much else.

Inigo Jones had built the Covent Garden piazza in the 1630s and it soon became the centre of style for everyone. It was 'the' place to be seen, parading around and boasting the latest fashion trends. This of course included hair fashions, and for both men and women, hairdressers' shops became popular destinations. The goings-on inside gentlemen's wig shops in the eighteenth century were many and varied, with barbers shaving, and then making and fitting perukes for their clients before applying endless colours and varieties of powders to the wigs whose tumbling ringlets had to be seen flowing down their owners' backs.

But Covent Garden had also become the centre of the capital's sex trade, with brothels, bawdy houses and bagnios commonplace. The high society of the early eighteenth century had moved west, leaving their offspring to inhabit the houses around the piazza, which soon descended into centres of vice. But the cash still flowed for the young entrepreneur wanting to set up a new business.

There is an anonymous account from 1779, well into the reign of George III, entitled *Nocturnal Revels* identifying Covent Garden as the centre of such activities:

> *The present reign, however, is that in which gallantry has attained its summit, and intrigue may now be pronounced in its zenith. Refinement is carried through every stage of life in this respect. The impotent, hobbling*

Peer who keeps half a dozen mistresses to support his reputation, though in fact he has not the least occasion for one, politely winks at his wife's amours. If, upon his return home in the morning, he meets his cornuter upon the stairs, still warm with her ladyship's embraces, his hair en papillote, and all his dress denoting his recent situation; nay, perhaps half his night-cap hanging out of his pocket; the only passe parole is, Bon jour, Monsieur - Bon jour, mi Lord. Punctilios being thus happily preserved, we never hear now of a duel, or a rencounter upon the score of a wife's infidelity - but when suspicions arise concerning a wife's honour, then satisfaction must be demanded, or a man's honour will be called in question, who lets pass unnoticed his mistress's inconstancy.

From kept-mistresses we shall descend a line lower, and consider those fair ones who are to be obtained at a minute's warning, for a stipulated sum. Before the modern institution of nunneries, the chief scene of action for promiscuous amours lay in the vicinity of Covent Garden. There are some debauchees still living, who must remember the nocturnal revels at Moll King's in the centre of Covent Garden market. This rendezvous was a general receptacle for rakes and prostitutes of every rank.

At that period there was a public gaming-table under the Piazza, called Lord Mordington's. To this association many families have owed their ruin. It was often the last resource of a failing tradesman, who repaired thither with the property of his creditors to make a push, when there were so many sharpers to surround him, and so many artifices used to defraud him, that it was a miracle if he returned with a guinea in his pocket. From this gambling sett, many a broken gamester has repaired to Moll King's to snore out the remainder of the night, for want of a shilling to obtain a lodging. If he should chance to have a watch or a pair of silver buckles remaining, whilst he was paying his devotion to Morpheus, the nimble-handed gentry of either sex were labouring in their vocation, and the unhappy victim to fortune became the still more unhappy victim to Mercury and his votaries. From this receptacle the son of Bacchus reeled home at daybreak; the buck took his doxy to a bagnio; and the blood carried off his Moll in triumph in a chair, himself at the top of it, with a broken sword, and a tattered shirt, escorted by link-boys, watchmen, and pickpockets. There is a print at the shops that gives a very natural and just representation of one of these scenes, which was actually taken from the life; it is so truly picturesque and descriptive, that anyone desirous of forming a perfect idea of such a frolic, cannot avoid being furnished with it.

There was even a publication produced and regularly updated called Jack Harris's *List of Covent Garden Ladies*. In the piazza, there was a thriving tavern called the 'Shakespeare's Head', where in the late 1740s Jack Harris was ostensibly the head-waiter, but in reality, a successful pimp. By the late 1780s, the area covered by his pamphlet extended well beyond Covent Garden and recognized Marylebone as the trendy new centre for such things, while Covent Garden remained Marylebone's 'elder sister'.

And so, it was into this maelstrom of activity, both above and below the surface, that Francis Day set up his barber's shop at 7 Tavistock Street, just off the south-east corner of the Covent Garden piazza and a far cry from rural Yorkshire whence he had come.

But sadly, Francis's personal life during his early days in London was full of tragedy, as was so common for those times. On 5 May 1770 in St George's, Bloomsbury, Francis married Elizabeth Parsons, who had come from a farming family near Lewes in Sussex. One of the witnesses at the wedding was Elizabeth's older sister Susanna. The following month, they were blessed with a daughter, also Elizabeth, but sadly the mother died in September 1771. At the age of only twenty-three, Francis found himself a widower with an infant child and trying to make his way in city life which was completely new to him.

Subsequent facts suggest that the Parsons family were a close and tightly-knit clan. Elizabeth's older sister Susanna had also come up to London and, seeing her brother-in-law in dire straits and with a young daughter on his hands, she seems to have taken pity on him and moved in.

By October 1774, he is listed in a poll book residing at Temple Bar, right beside the famous church of St Clement Danes where The Strand becomes Fleet Street and very near Covent Garden. He voted in a 'Poll for Two Citizens for the City and Liberty of Westminster' and is described as a peruke-maker.

On 29 July 1774, a baptism is recorded in the records of St Clement Danes: 'John Day, of Francis and Susanna' but on 12 May 1776, the child's death is recorded in the same records. On 9 March 1777, another baptism is recorded: 'William Day, of Francis and Susanna, born 16th of January', but again the child's burial is recorded later that year on 20 October. With child mortality being very common, it was quite normal for a couple to name their next child of the same gender after one who had previously died. On 6 October 1778, a further baptism is recorded at St Clement Danes: 'William Day, of Francis and Susanna'.

This child was clearly healthy and surviving and his parents must have realised that a legalisation of their relationship was now long overdue, especially as Susanna was pregnant again. The marriage took place in St Pancras Church but he was described as a parishioner of St Clement Danes. He was thirty-two and a widower. She was thirty-four and was said to be of the St Pancras parish.

Francis had been widowed, had lost two subsequent children and had a seven-year-old daughter, an infant son and another child expected. This had been a character-building first decade in the capital and he now deserved some stability with his new wife to help him support his two children and a new business starting up in the best possible location to make some money.

More children followed for the newly-married couple and they were all baptized in St Clement Danes. In April 1780, a daughter Susanna was born followed in October 1781 by another daughter Mary. However, soon after, tragedy struck again with the death of little Susanna. Their final child, a second Susanna, appears in the baptismal records on 9 October 1785.

However, between Mary and the second Susanna, another son was born. This was Charles. The parish records show a baptism on 25 January 1784: 'Charles Day, of Francis and Susanna' but there is no record of the actual date of his birth. However, the common practice of the times in Anglican churches was for infants to be baptized as soon after birth as possible, simply because infant mortality was common and it was believed that the soul could only have a safe passage if the child had already been blessed in baptism. It is therefore safe to assume that Charles's year of birth was 1784, as a gap of more than twenty-five days between birth and baptism would have been very uncommon.

By the time of the birth of the second Susanna, Francis was thirty-seven and his wife Susanna was forty. They had five children to support and must at last have felt fulfilled in their building of a family after so many set-backs. It was time to develop the barber's and wig-maker's business.

Shops such as Day's Rooms at 7 Tavistock Street, Covent Garden, were exciting and colourful places to be around. The clientele were lively people, outward-going and keen to socialize. The theatres in the vicinity of Covent Garden produced many thespians who, by their very nature, were anxious to see and be seen, parading all the latest fashions. The area also became a haven for artists, architects, bookbinders, printmakers and the associated shops and auction houses that go with such pursuits.

And there was competition. Francis Day was not the only barber to set up shop in Covent Garden at this time. Another was one William Turner whose shop was just west down Tavistock Street and straight on into Maiden Lane at No 21. He had come up from the west country and married a local girl from a prominent family, Mary Marshall. He was ambitious and full of stamina which, like Day, he channeled into developing his shop. The couple had a son in 1775 whom they grandly named Joseph Mallord William Turner, after Mary's younger brother. He was destined to become Britain's greatest painter of the nineteenth century. It is surely likely that young Turner would have mixed with the Day boys, William and Charles, up the road and compared notes about their fathers' shops. The Turners also suffered personal tragedy losing two daughters after their son was born, effectively leaving him an only child who probably sought his own contemporary company.

Charles was considerably younger than these two Williams and probably saw them as role models. During the 1790s, he developed into a handsome teenager capable of charming the wealthy patrons as he headed towards his apprenticeship in his father's trade, as had no doubt been the case with his older brother. But fortune smiled on him and his father, and a more lucrative alternative presented itself in the form of a diversification, probably brought about by economic necessity.

The start of the problems came in 1789 with the Fall of the Bastille in Paris and the Revolution that followed. The beaus of Paris either fled over the Channel or drastically changed their ostentatious ways, abandoning fashion and wigs in particular. Consequently, the hair-dressers and wig-makers found themselves on hard times and many followed their clients by finding ways to London and continuing their trade there. Their centre became Soho and they were prepared to trim their profitability to survive, thus undercutting the likes of Day and Turner, just to the east in Covent Garden. In addition, many of the former regular clients became very wary of what they saw happening in France, fearing that a spark could set off the same reaction in England. Perhaps a small way of avoiding such a dreadful occurrence would be to dumb down their lifestyle and in particular the hair coiffeurs and associated wigs, powders, ointments, salves and potions that went with them. Day's business began to suffer.

The last straw, quite literally, was the failure of the harvest in 1795 following the exceptionally hard winter that preceded it. Harvests had been diminishing for decades and much importing of wheat from Europe and America had become unavoidable. But France and Britain were at war again by 1793 and trade was stifled. A major constituent of hair powder was wheat and corn flour which was now in very short supply. And when the government imposed a hair powder tax, hairdressers had to take action to avoid financial ruin and attempt to diversify into other trades and commodities.

Francis Day had to find a new income stream and quite randomly, a chance presented itself in the nick of time around about 1799. This was in the unlikely form of boot-blacking, helped by what was turning out to be an exceptional entrepreneurial flair being shown by his fifteen-year-old son, Charles.

1. St Sepulchre Gate, Doncaster, showing in the middle distance on the right the King's Arms pub where the blacking recipe was exchanged in about 1800 (this photo dates from c1900).

In the late 1790s, a journeyman hairdresser, Benjamin Martin, joined Francis Day's business in Covent Garden. He had originally come from Halifax in Yorkshire, where he was baptized on 1 March 1774, the son of Andrew and Sally Martin. Andrew was a staymaker, a highly skilled tailor who specialized in making corsets. After Benjamin's birth, the Martins decided to move to Doncaster, but Andrew died in 1782, aged just fifty. Starting in 1788 and having decided to remain in his father's field of fashion and style, Benjamin served his apprenticeship as a perukemaker in Gainsborough, close by in Lincolnshire, under his Master, Matthew White. After he attained his status as a journeyman, he decided to head south to the metropolis. There the similarities with Francis Day end. There is no evidence that they were in any way related.

His sister, older by thirteen years, had married one Anthony Moore in Doncaster. In about 1799, Benjamin decided to take his annual leave by going back to Doncaster and stay with his sister and brother-in-law when the Doncaster races were on. Anthony Moore kept and lived over The King's Arms, a pub in St Sepulchre Gate, right in the middle of the town.

At the time, the French Revolutionary Wars were raging all over Europe, pitting France against the monarchies of Britain, Russia, Prussia, Austria and several others. The British Army needed to be served by a constant stream of recruits and recruiting was taking place all over the country. It was difficult to persuade men to go into the army for low pay when better wages were beginning to emerge as a result of the industrial revolution. Staying at The King's Arms was a low-ranking soldier named Thomas Florry, who was a servant to one Captain Wilson, then on recruiting service in Doncaster. Florry's boots were a gleaming and shining black. They were much admired by the landlord and his brother-in-law who asked Florry how he had achieved such a spectacular result. The answer was a recipe given him during his travels in the continental wars. Moore asked for it in exchange for a quart of ale, an offer which the thirsty and impoverished soldier accepted with alacrity. Benjamin was sure that such spectacular boot blacking would be highly attractive to the well-dressed gents of Covent Garden. Boot-blacking was a new commodity in London, the Warren brothers having recently set up their factory in Hungerford Stairs by Charing Cross, not far from Covent Garden. But Benjamin had not been greatly impressed by their product's results and what he had seen on the boots of the thirsty soldier was far superior. So, Moore happily gave Benjamin the recipe to take back to London with him.

Although they were nearly ten years apart in age, Benjamin had struck up a good friendship with his employer's son Charles. He told Charles about the recipe and they both discussed the possibility with Charles's father of experimenting with the recipe at the back of the shop, which was already set up as a workshop to make the powders, ointments and salves needed by Francis for his trade. Francis saw this as a possible diversification, given the difficult times that the hairdresser's trade was facing after the French Revolution, the changes in fashion and the influx of French hairdressers to London. He consented that the boys should try their experiment. They did and it certainly seemed to work.

Benjamin was twenty-five and Charles only fifteen. Even at that age, Charles had a natural flair as an entrepreneur and, with a father who had limited but enough means with which to help him, a new firm of manufacturers of Real Japan Blacking was soon up and running, operating at first from the back of 7 Tavistock Street.

Originating in India, China and Japan as a decorative coating for pottery, Japan Blacking made its way into Europe by the seventeenth century, the application being mainly to furniture. In the late-seventeenth century, high European demand and rumours that higher quality pieces were not exported, led to production starting in Italy. As the demand for all things 'Japanned' grew, the Italian technique for imitating Asian lacquer work also spread and was developed in Britain, France, Italy, and the Low Countries. Records indicate that people had been making their own recipes for 'Japan blacking' as early as 1761 to be applied to footwear. The streets of London were particularly filthy and a decent product for cleaning boots and shoes was in considerable demand. Benjamin and Charles came along with their secret recipe which seemed to be superior to anything else. It was a stroke of genius to call it 'The Real Japan Blacking'.

Initially the business traded as Martin and Co, presumably in recognition of the fact that the whole idea had originated from Benjamin and his family. Benjamin was the manufacturer with Charles and his father being responsible for marketing and distribution. But the address given was 7 Tavistock Street, the premises of Francis Day's hairdressing and wig-making business.

By 20 November 1801 (Charles was still just seventeen), they could afford to advertise in *The Morning Post*:

THE REAL JAPAN BLACKING

The proprietors now offer to Public notice this most valuable composition, which they warrant far superior in every respect to any Blacking hitherto manufactured. It possesses every quality that can possibly recommend its general use, and they are well assured, that no person can possibly use it without asserting it to be the best they ever tried. It produces the most beautiful jet and shining black ever seen, with one half the usual labour: a cambric handkerchief may be rubbed on the boot without its being in the least soiled; and it possesses this inestimable recommendation, that instead of injuring the leather, as other Blackings do, it is found an excellent preservative to the leather by rendering it perfectly soft and pliable, and impenetrable to the wet. The dirt on boots or shoes, after this Blacking has once been used, is removed with the greatest ease, and it will keep for any length of time.

Sold, wholesale and retail, at Day's, No. 7, Tavistock-street, Covent Garden; and retail, at Harding's, No. 213, High Holborn; Axtell's, No. 1, Finch-lane, Cornhill; and Lander's, No. 10, Devereux-court, Temple; in stone bottles, price 1s. 6d. each, with painted directions, affixed thereon,

signed Martin and Co.
N.B. A good allowance to sell again.

This exact same advert was repeated in the same paper on 3, 5 and 9 December 1801 and in the *London Courier and Evening Gazette* on 2 and 5 December 1801. Things were beginning to take off. The adverts went on through 1802, but by 23 November 1802, the firm was stated as Day and Martin and the number of retailers selling the product had expanded from three to nineteen, with the statement added:

… and by a respectable shopkeeper in every principal town throughout Great Britain.

Subsequently, it was revealed that a partnership agreement between Benjamin and Charles was drawn up and dated 14 December 1802, stating the firm's name as Day and Martin.

This was significant progress in the space of just one year and is perhaps explained by a particularly imaginative marketing ploy. Marketing was a concept in its infancy, but a method adopted by Benjamin and Charles must be an early example of best practice. They purchased one hundred surplus suits in Petticoat Lane, clothed one hundred recruits and sent them out to all the suitable shops in London to purchase a bottle of 'Day and Martin's'. After the perfumers, oilmen and grocers had been visited several times by different customers enquiring after the same product, the shopkeepers could only deduce that this must be something they had missed and immediately ordered significant levels of stock. Hence the rapid increase in the number of retailers.

The advertisements continued in the daily papers and their

eloquence is quite noticeable. There was even some gossip that Lord Byron had been engaged in drafting the wording. In his final Appendix to *The Two Foscari*, Byron gives Day and Martin some enviable publicity:

> *Whilst I have been occupied in defending Pope's character, the lower orders of Grub-street appear to have been assailing mine: this is as it should be, both in them and in me. One of the accusations in the nameless epistle alluded to is still more laughable: it states seriously that I 'received five hundred pounds for writing advertisements for Day and Martin's patent blacking!' This is the highest compliment to my literary powers which I ever received.*

Business boomed and by 30 December 1805, the following notice appeared in *The Morning Chronicle*:

DAY and MARTIN

Proprietors of the real JAPAN BLACKING,
Beg leave to inform the Public, that in consequence of the very great demand for their Blacking, they have built an extensive Manufactory, at No. 97, High Holborn, where they request all wholesale orders may be addressed. Retail as before, at No. 7, Tavistock-street.

It was recorded that the building costs were £12,000. Charles was still only twenty-one. However, he was single minded, very determined, with an extraordinary memory for detail, but not at all a 'partnership' person. Thus, in April 1808 Benjamin, by then in his mid-thirties, agreed to accept a pay-off from Charles for his half of the business, on the basis of which he could return to

Doncaster and live in comfortable retirement. The sum agreed was £7,000 for the goodwill attached to the recipe and £3,643 for Benjamin's share of his partnership capital. Benjamin gratefully accepted. He consented that Charles (by then at the ripe old age of twenty-four) should continue to trade as Day and Martin, the product now having been established under this household name. This was the advance notice that appeared in *The London Gazette* on 26 April 1808:

> *Notice is hereby given, that the partnership lately carried on between us the undersigned Charles Day and Benjamin Martin, as Manufacturers of Blacking, called Real Japan Blacking, in High Holborn, in the County of Middlesex, or elsewhere, under the firm of Day and Martin, has been this Day dissolved by mutual Consent; and that the said Trade of Manufacturers of Real Japan Blacking will be in future carried on by the said Charles Day only – Dated 29th Day of April 1808.*
> *Charles Day*
> *Benj. Martin*

Benjamin had married Hannah North in London in 1804 and the couple had six children. On the proceeds of his pay-out from Day and Martin, he built two houses in Doncaster, in one of which he lived for some time before moving to the Sheffield area, where he died in 1834.

2. Introductions in Regency times

On 23 July 1799, a wedding took place in St George's, Hanover Square, in the heart of Mayfair, London, between Pinder Simpson and Elizabeth Ollenranshaw, both of whom were said to be 'of this Parish'.

The bride came from a large family in Stafford. Her father was a Master Cordwainer (being the old word for a shoemaker) and her mother Abigail was from the Peake family who were well-known in 18th century Staffordshire as publicans in winter and 'bricklayers' (not the specialist term now used, but then meaning more generally what would now simply be called 'builders') in the summer. At the time of her marriage, Elizabeth was thirty and had come down to London to seek work, and perhaps a husband.

The bridegroom originally came from Retford in Nottinghamshire where he was born in 1773. His unusual Christian name, Pinder, was his mother's maiden name. But his grandfather, William Pinder, was born in Gainsborough (just twelve miles from Retford and twenty miles from Doncaster) and his marriage record describes him as a 'tonsor', another old word meaning barber or hairdresser. Subsequently, a certain Benjamin Martin was to train as a perukemaker in Gainsborough.

Pinder's parents, Ann Pinder and her husband John Simpson, relocated to Romford in Essex. From here, young Pinder sought work in London and underwent his training as a land agent and conveyancer. This he did in Mayfair where he made some excellent connections from the outset.

Pinder and Elizabeth's first child, a girl called Georgiana, arrived a year after their marriage and she was born in Piccadilly. They were living their early married days near Pinder's work. But when Elizabeth fell pregnant again the following year, they decided a more suitable base to bring up their family would be out in Essex near Pinder's parents. John was born in December 1801, followed by four more children over the next eight years, Charlotte, Marianne, Pinder Jnr and William. Pinder's work base remained in Mayfair and he can be seen advertising the rental of a large property in Hertfordshire in *The Morning Post* in 1807, giving his business address as 7 Old Burlington Street.

Pinder Simpson and Benjamin Martin were almost exactly the same age, just two months apart. With them both trying to find their way in the capital in the late 1790s whilst in their early-twenties, coming from nearby towns in the East Midlands, and with a shared background in the hairdressing trade, it seems quite possible that they knew each other. Through Benjamin, Pinder could have met the Day family in Covent Garden and friendships struck. Although Pinder was not a solicitor, he would have been able to give Benjamin and Charles some guidance on legal matters, if for nothing else to draw up their partnership agreement in 1802. Also, he could well have helped them identify a site for their proposed blacking factory. Whatever way their close family friendship started, the very strong bond between Pinder and Charles was mutually upheld for the rest of Charles's life.

By 1806, the twenty-two-year-old Charles was already a wealthy young man, with dashing good looks and a charming personality honed in his father's shop, with the constant flow of regular customers. Being ten years his junior, Charles looked up to Pinder and listened to his advice. But as a child of his time, the one glaring omission in his life was a lady on his arm. Pinder and Elizabeth must have noticed this and decided to lend their assistance with some introductions.

Back in Stafford, Elizabeth had many cousins, but in particular there were 3 sisters roughly the same age as Charles. Their mother was originally from Westminster and they probably all had a yearning for a life in London. The oldest sister was called Rebecca and an assignation with Charles could easily be arranged. Charles was completely preoccupied with his business which was expanding at a rapid rate. The new premises at 97 High Holborn had just been occupied at the end of 1805. All of Charles's energies were going into the manufacture of 'The Real Japan Blacking' in the new factory and its subsequent marketing. In his eyes, a romance was probably not something of any great significance. Getting married is just something that a man did. Rebecca Peake was the girl waiting for him and he duly reported at St Mary's Collegiate Church in Stafford for his wedding on 6 September 1806. The knot was tied and Rebecca of course became his 'dear wife' – what else? Simple!

There was certainly a dwellinghouse at the new factory and it is likely that this was Charles and Rebecca's first residence. To no one's surprise, it was not long before Rebecca was pregnant and their first child, a daughter Letitia Caroline (but always known as Caroline) was born on 17 June 1807, just nine months and a few days after the wedding. For whatever reason, they would have no more children.

With Charles living 'over the shop' and the business expanding at a rapid rate, he probably neglected the concept of fatherhood and put all his energies into his work. Rebecca had come from a completely different background and now found herself in a large and crowded city with little chance of escape. She did not understand and therefore had little interest in business. Connecting with her husband, who was obsessive and single-minded about work, became more and more difficult. She would have been homesick for Stafford, a relatively small market town, and its idyllic rural hinterland. Instead she was cooped up, albeit in acceptable and material comfort, living in a factory in a densely populated part of the capital, and trying to bring up her infant daughter. The emotional attachment between Charles and Rebecca, essential even then for the successful rearing of a family, simply was not there – and it probably never had been. He had seen her as an easy and convenient conquest, and she had been dazzled by his handsome charm and burgeoning wealth. The marriage was never destined to be a success.

Rebecca did however have some family connections in London, being her mother's home town. Her uncle Samuel Brookes had done well and become a King's Messenger. He had died in 1797 but his widow Lydia lived in Jermyn Street off Piccadilly. Rebecca would have enjoyed visiting her aunt as well as her aunt's sister in Chelsea. Also, she had an uncle on her father's side (originally from Stafford) called Samuel Peake. He had set up a retail shoe business in The Strand, very near to her father-in-law's hairdressing business. He never married but was keen to maintain his family connections and Rebecca would have found solace from her lonely world in making walking visits to him.

At this precise time, Charles would have been pre-occupied with negotiating an amicable deal with Benjamin Martin for his retirement from the partnership. This would have been a very delicate matter, probably involving long discussions with Pinder Simpson but excluding their cousin wives. Rebecca would not have been able to offer any helpful advice or to act as a sympathetic sounding board.

To be achieving what he was in his business, Charles must have had a big ego, an ego that would have needed some emotional release. And it is doubtful whether Rebecca could have satisfied that, with the distance that was developing between them. By the early nineteenth century, Covent Garden was not quite the centre of vice that it had been 40 years earlier. Harris's *List of Covent Garden Ladies* had been banned as a publication after 1793, but there seems little doubt that the necessary information could still be easily obtained 'underground'. Charles was living in the midst of this. He was young, handsome, and making large amounts of money. He could afford whatever delights he fancied and the temptation must have been irresistible. The royal family were leading the way and giving 'free living' a false sense of respectability. It is thought that between them the future Kings George IV and William IV, who were brothers, fathered at least 13 illegitimate children. The climate in London between the years 1808 and 1813 was as promiscuous as it has ever been. But the sexual freedom of Regency London had its associated dangers. Venereal diseases, and syphilis in particular, were rife. Contraception and protection, such as they existed at the time, were virtually ineffective. A product sold in his father's shop, of which Charles would have been well aware from his childhood, was the condom made from a sheep's bladder – an early attempt at contraception, but almost useless. Sexually transmitted diseases had been called the Gentleman's Diseases, but by Charles' time they were prevalent through all ranks of society. In 1813, it was estimated that 20,000 young men a year were becoming venereally infected through London's prostitutes. Charles was seeking pleasure and gratification in a very dangerous environment.

By 1813, he probably knew something was wrong. The first

signs of syphilis are painless sores around the genitals, anus or mouth – if these had appeared, he might have begun to fear the worst. Such fears would have been confirmed if he had subsequently had rashes, with a fever and general fatigue, being the secondary symptoms of syphilis. Such symptoms would have disappeared as the disease entered its latent phase and this could have given him a false sense of security. But around about 1813, Charles would have noticed some problems with his sight and this would have given him real concern as blindness was seen as a classic result of a syphilitic infection.

In 1806, Charles had become acquainted with John Weston who was running a warehouse business in The Strand. They became close friends and developed a mutual respect. Weston had given him invaluable assistance during his continuing actions against counterfeiters. After Benjamin Martin left the business, Charles was at the height of his powers, channelling all his energy into the development of his business, and probably to the detriment of his marriage. But with the onset of health problems resulting from his high living, he was stopped dead in his tracks and made to think. If his condition was going to deteriorate, he would need managerial assistance of the best quality in the business. John Weston fitted this description as perfectly as Charles could hope. In the midsummer of 1813, Charles tempted Weston with a package he could not refuse – a guaranteed salary of £1,000 per year, very big money for those times. Weston closed down his own business and accepted Charles's offer which had to include the residential accommodation at the factory. From that point on, John Weston did all the daily management and paid the forty men and boys employed.

2. Illustrations from 'A Day at Day and Martin's', *The Penny Magazine*, December 1842:
   a) Filling
   b) Sealing
   c) Labelling
   d) Packing paste-blacking

2   e) Packing warehouse

In 1811, Rebecca's father William had died in Stafford. He had three daughters by his wife Susannah Brookes, whom he had married at St George's, Hanover Square, in London in 1779. He had no sons and so, in 1792, he had passed on his business of operating The Goat's Head public house to his younger brother John. This had not worked out well. John had died young in 1798 leaving a widow and three small children who tried to carry on the business after the widow remarried. With William's subsequent death and one of his daughters now married in London to a wealthy young businessman, his widow (with her two other daughters Elizabeth and Susannah) was tempted to return to her roots. Charles, in an unhappy marriage with a baby daughter, found himself pressurised to open his doors to three more women – his mother-in-law and her two other daughters. A larger house was needed, especially as he had to move out of his existing abode to accommodate his new manager. Although not yet thirty, he was already wealthy enough to consider an extravagant option.

He found the solution in a new development to the north which was being named Euston Square. Back in the 1750s, what was to be the first of London's 'circular' roads was being built. This was what at the time was known as the New Road from Paddington eastwards to Islington. This New Road simply crossed fields in a patch of open countryside sited between what were to become King's Cross and Warren Street. In the later-eighteenth century, development from the south encroached upon the boundary of the New Road and a nursery was established at this point, known as Montgomery's Nursery Gardens. By 1812, plans were being made to enclose these gardens with a similar space to the north of the New Road, with new houses to form the enclosure under the new name of Euston Square. Although this was only about 1 mile and within walking distance from the blacking factory at No 97 High Holborn, it would be an entirely changed and improved environment for Charles' family. Charles also saw this as a wise investment for his growing wealth and decided to purchase five of the new houses, planned as the terrace bordering the north side of the square and facing south. These were Nos 1, 2, 3, 9 and 11 Euston Square and No 1 would become the new residence for his family.

With John Weston excellently fulfilling the role of production manager in the factory, Charles's business was in good hands and the profits continued to accumulate. Also, with the move to Euston Square, Charles's domestic arrangements were as good as they could be, given the addition of his wife's mother and sisters to the household. But there was still a gaping hole in Charles's life - the need for emotional fulfilment - and he was going to suffer greatly if that problem could not be solved. But worst of all, he knew he was losing his sight.

The historical period known as 'The Regency' officially began in 1811 when King George III's state of health, and mental health in particular, had sunk to a level where he was simply not able to rule the country, and all that that entailed. This final collapse (there had been others beforehand from which he had partially recovered) was largely brought on by the death of his youngest and favourite daughter, Princess Amelia. Parliament had no option but to appoint George Augustus Frederick, Prince of Wales, and first in line of succession to the throne, as Prince Regent, acting as monarch in all but name. George was already forty-nine years old and his father had been king for fifty-one years.

George had always been a man of extravagance and, with his new found status, he had no intention of changing anything. Outwardly, this was manifested by a lavish and opulent lifestyle that had resulted in mounting debts over the years. His residences were furnished and decorated with no expense spared, and he dictated a fashion of living which the public was eager to follow.

His private life was no different. Locked in a loveless but convenient and arranged marriage to his cousin, Princess Caroline of Brunswick, it was an open secret that George enjoyed the attentions of several mistresses and fathered illegitimate children, or to use the polite reference of the time 'natural children'.

His greatest passion, however, was architecture and building and he was determined to embark on some ambitious metropolitan improvements to the capital. With the help of his favoured government architect, John Nash, this was to be categorised by exuberance and experimentation. Nash had a similar easy-going approach to life and had been closely involved with the building and 'improvement' of Carlton House, George's main London residence. All styles were to be mixed together in a cocktail of liveliness and colour. If he was concerned about the country's judgement in pursuing such a course, he was given the ideal opportunity by the national sense of confidence following Wellington's victory over Napoleon at the Battle of Waterloo in 1815. Apart from anything else, this was an event which resulted in the abolition of income tax, such as it was at the time.

Various ambitious projects appeared. Property speculation at the seaside became the craze and Brighton in particular, being the nearest resort to London, developed rapidly. George wanted his 'seaside cottage' and gave Nash *carte blanche* to fulfil his wishes. The result was the bizarre Brighton Pavilion – an over-the-top confection of Indian and Chinese styles, where George could indulge in excess. After this, anything was possible. On the second anniversary of the Battle of Waterloo, 18 June 1817, a new crossing over the River Thames was opened and named Waterloo Bridge. For the Prince Regent, this was another excuse for a massive party, captured in Constable's famous painting. With the dubious importing of the Elgin Marbles from the Parthenon in Athens finally achieved in 1812, influences from ancient Greece were also introduced, notably in Sir John Soane's remarkable design for the imposing Bank of England. This was most noticeable in the St Pancras New Church, built right opposite Charles Day's new house at 1 Euston Square in the decade following his arrival there. The Greek revival design of the Inwoods, father and son, was selected and Frederick Duke of York, who was next in line of succession after the Prince Regent, laid the foundation stone on 1 July 1819. The church was built to serve the prosperous new developments on the northern boundary of London and in particular the well-to-do district of Bloomsbury. It was completed by 1822 at a cost of £76,679 and could seat 2,500 people. Its most striking feature were the four famous caryatids, statues of maidens fulfilling the role of supporting columns, who as it happened stared straight at 1 Euston Square.

There was also a flowering of the arts. Jane Austen published *Pride and Prejudice* in 1813 followed by Mary Shelley's *Frankenstein* in 1818 and Sir Walter Scott's *Ivanhoe* in 1819. John Constable was at the height of his powers but was being challenged by Charles Day's boyhood acquaintance J M W Turner, the barber's son from Covent Garden, who was receiving commissions all over the country with his new and experimental style. In 1820, as Constable was starting work on his most iconic painting *The Hay Wane*, the National Gallery was being founded. On the scientific side, the profound effect of the invention of the steam engine was being noticed. Steam-powered ships would soon be crossing the Atlantic and the era of railway travel was dawning. Another event in 1812 which would have passed completely unnoticed at the time was the birth of an infant named Charles, the son of John Dickens, a naval clerk in Portsmouth.

After 1815, with the new found national sense of certainty and prosperity, there was a boom in house building, causing the boundaries of London to expand towards, what for centuries had been known as, Marylebone Park. This had been in the ownership of the crown and let out to tenant farmers for the previous 150 years. In 1811, the crown spotted a financial opportunity. With the rapid expansion of London, more money could be made by building on Marylebone Park than by farming it. At the same time the new Prince Regent, being determined to make his mark, wanted a new summer palace in north London set in exclusive grounds. The leases on Marylebone Park were not renewed and architects were invited to produce designs for the area.

John Nash produced a scheme that was bold enough to appeal to the Prince. The area, renamed The Regent's Park, was designed as a huge circle with a lake, a canal and the new royal residence inside. It would be linked to the Prince's other home at Carlton House by a fine processional road, to be named Regent's Street. To pay for it, Nash planned fifty-six villas in the park and a series of grand Regency terraces around it.

The complete plan was never implemented because the Prince turned his attention away from Carlton House, which he eventually demolished, to the subsequent development of Buckingham Palace. The idea of a summer palace was dropped and only eight of the planned villas were built. But many elements of Nash's scheme survived. Regent's Street was built with shops covered by arcades, attracting men of rank and fortune. With the newly invented gas street lighting, commercial activity went on well into the evening. It was 'the' place to be seen for those aspiring to be 'dandies'.

The Regency dandy was a man obsessed with his sartorial elegance and appearance. He was probably self-made and keen on rising up the social ladder. He would strive to sound refined and indulge in leisurely pursuits. He would also be able to afford an aristocratic lifestyle, despite coming from the middle classes. And an essential part of his image would be his gleaming footwear - shining black boots and shoes.

About thirty years earlier, the development of 'the gentleman's club' had begun, particularly around the area of Pall Mall, conveniently close to the Prince of Wales' Carlton House. Leading the way were Boodle's and Brooks's which had emerged from Almack's, a well-known coffee house and meeting place of the well-to-do. The clubs soon became centres of gambling and drinking, where gentlemen could enjoy themselves away from their domestic restrictions at home. And a wild night could culminate in a risky trip down the back streets and alleys off St James's Street, where brothels and their associated dangers were commonplace. The cult figure in all this and the leader of contemporary male fashion was Beau Brummell who had managed to cultivate a friendship with the Prince of Wales himself. However, Brummell's excessive living finally caught up with him. He fell out of favour with royalty and eventually died in poverty in France. The cause of death was, not surprisingly, syphilis.

Whilst Charles Day probably was himself no dandy, being obsessively devoted to the unlimited prosperity of his business, there is no doubt that it would have been in his best interests to be seen to promote 'dandyism' and to identify with it – and a visit to the clubs of Pall Mall to escape from his domestic stalemate was probably a temptation he could not resist. But having a desirable residence near to the West End epicentre of 'dandyism' was essential and '1 Euston Square' was undoubtedly an address with status.

Following his move to Euston Square, Charles Day shows the first of several signs of a strongly philanthropic side to his character. In the 1813 report of 'The Northern Dispensary', he is shown on the List of Governors as subscribing two guineas per year and as a Member of the Committee. The Report begins:

The Committee, in presenting their fourth annual statement of the funds and resources of the Northern Dispensary, together with the number of patients who have received the assistance which it offers, in the different departments of medicine, surgery, and midwifery, are anxious to call the attention of the public to an Institution which has already accomplished much towards relieving the distresses of the lower classes, but which is capable of effecting a great deal more. At a time like the present, when the extraordinary severity of the winter has borne peculiarly hard upon those who depend for subsistence on their own labour, and still more upon those who are out of employment, and whom the high price of fuel and other necessaries of life has reduced to the extremity of want, the numbers who fall a prey to disease increase at an alarming extent.

In that year, 1,172 patients were taken in of whom 926 were cured and only twenty-four died. A Governor was any person subscribing one guinea per year and during that year was entitled to have one person continually on the books. The adjective 'Northern' in the title referred to the area immediately north of the City as far as Camden Town, Euston Square being central to this area, and patients had to come from within it. In other words, Charles Day was paying for the medical needs of two poor people in his vicinity for a whole year and was helping to govern the charity. These were of course the days before any welfare state when the poor were entirely reliant on the charity of the rich.

In 1815, another burden was placed on Charles' domestic circumstances. His older sister Mary had married a cousin, William Claughton Dey, in 1802 and the couple had settled in Doncaster. Between 1803 and 1813, they had four children but the marriage was never happy. By 1815, a separation was unavoidable because, as Mary later put it, William's behaviour 'was without reason harsh and violent'. She left Doncaster with the four children and went to London, falling on her brother Charles' benevolence. He made her an annual allowance which enabled her and her children to live independently but he still had the burden of responsibility.

All through this time, Charles's eyesight continued to deteriorate and by 1816 he was, to all intents and purposes, blind. Mercifully, John Weston was undertaking his managerial role at the factory to Charles's complete satisfaction and the business continued to be highly profitable. Charles was still only thirty-two but had probably deduced that he was a victim of syphilis. It was known even then that the disease was only contagious in its primary and secondary stages. These had happened over three years earlier and he was now well into the latent stage. This could give him a certain amount of freedom as he was safe in the knowledge that he could no longer pass on the disease. However, with his blindness, his movements were severely restricted and any further excursions to the clubs and beyond would be very difficult if such activities were still to remain clandestine. He was trapped and had to start thinking about a solution.

3. Competition and intellectual property

After Benjamin Martin retired from the business in 1808, Charles was clearly relishing being in charge by himself. He was already, at the tender age of just twenty-four, showing the characteristics that were going to be stamped on his entire career – a single-minded determination to achieve his goals within the bounds of fairness and ethical correctness, allied with an extraordinary mind for retaining every detail about the business and its administration. Nevertheless, from about 1811 onwards, he seems to have become increasingly frustrated by some of the behaviour of his so-called competitors.

It is almost certain that, as soon as any good commercial idea or product appears on the market and quickly becomes popular and successful, it will attract those who try to copy it. The 'Real Japan Blacking' produced by Day and Martin was no exception. Cases of counterfeiting began to emerge and Charles Day was quick and merciless in taking legal action. He could be described as ruthless, but in fact, his actions were quite justifiable and driven by his high standards of correct business ethics.

Charles Day was very able at using the most modern media advances to disseminate information. By 1810, he was advertising extensively in newspapers up and down the land. The following appeared in numerous local newspapers as well as the national press:

THE REAL JAPAN BLACKING

Made by DAY & MARTIN, London
This invaluable Composition, with half the usual labour, produces the most brilliant jet black ever beheld, affords peculiar nourishment to the leather, will not soil the finest linen, is perfectly free from any unpleasant smell, and will retain its virtues in any climate. – Sold, wholesale, by DAY and MARTIN, No. 97, High-Holborn, London; –
AND RETAIL BY THEIR AGENTS,

There would then follow a list of retail agents (ie shops) local to each specific newspaper.

But the counterfeiting was becoming extensive. His initial action was a warning to the perpetrators. This took the form of a notice dated 20 August 1810 published in over one hundred newspapers from Cornwall to Aberdeen over the forthcoming months, with the following colourful wording:

TO
COUNTRY SHOP-KEEPERS AND OTHERS.
WHEREAS a set of SWINDLERS are now travelling the COUNTRY to solicit ORDERS in the names of DAY & MARTIN, Blacking Makers, 97, High Holborn, London. Shopkeepers and others are, therefore, cautioned from the fraud that is attempted to be practiced on them, as by paying attention to the No. 97, it will easily detect the counterfeit, many of them having no number at all; and prosecutions, after this notice, will be commenced against any persons offering the counterfeit for sale.
N.B. No HALF PINTS made.
London, 20th August 1810.

But the problem persisted, and Charles tried one final approach before taking legal action, being a warning to the general public, rather than the shopkeepers. In 1812, this appeared:

DAY AND MARTIN,
Beg leave to acquaint the public that by attending to the following particulars they will avoid being taken in by the vile Compositions that are offered as the genuine BLACKING, prepared by them at 97, HIGH-HOLBORN, LONDON. After the word BLACKING, in the first line of the Labels, the Counterfeits have a small (as) some have the same before the word MADE in the next line, and others put a small (nr) immediately before the Number 97. Purchasers should observe that the whole Address is clear and distinct.

But it seems that this made little difference either and Charles had no option but to start taking some serious action as a deterrent to those who were doing wrong. With recent case history suggesting the best approach, Charles's solicitor, Richard Stephens Taylor, and barrister, Edward Wilbraham, advised that an application should be made to the Court of Chancery for 'injunctive relief'. This effectively would put a temporary stop, pending a full hearing, to any activities that Charles maintained were wrong. The defendant could only get this lifted if he had the energy to put a good case to the Court. Unlike its reputation for full hearings in the early nineteenth century, the Court of Chancery allowed these preliminary applications to be obtained quickly.

Matters came to a head when Charles Day lost his general manager, Peter Statham, on 27 May 1813. Statham went into business with one Samuel Slee and started producing blacking with the secret recipe used by his former employer. At the time, the law had little redress against former employees who did this, but Slee and Statham made the mistake of labelling their product so as to indicate that it was actually made by Day and Martin. Charles filed his bill to the Court on 5 July 1813 together with evidence from himself and, among others, one John Weston, a perfumery and medicine warehouse manager from The Strand who will feature large in Charles's business in the years to come, and the decision was briefly reported in the Morning Chronicle on 9 July 1813:

COURT OF CHANCERY.
DAY v. SLEE AND STATHAM.
Yesterday an Injunction was obtained to restrain the Defendants from affixing Labels to their Blacking, being copies used by Day and Martin, or any other Labels or description representing the Blacking to be actually made by Day and Martin.

The speed with which this was achieved must have taken everyone by surprise. Statham did put in an answer in August 1813, but it was ineffective. Matters dragged on to 1815, that being the way of things in the Court of Chancery then, and there were even letters of support for Statham and Slee in the press. But by then Statham and Slee had ceased to trade. Charles did not achieve a totally satisfactory result, but the competition had dissolved which was the main object of the exercise and his competitors now knew that he was not afraid to take legal action. In fact, this is exactly what he did, commencing six further cases between January 1814 and July 1815. In all these, injunctions were granted and none needed to be taken any further. The tactics seemed to be working.

3. A Day and Martin blacking bottle (c1815) showing the label that became intellectual property.

But the next infringement on Charles's growing enterprise turned out to be the most significant and attracted the most attention in the press. It is now seen as a landmark case in the early days of intellectual property law; and, as we shall see, there was great public interest and heavyweight argument from Charles's counsel, Anthony Hart. The decision, however, never reached the Law Reports, probably because it was made at the preliminary or interlocutory stage, i.e. before a full hearing. Determinations at the preliminary stage had become a bit of a habit in the Court of Chancery during Lord Eldon's reigns as Lord Chancellor, 1801-1806 and 1807-1827. His Lordship gained a reputation early – whether fairly or unfairly – for being slow to decide after full hearings, or indeed to hear many cases at all. But in this heavily charged political time, it was, of course, his political adversaries who levelled the charges. Even so, an extensive practice began to prevail where litigants brought major issues as motions rather than go to the delay and expense of full hearings, for the purpose of getting Lord Eldon's immediate, if somewhat gut, reaction.

In September 1815, Thomas Day (no relation) took a lease on a property at the back of 87 High Holborn, a matter of yards from Day and Martin at No 97. He then sublet the property to his son John Day who had established a partnership with Peter Martin, an illiterate gardener from Warwickshire who soon and very conveniently disappeared, being sent a very modest and occasional drawing from the business. Not surprisingly, their business was the manufacture of blacking. The labelling on the bottles was almost identical to that being used by Charles, which had now been standard for several years. There were some changes in the actual wording and the 'No 87' was substituted for the 'No 97', but otherwise the overall appearance was very similar with an almost identical typeset. Charles collected various affidavits (one of them again from John Weston) and lodged his bill with the Court of Chancery on 27 June 1816 and, as usual, the interim injunction was given pending an answer from the defendants. This, unlike many others, they did on 13 August 1816 and immediately sought a hearing to have the interim injunction lifted. The hearing took place on 16 August and the Court (the Lord Chancellor, Lord Eldon) pronounced immediately in favour of Charles; but not perhaps as straightforwardly as Charles might have wished. The next day there was a very extensive report in *The Morning Chronicle*, a full column, over 2,000 words, with which Charles must have been delighted because of the free publicity – even then, the adage 'there's no such thing as bad publicity' applied, with the attention-seeking first sentence:

> *This case excited considerable interest in the Court from some important law points connected with it, and also afforded much amusement.*

'Amusement' was not a word normally associated with the Court of Chancery and the public would have been encouraged to read on.

Charles had strengthened his legal team by adding Anthony Hart, an experienced counsel in such cases, to Edward Wilbraham, the counsel he had already engaged. The lead for the defendants was taken by Sir John Leach.

The report continued:

> *LORD CHANCELLOR – Show me the blacking bottles. It is the first time I had ever the pleasure of seeing such evidence in Court. I see you have got them labelled. Mr Hart, are your bottles also labelled?*
> *Mr. HART – Yes, my Lord. We can give chapter and verse for our statement, our bottles being signed by Mr Cox* [The Master of the Court].

LORD CHANCELLOR – I have looked at them, Mr Leach. Now I see some difference in the labels. You say, 'Stir, the blacking well,' they say, 'Stir it well with a brush or stick.' You say, 'in one minute it will make the finest jet black ever seen,' they say, 'in one minute you will have the finest jet black ever beheld.'

Mr. LEACH proceeded – Generally speaking it was no doubt impossible for two individuals accidentally to use the same terms in describing the same thing, but it was obvious that when any article of trade, in consequence of its peculiar quality, acquired a familiar name, that name or that particular mode of expressing the quality would be common to all who dealt in the article. Yet the defendants knowing the charge likely to be made against them did set their wits to work, they knew as the label of the plaintiff was entered at Stationers' Hall, and had thereby become a literary composition, they might be charged with piracy, and they therefore tried all they could to invent new terms, which he would by and by state to his Lordship. The type of both parties, however, he begged leave to say was different, the plaintiff using one forming an obtuse angle somewhat Italic, the defendants using the good old-fashioned Roman character. To show his Lordship the invention and literary talents of his clients, he would now compare the labels of both parties.

(Here the Learned Gentleman in a very humorous manner commented on both the labels to the great amusement of the Court and audience. The plaintiff called his blacking 'inestimable', the other said theirs was 'excellent'. The one that his blacking 'nourished' the leather, the other that his 'cherished' it. The one that his would keep in any 'climate', the other 'in any part of the world', &c. &c.).

It would be a new doctrine for the Court to say that a man was to be judged for his intentions, and not for his actions. When a plaintive had a monopoly by patent, let him exclusively sell - but when he has not one, let others certainly be allowed to compete with him. He asked whether his lordship thought that part of the injunction prohibiting his clients from using the words '87, High-Holborn' could stand?

LORD CHANCELLOR – 'It cannot stand, Mr Leach' – His Lordship then gave his judgement.

The Court never had or indeed could it exercise the power of preventing any man from endeavouring, by honest, fair competition with others, when no patents existed, to gain livelihood; but it never would sanction that individual selling his own articles as the manufacture of others.

He had heard a good deal today about blacking, and he confessed he had been much amused with it; but let the parties remember, that whatever the conduct might have been which called for the first application, that conduct would not in the smallest degree influence his decision now.

He was very glad to see blacking was such a valuable article now; for, if he was not mistaken, when the original partnership between Day and Martin was dissolved, the firm of the Company was mutually agreed to remain, and Martin received £10,000 as his share of the concern.

The defendants could not be prohibited from using such a firm, provided they had partners of the name to justify their using it; and it was absurd to say they were to be prevented from carrying on their business in 87, because the plaintiff carried on his at 97. They might carry it on at 96 if they chose; but still they must sell their blacking as their own, not as the plaintiff's.

Yet he (Lord Chancellor) could not help the public being misled if the defendants acted fairly; for example, on one of the bottles he had seen today, the lower part of the figure 8 was so erased as to prevent its been distinguished from a 9. The celebrity of the original Company had led them to a very great wholesale business, and persons, either in London or Edinburgh, buying retail were not always to know which Company lived in 97, and which in 87.

He knew no man who had more genius and invention than Mr Leach had; but when he gravely stated that his clients could not invent an advertisement or label totally different from the plaintiff's, he (Lord C) thought

Mr Leach did not give those clients so much credit as they deserved for their ingenuity, for they had actually shown they had some ingenuity in trying to get an injunction of this Court off their shoulders, which was a measure not very easily done, and which consequently required skill.

He disliked an expression used by Mr Wilbraham, namely, 'that the injunction would do the defendant no harm,' and he never wished such an expression to be again used. The court did not try the propriety of an injunction, by the harm it might do or not do to his Majesty's subjects, but they tried it for the purpose of preventing fraud.

As an honest man then acting with a sincere desire to do justice between man and man, he declares his firm conviction of the fraudulent intentions of the defendants, in using this firm and label.

He now, therefore, gave his decision, that the injunction should stand, but as some expressions in it might require an amendment, he would take it home with him, and return it tomorrow morning, but if the parties were dissatisfied with it, he tendered them the alternative of an issue by Jury. They might accept of either, but he declared that this was his decision.

Mr LEACH said, the solicitors on both sides would consult what they should do respecting the issue, and give an answer tomorrow.

LORD CHANCELLOR. Give me the injunction meantime, that I may erase the words, '87, High Holborn', which cannot stand, and make any alteration I see necessary, but remember it still remains in full force.

Four days later, the same newspaper reported as follows:

DAY v. DAY AND MARTIN.

Mr. LEACH said his clients had taken his Lordship's offer of allowing them to take the advantage of trial by Jury into their serious consideration, but had declined that offer, in consequence of being satisfied with his Lordship's judgment.

LORD CHANCELLOR – 'Mr. Leach, I have also duly considered the judgment I formerly gave in this blacking business; and, after the best attention I could possibly bestow on it, I see no cause whatever to alter it, as I am persuaded it is well founded. I have further to add, that I have made such alterations in the Injunction as I deemed proper and just; and, while I have altered it so far as respects the signature, I have taken care to preserve the legal rights of the new company, and at the same time to guard the original Company from being again imposed on'.

This could have been said to be a Pyrrhic victory for Charles Day. But the main objective of eliminating the competitive threat of another firm making the same product almost next door under the same name, which the Lord Chancellor said the Court of Chancery could not stop, was achieved. This was mainly because the new firm had been prohibited, in a decision which the Court of Chancery could and did make, from marketing its product in bottles with labels that could be confused by the unsuspecting public with those of Charles Day's original firm. The costs of the whole case would have also weakened the new firm far more than the established firm of Day and Martin. So, the new firm seems to have just faded away.

But the case of 'Day v Day, Day and Martin', which over the years had dissolved from public attention following stronger and perhaps more relevant cases presenting themselves as the concept of intellectual property law developed, has now been re-established as a landmark case in this field, the intellectual property being the actual wording used on the blacking bottle labels.

After this case, Charles embarked on another national campaign in the press to keep the public informed. The following appeared in *The Public Ledger and Daily Advertiser* on 25 January 1817:

FRAUD PREVENTED.
To counteract the many attempts that are daily made to impose on the unwary a spurious composition instead of the Genuine Blacking prepared by DAY and MARTIN, they are induced to adopt a new Label, in which their address,
97, High Holborn,
is placed so conspicuously, that they trust an attention to this, and the difference of the type, which is unlike all letter-press, will enable purchasers at once to detect the imposition. The Real Japan BLACKING, made by DAY and MARTIN, 97, High Holborn, will in future be sold in Bottles at 6d., 1s., and 1s. 6d. each, and a copy of the label left with all venders.
DAY and MARTIN, 97, High Holborn.

But the counterfeiters carried on. There followed seven more cases between 1816 and 1822 being presented by Charles Day in the same way, seeking injunctive relief from the Court of Chancery. The various proceedings had their interesting moments. One was based merely on a spelling mistake, the defendant having mis-spelt 'inestimable' as 'inestmiable'. In another case, Charles's counsel came out with the wonderful quote:

For who, with the slightest pretention to polish, could be unacquainted with the names of Day and Martin? Could it be necessary of those gentlemen to say, that, by stooping to the feet, they had raised themselves to the head of society?

Charles succeeded on every occasion and eventually such necessary actions became less frequent.

However, there was a further case which has become perhaps more celebrated, simply because the counterfeiter was none other the Charles's own nephew, William Charles Day, the son of Charles's older brother William. This took place in 1843, some seven years after Charles had died, but the circumstances were very similar to the case that had taken place twenty-seven years earlier, ie two different Day and Martins setting up in partnership to manufacture blacking very near to No. 97 High Holborn and using labels that differed only very slightly from those of the original business. The original business of Day and Martin had carried on after Charles's death to benefit the various annuitants mentioned in Charles's Will. The action was taken by the executors of Charles Day's estate, of whom the first mentioned was William Croft, a retired civil servant who had been responsible for the finances of the Army. The case therefore became known as 'Croft v. Day'. Inevitably, the judgment of the Court of Chancery was exactly as before, with the memorable statement being given in the judgment by the Master of the Rolls, Lord Langdale:

'No man has a right to sell his own goods as the goods of another'.

4. Edgware and the Peake sisters

By the time he was going blind in 1816, Charles was beginning to realise that living at 1 Euston Square was not providing the ideal solution for his wife and her family. What had appeared to be a location on the edge of the city in 1812 was fast being swallowed up by the creeping urban development northwards. Added to that, the extravagant living of the Prince Regent was becoming more and more unpopular, causing considerable unrest amongst the working classes. With the effects of the agricultural and industrial revolutions, working people were flooding into the cities and forming themselves into organised groups. Social reform, and electoral reform in particular, was being demanded. 'Rotten boroughs', with hardly any inhabitants, may have two representatives in parliament, whereas huge cities such as Manchester may have none. The ruling class formed a minute part of the population and they were incapable of coming forward with sensible solutions. Revolution had already happened in France and they were terrified that it would hit Britain. If there were going to be any riots, they could be happening right outside the Days' front door and this would have been of serious concern to the inhabitants of 1 Euston Square, all of whom were female apart from Charles.

People were being deprived of jobs by all the newly invented machines. Gangs of workers went about smashing up the offending contraptions. These were the Luddites, the origin of the name being uncertain, whose movement began in Nottingham and who counted Lord Byron, no less, as a sympathiser. His family seat was at Newstead Abbey in nearby Sherwood Forest. He spoke in their support in the House of Lords. Public unrest was fuelled by other unrelated factors. A volcanic eruption in 1815 on an Indonesian island was so massive that it had an effect on world climate the following year, causing disease and crop failures. The 1810s were and remain the coldest decade on record. In addition, the Prince Regent's only legitimate child, Princess Charlotte, who enjoyed considerable popularity and was seen as a future ray of hope for the monarchy, died in childbirth with her infant son being stillborn. Crowds were being whipped into a frenzy by speakers at public meetings such as Henry 'Orator' Hunt (non-violent) and Arthur Thistlewood (violent). Appalling policing at a rally featuring Hunt in Manchester resulted in the Peterloo Massacre. But even closer to home for the Days was the Cato Street Conspiracy, led by Thistlewood, which cost him his life by execution. Cato Street, where the plot to assassinate cabinet members was hatched, only to be uncovered by a double agent, was in Marylebone and uncomfortably close to Euston Square.

Charles was unwilling to relinquish a base near his work in central London but was beginning to think that an alternative country base within easy reach would be desirable, not only for his wife and family but also to give him some privacy whilst in London to indulge his 'other life'. But he would also be happy to escape occasionally from the city and enjoy the peace of the countryside.

Throughout all the preceding years of meteoric expansion of his business, he had kept in close contact with Pinder Simpson, partly because of the family connection, but principally to advise him on the investment of his excess profits in property. It is almost certain that Pinder would have helped with the Euston Square purchases and Charles's property portfolio continued to expand with the purchase of several addresses in Eagle Street at the back of the blacking factory. There were very sound financial reasons for investing in landed property. Legacy Duty had been reformed at the end of the previous century and William Pitt the Younger, the Prime Minister of the time, had initially tried to extend the tax to include landed property, but this was rejected and the duty remained only on personal property.

Pinder would have been asked by Charles to look out for any promising houses and small estates in the environs of London. He was aware of some interesting properties coming on the market around the area of Caterham in south-east Surrey. Whilst this interested Charles, the communications between northern London and Caterham were not the easiest. But this could provide investment opportunities in the future.

However, something then came on the market which seemed to fit the needs of the Day family perfectly. This was a small fifteen-acre estate to the north of London in the village of Edgware, known as Edgware Place but containing Edgware House. It could not have been more convenient for travel from London and Euston Square in particular, being situated on the old Roman road of Watling Street, a dead straight route leading out of London to the north-west. To get from Euston Square to Watling Street (later Edgware Road) was a simple route westward along the New Road (later Marylebone Road).

When the estate was being subsequently valued, the house was described by the valuer as follows:

A genteel Villa Residence, stuccoed and slated roof, with entrance portico and handsome stone steps comprising, on entrance floor, two drawing rooms with folding doors and handsome statuary chimney pieces, a good dining room and small breakfast parlour, a water closet and back steps and door into the yard. Two good bedrooms and a light closet adapted for a dressing room with a water closet adjoining, which is adapted for either of these bedrooms. Three other bedrooms, two attics and a linen closet on the stairs.

A good basement, servants hall, kitchen, scullery, larder, dairy, butler's pantry and good wine and other cellars.

There is a dry area round parts of the house and under the colonade. A way entrance door to the enclosed drying yard, which leads to an ornamental building, which is detached, with a flight of steps leading to the upper part, which comprises a billiard room, a model room or bedroom, another bedroom. Between these a washing house or laundry on one side and a four-stall stable on the opposite side and a coachhouse for two carriages. In the pleasure grounds is an ornamental dairy, well fitted up. An enclosed farm yard with a chaise house and harness room, a cow house and poultry yard, a thatched cattle lodge and a granary timber, built, boarded and tiled, and a piggery. Adjoining the above building is an apple room and gardener's room. Enclosed rick yard, kitchen garden with fish pond. The Temple at the entrance from the town of Edgware is a gardener's house, stuccoed, with a porch entrance and a garden room.

The whole area is about fifteen acres with pleasure ground and a gravel walk to lead round the paddock with a border of flowering shrubs and handsome timber and other trees, the interior containing about eight acres is luxurious meadow land.

It was the perfect fit. Charles could come and go, to and from London, conveniently as he pleased. He had his own horses and carriages and there was plenty of accommodation for them. For visitors, there were frequent mail coaches and other transports going along Watling Street between Edgware and London. There were enough bedrooms for his female retinue of wife, daughter, mother-in-law and two sisters-in-law, and spacious grounds for them to enjoy the rural atmosphere on short walks from the house. There was also ample room for the necessary servants.

The 'Temple' referred to in the above description would have been the gatehouse built subsequently by Charles and known locally as the Blacking Bottle Lodge, being built in the shape of one of Day and Martin's blacking bottles. The circular, domed-roofed lodge was surrounded by a verandah with windows on each side of the door. The chimney stack resembled the neck of the bottle, the chimney pot the cork, the door the main label and the windows were the labels extolling the merits of the bottle's contents.

4. Blacking Bottle Lodge, built about 1830 by Charles Day at the entrance to Edgware Place (this picture taken c1900) Barnet Libraries' Archives and Local Studies Centre.

The purchase was secured in 1817, to the universal delight of the whole family, with the possible exception of the ten-year-old Caroline who was beginning to appreciate and enjoy the social attractions of the city, so different for her to the boredom of life in the country.

Edgware was a staging post on the old pilgrim route between London and St Albans. As such, the central feature was very much the ancient medieval church of St Margaret of Antioch. The family were happy to identify with the farming community and they became regular attenders of the church. They began to make friends in the village and in particular, their neighbour and local physician William Foote and his wife Sarah. Let it not be forgotten that Charles achieved this move to Edgware in his new state of blindness. He never actually saw the property. With his knowledge of the likely cause of his blindness, it was probably no coincidence that he decided to befriend the local doctor.

1 Euston Square still had to be maintained as the main family residence. Charles would be there regularly attending to the affairs of Day and Martin. Although he was blind, he was still very much in charge, with John Weston being his 'eyes' in the factory. Charles would be taken to the factory whenever he could, but as a regular discipline, he and John Weston would have a meeting at the house every week to discuss current developments and to plan for the future. They would also go over the bookkeeping together. Charles had always had a good memory but, with his blindness, this if anything had been intensified. John Weston and Pinder Simpson were astonished at his ability to retain the smallest details of transactions that had taken place.

The ladies did not always stay together. Rebecca and her mother, with the complaining Caroline, became very attached to Edgware and probably spent more time out there than in the city. However, Rebecca's two sisters, Elizabeth and Susannah, welcomed the chance to have some time to themselves and quite often remained in London with Charles. Until then, Charles had not really been able to form much of a friendship with either of them but, with these new circumstances, that soon changed.

John Weston was widowed in 1818, leaving him with a son James who was then eleven years old. On his frequent visits to Euston Square, John became well acquainted with the Peake sisters, he and Elizabeth being very close in age. Elizabeth was nearing forty and single. Charles could see the sense in encouraging this friendship. If it were to blossom into something more permanent, it would establish John firmly in the family as well as the business and ensure that he would never cease to be the manager of the blacking factory. This would be very good news for Charles who had been delighted with John's performance as his manager since he had taken up the post in 1813. John and Elizabeth were duly married on 13 October 1821 in the St Pancras Old Church (the new church was under construction at the time), with Charles Day and Susannah Peake being the witnesses.

Susannah had acted as Charles's guide for the whole day, but this was not the only assistance that Susannah would be giving Charles.

The times in Euston Square with Elizabeth and Susannah, who had left Rebecca and their mother back in Edgware, gave Charles an ideal opportunity for getting to know them both much better, and he soon began to realise how different they were from his wife, especially Susannah. Rebecca and Elizabeth were very close in age – only eleven months apart, having been born in the same calendar year. But Susannah was four years younger than Elizabeth (there had been a boy William born a year before Susannah but he did not survive) and consequently she was quite an independent spirit. It soon became quite clear to Charles that, of the three Peake sisters, Susannah was by far the most intelligent, with an active brain that needed stimulation. They quickly made a strong connection and Charles soon began to realise that perhaps he had been matched with the wrong sister.

A very strong bond of friendship developed between Charles and Susannah and it was not long before Charles began to pour out his pent-up emotional feelings to her. In turn, Susannah could not conceal the fact that she had very little time for her oldest sister and that they had never been close. In fact, Rebecca had shown considerable animosity to Susannah over the years, probably revealing a certain amount of envy for her intellectual abilities. As a result, both Charles and Susannah decided not to reveal their developing friendship to Rebecca. It was best left a fairly clandestine relationship, away from the family in Edgware and reserved for London.

Susannah could see that Charles's sexual needs were not being satisfied following the cooling of his relationship with Rebecca. This had been the case since Caroline had been born more than ten years earlier and had driven him to fall prey to the dangers of the London sex trade, with the result that he was now blind having contracted syphilis. But because he was blind, his wings were clipped and the daily practicalities of moving around the city could not be achieved without considerable personal assistance.

Charles and Susannah's friendship blossomed and they became very close. There is no doubt that there was an absolute meeting of minds on an intellectual level. Unlike her sister, Susannah had an inherent understanding of business and what was entailed in the creation of added value and the consequent generation of profit. At last, Charles had found a kindred spirit – someone who understood the way his mind worked and could tolerate his obsession with his work. What is more, he realised that Susannah could understand that he was not ruthless, but fair. She could see that he had a generous spirit and conducted his affairs on the basis of a strong ethical code. He knew how to make money by sheer hard work, endeavour and a natural flair for entrepreneurship. He would only indulge in struggles against his competitors, if such struggles were motivated by self-defence. However, in such circumstances, he was merciless in his pursuit of victory, safe in the knowledge that he was morally in the right and his opponents deserved their fate. Susannah could understand this completely and would have been happy to become involved with Charles's affairs and offer her advice in the many discussions they would have and enjoy. After what had gone before, Charles would have found this extremely fulfilling. She also appreciated his generosity of spirit and philanthropy. He realised that he had a special gift for wealth creation and was prepared to give back some of this wealth to causes which he considered deserving and worthy. He was already supporting the Northern Apothecary, giving medical assistance to the needy in his area around Euston, and was beginning to formulate some ideas how to help the poor in the parish of Edgware. His blindness had also started to make him think how he could aid fellow sufferers who had been struck down under circumstances they could not control, unlike himself. He could see that, with the industrial revolution, a period of huge prosperity lay ahead, but that much of the resulting riches would stay with those who were already wealthy, and that the gap between them and the working classes would widen. He could see that social reform on a huge scale was essential but unlikely to happen in the short or even medium terms, purely as a result of human greed. In Susannah, he had at last found someone who could appreciate his point of view and behaviour.

It will never be known whether Charles and Susannah were sexually attracted to one another. If they were, it must have been a great temptation to take things a stage further and have a clandestine affair. But this would have been ridiculously risky. In Edgware, they were still spending half their lives under the same roof as Susannah's mother and sisters (one of whom was Charles's wife), who in turn made several visits to the house in Euston Square. Divorce was not an option. Apart from the fact that it would be completely unacceptable from a social point of view, the legal practicalities were problematic. The Matrimonial Causes Act, which reformed the divorce law considerably, was still nearly forty years in the future. Around 1820, divorce demanded either a complex annulment process or a private parliamentary bill, both at great cost. If anyone, Charles could probably afford this, but a private bill sometimes entailed lengthy debates about a couple's intimate marital relationship in public in the House of Commons. Nothing could be more undesirable.

But Susannah realised that something had to be done for Charles's sake. A solution had to be found and she was the only person who could find it.

Susannah tried to make trips back to her home town of Stafford as frequently as she could. This was helped by the fact that Charles had made several business connections there as retail outlets. In the late-eighteenth-century, the main industry of Stafford had become shoemaking and Pinder Simpson's father-in-law, John Ollenranshaw, was a master cordwainer in the town. The newly available product of boot-blacking would have sold well there.

The Peake surname was common in Stafford and Susannah had many relations to visit. She would have started at The Goat's Head, a public house at 91 Eastgate Street, which had been her childhood home, and the house next door at 92 Eastgate Street, both of which were now owned by her uncle Samuel Peake – he of the shoe shop in The Strand in London – but had been in the family since 1748.

Rebecca had never told Charles much about her family – she really was not very interested. Since her father's death and the move to London of her mother and sisters, she had had no reason to return to Stafford. Charles had met her uncle Samuel in London and had agreed to provide a mortgage for a property purchase in Stafford, but had not been given any of the background information. However, Susannah had always taken a keen interest in her family and Charles was eager to hear from her the full history. In another meeting of their minds, she was delighted to enlighten him.

5. The Peakes of Stafford, a likeness and lavish living

In August 1748, William Peake, a twenty-seven-year-old bricklayer, purchased two houses in his home town of Stafford, Nos 91 and 92 Eastgate Street. He paid £55 for them, a modest amount even for those times, suggesting they were in poor condition. He raised the money with a mortgage. One house had a sitting tenant, but when they both became vacant, William moved into the larger house (No 91) and between 1753 and 1755 obtained a license to sell ale and beer. This was to give him a winter income to supplement his principle income as a bricklayer or builder, which inevitably was mainly a summer activity. He renovated No 92 before letting it out to a widow.

William's personal life had been full of the usual sad events that were typical of the times. He had married a local girl, Elizabeth Foden, in 1744 and the couple had four children. But Elizabeth died after the birth of the fourth child in 1751. Of the children, only one survived into adulthood. This was Abigail who married the Stafford master cordwainer John Ollenranshaw and whose daughter Elizabeth was to marry the young Nottinghamshire land agent, Pinder Simpson.

William remarried in early 1753 just as he was establishing his new trade as a publican at 91 Eastgate Street. His bride this time was another local girl, from the nearby village of Stone, called Elizabeth Shelley and before the year was out, their first child William had been born. There followed Samuel (1756, who never married but moved to London where he operated a shoe retail business in The Strand), Jane (1758, who married Hugh Knight, a clockmaker in Stone), Michael (1760, who died as a boy in 1772) and John (1767, who would follow into the family businesses).

In 1771, William increased his mortgage to £100 and used the cash for a major renovation and enlargement of the pub, which had now gained the name of The Goat's Head. This name had been derived from the arms of the Worshipful Company of Cordwainers, dating back to 1272 when the first ordinance was set up governing the rules of the trade of shoemaking in the City of London and when cordwainers made boots from goatskins imported from Cordoba in Spain. The shield in the arms bears three goat's heads and the whole is surmounted by a further goat's head. The Eastgate Street area housed many cordwainer's workshops, whose labourers were in constant need of refreshment. William's chosen pub name was a clever piece of marketing.

He also gave No 92 a brick front and when in 1776 the house became vacant, William's oldest son William, by then aged 22, moved in. This was to fulfil an agreement that had been made after William married his second wife that No 92 would become the property of their eldest son after he and Elizabeth had both died. Young William was following his father into the bricklaying trade and No 92 had a substantial yard at the back, nineteen-feet-square and ideal to use for the storage of building materials with a lime house recently erected there (lime was an essential material both for mortar and limewash).

But young William was still single with an adventurous spirit. So, he set off for London, probably at about the same time as his younger brother Samuel. He met a girl, Susannah Brookes, and they were married in what was probably a quiet affair on St Valentine's Day, 14 February 1779, at St George's, Hanover

Square, in wealthy Mayfair, where his niece Elizabeth would marry Pinder Simpson twenty years later. There were four weddings in the church that day, all with a witness in common (probably the verger). But with a house and a trade waiting for him back in Stafford, and having achieved the main reason for his time in London, young William took his bride back to his home town. Their first child, a daughter Rebecca, was born in January 1780, very quickly followed by another daughter Elizabeth in December of the same year. Their third pregnancy produced the long-awaited son called (not surprisingly) William in January 1783, but tragically he died soon afterwards. A third daughter, Susannah, was born in January 1785.

Amongst all this family activity and with The Goat's Head going very well, in 1783 old William, by then aged 62, decided to hand over his bricklaying business to young William and concentrate on the pub at No 91. Young William and his family were established in No 92, which was still owned by his parents but held in trust for him until after their deaths.

However, old William was ageing and wisely decided to make plans through his Will. With his eldest son well established, he needed to allow for his other three children. Samuel was running his own business in London and (in the terms of the earlier settlement) would inherit No 92 if young William did not have a son. Jane was married to her clockmaker in Stone and quite safe. This left the youngest son John and consequently he made careful provision for him in the Will.

John had been working in the bricklaying business with his brother, but old William directed in his Will that after his death, his friend Charles Clark should decide how long his widow Elizabeth was capable of managing The Goat's Head, implying that she was clearly doing so up to that point, without diminishing the value of the business. The Will further said that, when her capability ceased, the business should be offered to John at a fixed price of £190.

The Will was dated 14 January 1789 and old William died on 2 April 1789 at the age of sixty-eight. In fact, his wishes were only partly carried out. Elizabeth only held the license until the following year when John took it over at the age of only twenty-three. However, he did not own the property. The Will was never proved formally and the executors (son Samuel Peake and son-in-law Hugh Knight) technically continued to hold the titles in trust for Elizabeth.

On 7 March 1791, in St Mary's Collegiate Church, Stafford, John married Sarah Hammersley, the daughter of another family of local pub and shop owners but with Quaker origins dating back to the English Civil War. She was pregnant at the time and their first child, a healthy boy called William (the family tradition had to be continued) was born 4 months later. In 1793, another son John was born but he only survived for four months. In 1794, they were blessed with a daughter Mary but she barely survived three months. Another daughter Sarah was born on 26 June 1795 and she showed all the promise of a healthy future, to the great relief of the parents. A further son John, named after his father and deceased elder brother, arrived on 7 July 1797. The Goat's Head had a content young family *in situ* with grandmother Elizabeth happily helping with the day-to-day running. But further tragedy struck in April 1798 when the young father John was taken from them at the age of only thirty. He left his wife Sarah, and their three children aged only six, two and 9 months.

Meanwhile, young William continued to run the family bricklaying business successfully and was now describing himself as a mason rather than a bricklayer. He had benefitted from a better education than his father (who could only sign his Will with his mark X) as can be seen from the flowing signature on his marriage document. Soon after his father's death in 1789, he was able to move out of the fairly small No 92 with his wife and three daughters into a larger house, leaving No 92 to be let and his mother to benefit from the income. But with John's death in 1798, fresh arrangements needed to be made and the mother decided to move out of The Goat's Head into No 92, where she could be independent but still offer help to her grieving daughter-in-law, who took over the license.

Grandmother Elizabeth eventually died in 1802 and so young William finally inherited No 92, where he used to live but which was now too small for his family. Consequently, for a short while the house was let.

Not surprisingly, and probably out of a certain necessity, Sarah remarried in 1799, her new husband being John Matthews, a local blacksmith and fourteen years her junior. The Goat's Head already had extensive stables at the rear, probably linked to the horse fairs held in Eastgate Street several times a year. John Matthews added a shoeing forge and continued to work as a blacksmith as well as becoming the licensee of The Goat's Head in 1800. But old William's executors finally had his Will proved and decided to proceed with the long overdue sale of the premises to repay the outstanding borrowing on the mortgage. In June 1803, the following notice appeared in the Staffordshire Advertiser:

татTO BE SOLD BY AUCTION
By Mr. Henshaw
At the Goat's Head in Stafford, on Monday the 25th
day of June, 1803, at 4 o'clock in the afternoon.

All that the said Public House known by the sign of the Goat's Head, situate in or near the Pig Market. The House contains good cellaring, two parlours, kitchen, brewhouse, five chambers and two attics. The Yard is entire and contains stabling for near twenty horses, and a Blacksmith's Shop. The whole are now occupied by Mr John Matthews, who will shew the same.

The house is eligibly situated for market and other business, and has been well frequented for more than half a century.

Further information may be had from Mr SECKERSON, Solicitor, Stafford.

The auction did not go according to plan and the reserve price was not achieved. This gave Samuel Peake the opportunity to raise the money and purchase No 91, knowing that he would eventually inherit No 92.

Meanwhile, life in the Goat's Head continued to be a struggle. Over the next ten years, Sarah and John Matthews had four sons, two of whom died as small children. John was more interested in his blacksmith trade, leaving Sarah to run the pub. By 1805, it was too much for her and they relinquished the license, moving into No 92 with the blessing of young William (her brother-in-law and landlord), the blacksmith business being based in the back yard. However, tragedy struck again for Sarah in 1814 when John Matthews died at the age of only thirty-seven, leaving her a widow for the second time. By this time, her two Peake sons, William and John, were twenty-three and seventeen respectively and making their own way in the world (they both set up small businesses in Coventry, William as a shoe retailer and John as a grocer). This left the Peake daughter, Sarah aged nineteen, alone with her mother. They needed income from work, and it must be fairly certain that they continued to be employed in the pub by the latest license holder, Thomas Lea.

In the meantime, in 1806, young William's daughter Rebecca, by then aged twenty-six, had married Charles Day, the dashing young businessman from London who was doing extremely well for himself in his fast-growing business. Rebecca had always been a quiet girl and the family were slightly surprised by the union. Nevertheless, Rebecca left the comfortable home of her parents, who had now retired from their own businesses, and began her new married life in London. Her two sisters, twenty-five-year-old Elizabeth and twenty-one-year-old Susannah, were left behind with their parents, somewhat jealous and frustrated. That situation continued for five years until the father died in 1811, leaving behind his widow and two spinster daughters. They soon decided that life would offer them more if they moved to London and shared the new house being built by Charles in Euston Square.

On his older brother's death in 1811, Samuel inherited No 92 but was happy for his sister-in-law to continue to live there, especially after her second husband, John Matthews, died in 1814.

And so it was that, towards the end of 1820, Susannah Peake came back to Stafford from London to visit her family and her old haunts, finding her cousin Sarah, by then aged twenty-five and still single, living with her mother and with her life going nowhere. Although there was a ten-year difference in age, they had always had a good relationship growing up together, with their fathers working side by side in the same family business (although Susannah's family had moved out of the pub before Sarah was born). Susannah was pleased to discover that she and Sarah were still soulmates, sharing the same realistic and progressive outlook on life. They realised they could be a team, making a virtue of the fact that their differing personalities, Susannah the extrovert and Sarah the introvert, could be complementary to each other. During the visit, they had long chats together and Sarah's frustrations at being restricted to a life in Stafford became all too clear. Susannah began to formulate a plan for her and Sarah's future, which, if it were to reach fulfilment, could provide happiness for more than just the two of them.

Susannah suggested to Sarah a move to London and she had no hesitation in accepting. They returned to the capital together to start what would be a new life for both of them.

5. Sarah Peake 'Price', a photograph taken in her brother's home town of Lichfield, probably in 1868 on her journey north to her new home in Scotland

During the Regency, it was fashionable with those in the moneyed classes to have their portrait painted. Photography was still at least twenty years away and those who could afford it would naturally wish their likeness to be preserved for future generations. Charles Day was no exception.

Quite an industry had developed around portraiture at that time. Most artists considered history painting a higher art form than portrait painting. But portrait painting was significantly more lucrative, so many swallowed their pride and applied themselves to portraits. A few of the more talented artists, most often members of the Royal Academy of Art, did not wholly abandon history painting. In between portraits, they plied their brush on grand history paintings, which they might submit for the Academy's annual exhibition. Having a portrait painted by an artist who was a member of the Royal Academy was quite expensive, which meant that only the wealthy could afford such portraits. Those of the lesser gentry or the merchant classes might have their portraits painted by professional portrait painters who worked exclusively in that genre. Such artists were skilled enough to capture an adequate likeness of their subject, at a much lower cost than an Academy painter might charge. In most cases, these portraits would not be considered great art, but in the absence of photography, they were often cherished as the only image of a loved one. There were also itinerant artists who made their living travelling the country, stopping here and there to paint a portrait wherever they could get a commission.

Charles Day decided to have his portrait painted. The result was a very fine, short half-length, oil portrait on canvas. Unfortunately, even accomplished artists rarely signed their work, so it will probably never be known who created this likeness. It goes without saying that Charles would have spent a considerable sum of money on commissioning this portrait – probably several tens of guineas, or more. Given that he was very wealthy and expected to have the best of everything, it seems quite likely that he would have commissioned a member of the Royal Academy to undertake the task. It was however ironic that he could never actually see the result because of his blindness.

The most famous portrait painter of the Regency was Sir Thomas Lawrence. From humble origins in Wiltshire, he had risen to be the chosen portrait artist for monarchs, aristocracy and statesmen. And his fame spread beyond the UK, with an extensive European tour being undertaken from 1818 to 1820. From 1814, his studio was in Russell Square, a mere ten-minute walk from Charles' home at 1 Euston Square. With money no object for Charles, we could expect him to go for the best, especially when the best was just down the road. But tempting as it might be to adopt this theory, the style of the painting definitely does not fit with that of Lawrence or his studio.

Having commissioned the artist, Charles was likely to have been taken to the artist's studio for two or three sittings of about a couple of hours each. He probably changed into the very smart clothes depicted, and left them with the artist after the sittings so that the non-facial elements of the painting could be completed in the artist's own time. Charles would have been given the option of choosing the size of the portrait as well as its extent (from only the head to full length). Its modest size ($22\frac{1}{2}$ ins. x $18\frac{1}{2}$ ins.) and subject matter (short half length) suggested a certain economy to be offset against the quality of the artist.

Charles was depicted as a handsome and confident young man about town – the archetypal Regency 'dandy'. The artist had not shied away from displaying something of his visual impairment. There was a slight squint between the eyes and it would appear that one of them may have been artificial. Quite likely, the artist had flattered his appearance somewhat, and only a guess can be made as to the extent of his blindness from the portrait.

It is impossible to be precise in dating male images from the early nineteenth century simply from the dress worn. The rise in the wearing of trousers from the late 1810s onwards helped to date full-length portraits, but most paintings, like this one, portrayed only the more standardised upper dress items. Going by Charles's overall appearance and the more detailed features of his attire – his oiled hair, prominent sideburns and form of his garments, especially his waistcoat colour and narrow style of his coat - it is most likely the portrait dates from the period 1813-1820.

At this time, fashionable male dress, as worn by the urban moneyed classes, reached unprecedented heights of style and quality. The principle elements were the frock coat, inner waistcoat, shirt and neck cloth or cravat. The coat, invariably black or dark-coloured, was often double-breasted, fastening with metal buttons, as here. The coat skirt would be cut away at the waist or sloped back to a tail behind. No doubt, Charles had his coat professionally made-to-measure from the finest English broadcloth, which was the best cloth for tailors to work with and gave the smoothest fit. It was probably tailored in the Savile Row district, emerging in the early 1800s as the centre of superior male tailoring throughout Europe.

The inner waistcoat, also a bespoke garment, was often buff-coloured, as here. The shirt was made of the finest linen, such as lawn, the starched collar set high, resting on the jawline. The cravat/neck cloth, also of fresh white linen, would be expertly tied and arranged. Here Charles had a plain neckband above a frill. Spotless white linen was recognised as the mark of a gentleman and a key element of the impeccable, understated elegance so admired at this time. Charles looks to be aged here in his thirties, or thereabouts, and this confirms the date of the portrait as around 1820 when Charles would have been thirty-six.

So, it is likely that this portrait was a recent acquisition when Susannah Peake returned from Stafford with her twenty-five-year-old cousin Sarah, and admired it hanging proudly in the drawing room at 1 Euston Square. Susannah would have shown her great pleasure at the outcome of Charles' commission, reassuring for Charles in his blindness, and at the same time would have introduced him to her cousin Sarah. Apart from the servants, Charles was alone in the house at the time, the rest of the family having remained in Edgware where they felt safer. He was having to attend to the flourishing business of Day and Martin and working closely with John Weston, his manager who was still fairly new in the job.

Susannah had realised that Charles needed a permanent attendant when he was alone in the house in London, away from the family. He was blind but, being only in his mid-thirties, was still physically active and certainly no invalid. He required someone to be in the house at all times when he was there, to guide him around, fetch things that he required and generally to be at his beck and call. Susannah was far too engaged with diverse matters, both in London and with her ageing mother in Edgware, to fulfil this task, nor did she really want to. Sarah seemed the ideal candidate. They had discussed this before leaving Stafford. Although the work would not be particularly taxing, Sarah was so much in need of a change that this job, with the added benefit of living in comfortable surroundings in London, was particularly attractive. Susannah was confident that she could persuade Charles to take Sarah in as a member of his household staff, but with a specific job to do. She discussed the matter with him later in the day and he accepted the idea immediately, seeing the necessity for the post and particularly confident as the recommendation had come from the respected Susannah.

Susannah had to admit to herself that an extra benefit had crossed her mind. Such a role would have normally been undertaken by a manservant. But there was no reason whatsoever why the duties could not be undertaken by a woman and Charles had a particular need for female company. Sarah was no great beauty – Charles was blind – but anything she lacked in physical appearance was made up by a caring and attractive personality.

There was a spare room in the servants' quarters and Sarah moved in that night, starting her duties the next day. Susannah was able to stay around initially, but Sarah learned the geography of the house quickly and was soon able to do anything Charles requested. After a few days, Susannah was confident to leave them alone. Sarah soon realised that, if Charles had a visitor (be it John Weston, Pinder Simpson or any other of his advisers), she could leave him with them. If the visitor was a stranger, she would take them into the room, introduce them to Charles and then wait for Charles to dismiss her. Otherwise, she would always remain in the room with Charles and do anything he requested. Charles seemed to enjoy her company. They chatted all the time and he was gratified by the interest she showed in him and his affairs – something his wife Rebecca had never done, with her limited intellectual capacity. It was very rare that Charles asked to be left alone. In effect, Sarah soon became his companion, just as Susannah had hoped.

Charles did, of course, make regular trips back to Edgware to be with his family – wife Rebecca, daughter Caroline, mother-in-law Susannah and sister-in-law Elizabeth – and his other sister-in-law Susannah usually went with him. Sarah merely remained at her new home in Euston Square to await Charles's return and the resumption of her duties. In Edgware, Susannah told her family how cousin Sarah had come up to London from Stafford with her, and Charles had taken her into his employment as a personal attendant. Rebecca had not seen Sarah since she had left Stafford in 1806 when Sarah was merely eleven-years-old – she could hardly remember her. Whilst she felt slightly uncomfortable about having a member of her family being on the household staff, she realised the necessity of the appointment and the advantage of knowing the background of the person filling it. On the rare occasions she visited London, she was aware of Sarah's presence but hardly acknowledged it. This was not a rebuff in any way. She merely did not have the confidence to decide what to call her – 'Peake' as a member of staff or 'Sarah' as a member of the family. It was easier just to ignore her. Susannah had a quiet word with Sarah, who quite understood the situation and was in no way offended.

Quite often, when Charles and Susannah returned to London from Edgware, Elizabeth would go with them, needing some relief from the slightly suffocating family atmosphere at Edgware Place. She enjoyed London and the freedom of being able to go about the city as she pleased and in complete anonymity. In this way, in 1821 she had met and married John Weston, who had thus become part of the family to Charles's particular delight. They lived in the domestic accommodation at the blacking factory in High Holborn.

But Susannah could tell that Charles was needing another project to provide stimulation. He had now been living at 1 Euston Square for about 8 years. London was expanding rapidly to the north and the property was already much less desirable than it had been. The main reason for this was the advent of the newest from of transport – the railways. The United Kingdom was now in the grips of the Industrial Revolution and the ability to transport goods in bulk quickly from one destination to another was essential for the country's economic growth. The railways were the perfect solution and the technological development of the steam engine was encouraged as a top priority. The capital city, London, would obviously be the hub of any railway network and terminuses in the city were essential, especially on the north side to serve the great industrial areas in the north of England. Euston was soon identified as a perfect site for such a terminus. As a result, Charles was to find himself living in a hive of activity rather than on the quiet outskirts of the city. The house would remain a good investment property, being an ideal residence for railway executives, but not one for the London residence of Charles and his family. Something else had to be found, and the answer was not that far away.

John Nash had planned Regent's Park with fifty-six surrounding villas, but only eight had been built. Charles soon identified a suitable site at the north side of the New Road (now Marylebone Road) where it met Harley Street. The site was right on the edge of Regent's Park which was clearly going to be preserved as a park with no prospect of development. There was room for a small mansion house and a sizeable garden. It was perfect and would showcase Charles's status as one of the most successful businessmen and entrepreneurs in London. On 18 June 1823, the following notice appeared in the London newspapers:

> *The first stone of Harley House, in the New-road, for the town residence of CHARLES DAY Esq. was yesterday deposited by his daughter, to commemorate her birthday, officially assisted by the architect and the respective artificers; upon which occasion she ordered the men to be treated with good old English Cheer.*

It is believed that Charles laid out between £60,000 and £100,000 (approaching £10m in current values) on this whole project. The obvious name for the new residence would be 'Harley House'. Charles was making a big statement – he had arrived.

6. Harley House, Regent's Park, built by Charles Day in 1824 as his London residence. This etching appeared in the Illustrated London News on 11 October 1856 when it was the leased residence of the Queen of Oude (part of modern India) during her visit at that time.

In addition to the thriving business of Day and Martin, the planning and execution of the Harley House project would have kept him well occupied in the years between 1820 and 1824 when the house was ready for occupation. This was the public image of Charles Day. However, he also had a private life which was due to blossom, but could only do so under the cover of complete anonymity.

6. Births, deaths and almshouses

Life settled down quickly after Sarah's arrival in London. She realised the extent of her duties and would never be afraid of taking initiative if it was required. She and Susannah spoke on a regular basis and Susannah was delighted with the way the arrangements she had planned were falling into place.

More importantly, Charles was also very pleased with his new personal assistant. Inevitably, Sarah's work involved a certain amount of physical contact with Charles in guiding him around the house. Charles could not deny that he enjoyed this as well as Sarah's general feeling of companionship. Before long, they both began to realise that there was perhaps more physical contact between them than there needed to be and neither of them wished to show any resistance. They became the best of friends and inseparable when Charles was at Euston Square. What is more, Charles had every excuse to stay in London because of his business and also the overseeing of the construction of Harley House. He did of course visit the family in Edgware occasionally but his eagerness to return to London was not just explained by responsibilities at Day and Martin and Harley House.

And so, 1820 passed followed by 1821 with a highlight towards the end of the year when John Weston married Elizabeth Peake. But all through this time and into 1822, Charles's relationship with Sarah gradually developed. His family in Edgware observed him as being happier than ever, despite his blindness, but they were in the dark as to the real reason.

Early in 1822, Charles decided to revise his Will which he did through discussions with Pinder Simpson. Being solely a conveyancer, Pinder was not able to draft the Will, but with Charles's permission, he approached a respected attorney, Alexander Sidebottom, to finalise the legal document. The Will was complicated and left many annuities to his wife, daughter, parents, siblings and his mother's relations, but Pinder was also intrigued that a generous annuity of £200 was included for Susannah Peake as well as an annuity of £20 for Sarah Peake. He asked no questions.

It was not long before Charles's inevitable invitation to Sarah to come to his bedchamber at Euston Square. They had to be careful – there were other staff sleeping in the servants' quarters – but Sarah crept out of her room at dead of night and was welcomed into Charles's open arms.

In August 1822, Sarah whispered in Charles's ear the news that in turn made him thrilled and worried – she was pregnant. Quick decisions had to be made as to how scandal was to be avoided and the whole affair covered up. Sarah had to disappear quickly before her pregnancy became obvious. Charles would have to rely on Susannah to be the mastermind behind the meticulous arrangements.

Charles could only confide in the people who were closest to him and whom he knew he could trust. Like most people, that would firstly mean his parents. Francis Day had by now retired from his hairdresser's business in Covent Garden and was living in Greenwich with his wife Susannah. They knew that Charles's marriage was not particularly happy and were not at all surprised to hear of his fruitful relationship with his wife's cousin. They were also relieved that the illness that had caused their son's blindness had not affected his fertility.

Susannah Peake asked Charles whether his more distant relations could perhaps help. She certainly knew there were no options open in her family back in Stafford. Francis's family, with whom he had largely lost contact after moving to London over fifty years earlier, were based in far off Yorkshire and could offer no solution. Charles's siblings were all busy with their own families and still largely based around London which was too close for comfort. So, the focus inevitably moved to his mother's family, the Parsons from Lewes in Sussex.

Charles's mother Susannah came from a large family. She was the third on ten children. Her next sibling had been Elizabeth, Francis's first and late wife. After Elizabeth came Ann, and in their childhood, these three sisters were close and built up a lasting bond. Elizabeth's death fifty years earlier had shocked Susannah and Ann and they had always maintained close contact thereafter, although Susannah was in London and Ann in Brighton.

Ann had married one Samuel Virgo, also from Lewes and a trunk-maker by trade. They had settled in Brighton and had had five daughters and a son, Samuel. This son had always been a 'black sheep' in the family, a reputation that had certainly been transmitted to Charles over the years. He had been disowned by his family and little was now known of him. Of the five daughters, the youngest had died as an infant, two were still unmarried, one was married in London, but the oldest had just returned to Sussex from Suffolk and her family was still expanding.

Ann Virgo was by now a widow aged sixty-eight, but an experienced mother and grandmother. Her oldest daughter, also Ann, was now back in Brighton with her young but growing family. To Charles's mother, Susannah, this seemed a perfect situation to where the pregnant Sarah Peake could be sent to have her child under complete cover, away from London but not too far away.

Susannah approached Ann with her proposition and Ann loyally agreed to fulfil the plan.

Hurried arrangements were made and Sarah left for Brighton almost immediately. A story had to be invented as to why she had left Charles's service so quickly. This was easy. It was said that she had found the work somewhat tedious and was looking for something more interesting. It was maintained that the employment with Charles was always a fairly short-term arrangement until she became more established in London. But this story only needed to be used if Rebecca and the rest of Charles's family were to ask what had happened to Sarah. Susannah Peake was of course masterminding the whole operation.

Meanwhile, Rebecca's attentions, and to a lesser extent Susannah's, were being taken up by a major domestic upheaval at Edgware – the final illness and eventual death of their mother who had moved down to London after her husband's death in 1811. She died on 4 October 1822. Charles had already thought about opening a family vault in the churchyard at Edgware with his ageing parents in mind. But he thought it might be an appeasing, not to say diverting, gesture to do this now and make his late mother-in-law the first occupant. He commissioned an impressive stone sarcophagus and a site was chosen just beyond the east end of the church. The committal took place a fortnight later. A plaque was placed on the tomb and the Peake sisters were duly touched. But the effect on Rebecca of losing her mother was quite profound. For nearly ten years, she had had the constant companionship of her mother and two sisters. However, since the acquisition of Edgware Place, she saw even less of her husband, whilst Susannah, to whom she was never close, also seemed to spend most of her time in London and Elizabeth had moved there permanently on her marriage the previous year. Now her mother had died, leaving her alone except for the slightly trying company of her precocious fifteen-year-year-old daughter Caroline. As a result, she retreated even more into herself and became even less attractive to Charles.

7. The Day Tomb, St Margaret's Church, Edgware, in its current state. The vault was opened by Day following the death of his mother-in-law Mrs Susannah Peake on 4 October 1822.

However, the most urgent arrangement for Susannah to make was the eventual living accommodation of Sarah and her child. Charles was adamant that Sarah should remain part of his life and that he should be a caring father to her child. This could only mean that she lived somewhere in the vicinity of Marylebone and not too far from Charles's new residence of Harley House, by now well under construction.

To the west lay the land which formed the Portman Estate. This dated back to the sixteenth century, when Sir William Portman, Lord

Chief Justice to King Henry VIII acquired 270 acres of the Manor of Lileston (which became Lisson). Most of the land remained farmland and meadow until the developments of the mid-eighteenth-century when Henry William Portman, a descendant of Sir William, created Portman Square in 1764, with buildings by James Wyatt, Robert Adam and James 'Athenian' Stuart.

Portman Square was the focus of the new estate and was followed by the building of Manchester Square during the 1770s and Bryanston and Montagu Squares thirty years later. The area remained largely residential, attracting the prosperous middle class who wanted to live near the centre of London. There were also mews for tradesmen and servants. Development of the area north of the Marylebone Road around Dorset Square continued after 1815, and to the north west in Lisson Green, workers' cottages were built from 1820 to 1840.

Whenever Susannah Peake and Charles Day commuted between Euston Square and Edgware, they noted all these developments progressing quickly, Susannah describing them in great detail to the blind Charles. In particular, after they turned north off the New Road and onto the Edgware Road, she could see the start of the building of the workers' cottages in a new street that was named Earl Street. She reckoned that this would be an ideal place to house Sarah and her new child. It would be in the vicinity of Harley House and not far off the route between there and Edgware. In fact, the houses were not cottages as such, but rows of terraced two-storey houses. Individually they were incongruous and thus inconspicuous, one from another. This would be ideal for the required purpose. It was just a question of approaching the Portman Estate office and arranging a lease, a task that was achieved with relative ease. However, it was a question of being put on a waiting list as the houses were still being built.

9. The likely appearance of 29 Earl Street (now Broadley Street), Marylebone, the first residence from 1823 of Sarah Peake 'Price' with her infant sons Henry and Alfred.

There was another serious and significant problem that had to be solved – the child's identity. It would be far too risky to use Day as a surname, and the mother's name of Peake was also out of the question, being the maiden name of Charles's wife from whom all knowledge of the pregnancy had to be excluded. The only option was to invent a new name, which would also have to be adopted by Sarah as a new surname. A common surname for the time would seem a sensible idea, and Charles and Susannah decided on Price as a suitable choice, there being an abundance of Prices in London at the time. Using the same theory for a Christian name, the child's father would be referred to as John Price and the lease for the house was therefore made under this name. The fact that the Portman Estate seem to muddle this with 'Pierce' was an error that Susannah made no effort to correct, improving the smokescreen even more. Henceforth, Sarah Peake was to become Sarah Price.

With these arrangements being determined, Sarah disappeared to Brighton and the safe haven of Ann Virgo's modest and obscure home. Sarah kept in touch with Susannah by letter and Ann also kept her sister, Charles's mother, in the picture. Charles was very anxious to hear any information from any source as Sarah's pregnancy progressed. Charles ensured that the Virgo household in Brighton was kept well-endowed as a mark of his gratitude to them. But because of his blindness, this could only be done with the help of the only other person who had direct access to his money, his loyal and faithful clerk, Robert Barbrook, who was based at the blacking factory at 97 High Holborn. Charles and Susannah agreed that Barbrook had to be trusted and should be taken into their confidence. A local boy, he had worked for Charles since an early age and Charles had spotted his ability with figures. He was now in his mid-twenties and had worked his way up to being Charles's clerk and bookkeeper, and as such the necessary confidentiality had been impressed upon him. Barbrook accepted his instructions and understood the complete discretion that was required of him. He undertook to make the payments to the Virgos of Brighton as required.

Eventually the eagerly awaited news arrived. Sarah had given birth to a healthy boy on 20 February 1823. All had gone very well and Sarah had derived much comfort and support from Aunt Ann's daughter, also Ann, who was slightly older than her but had given birth to her fifth child Martha just a year earlier. It was decided that the boy would be called Henry, being a name not common in either the Day or the Peake families, and should be brought up and known as Henry Price. If anyone were to ask about his father, John Price, it could just perhaps be said that he was a seaman and was always away on voyages.

There was no rush to return to London. The house in Earl Street was still under construction and would not be ready for occupation until after July. Charles insisted that, with the approval of the Virgo family, Sarah and the baby should stay on with them in Brighton, or Brighthelmstone as it was still known at the time. This approval was readily given, encouraged by the continued financial support from Charles. Sarah and the baby benefited from the summer sea air. She regained her strength whilst young Henry thrived.

However, amongst all this joy, some sadness came into Charles's life. His father had worked on at his hairdresser's shop in Covent Garden until 1820, latterly describing himself as a 'perfumer'. He had retired to Greenwich, but died there on 17 September 1823 at the age of seventy-six. His had been an extraordinary life. The second son of a master joiner in Yorkshire, he had had to seek his own trade and then, in just his early twenties, had ventured to London and set up his own business. Personal tragedy with the death of his first wife did not dampen his determination to succeed and he carried on his business for nearly fifty years, never afraid to move with the times nor to help his son with the risks taken in his early entrepreneurial career. Charles, in whom his father's genetics had been amplified, had had an inspiring example to follow and now wanted to show his gratitude with a fitting burial and memorial. His father would be interred in the new family vault at Edgware with a suitable plaque being added to the side of the sarcophagus. Francis's mortal remains were laid to rest there on 4 October 1823.

By the autumn, the Earl Street house was ready and, with Charles's eager anticipation, Sarah and her baby son returned to London to start a new life. Susannah suggested that she should move in with them and Charles readily agreed. The house did not have the status that would merit servants living in, but Susannah was happy to fulfil this function. This resulted in her having to spread herself thinly, as Charles needed her assistance and company at Euston Square whilst her mother and sister still expected to see her in Edgware. It was imperative they knew nothing about the Earl Street house and Charles's second family.

Charles naturally wanted to visit Sarah and his baby son as often as possible. But the staff at Euston Square must be kept in the dark about what was happening. Conveniently, he was having to go regularly to oversee the work at Harley House and Susannah would arrange to go with him on some of these visits. He was blind but otherwise fit and, with her guiding him, he could easily manage the mile's walk from Harley House to Earl Street and back. His coachman would take them to Harley House early in the morning with instructions not to collect them until the early evening. As a result, Charles was able to spend many happy days over the winter of 1823/24 with Sarah and their new son, away from any prying eyes. Susannah would tactfully leave them alone whilst busying herself with household tasks.

Everything went perfectly and it was no surprise in the summer of 1824 when Sarah announced to Charles and Susannah that she was expecting again. This time, with the clandestine arrangements at Earl Street well established, there was no need to evacuate to Brighton. Sarah was confident that, with Susannah's help, her confinement and eventual childbirth could be managed by her remaining in her new home. This would also be much easier for Henry's care in the meantime. Charles agreed, but was prepared to enlist the best medical help if necessary.

The rest of 1824 up till Christmas passed by in expectant domestic bliss.

It was thought that Sarah's second child would be due towards the end of December 1824. Consequently, without the rest of the family knowing his ulterior motive, Charles decreed that Christmas should be spent at the newly-completed Harley House. What better way to celebrate moving into their new high-status residence on the edge of Regent's Park? He was, of course, wanting to be as near to Sarah as possible for the imminent birth of the child. Susannah made excuses for frequent visits out of Harley House. She was of course going to visit Sarah to make sure all was well.

On Christmas Day, Susannah was able to tell Charles quietly that she thought the birth was going to be soon. By Boxing Day, she knew she had to be with Sarah constantly and absented herself from the family walks in the park, and the visit from John and Elizabeth Weston, it being Elizabeth's birthday. She returned to Harley House late that night and waited for the rest of the family, except Charles, to retire. She could then whisper to him the great news that he had another son and all was very well.

The family were soon dismissed back to Edgware, with Charles remaining in London for the good reason that he would be having his usual annual inventory of all his property and monetary assets with Pinder Simpson, which happened at the end of every calendar year. Pinder had asked that they could be joined by his son John who was now training as a solicitor and whom Pinder was already seeing as his successor. Charles was happy to accede to this request, helped (unknown to the Simpsons) by his own high spirits.

At the first opportunity, he and Susannah set off by foot to Earl Street. Neighbours in the nearby houses, all good working folk who would have had no idea with whom they were dealing, were rallying round and giving Sarah some immediate help when Susannah was absent. Apart from anything else, care had to be given to young Henry, by now approaching his second birthday. Charles was overjoyed to hold his new son in his arms. Again, they wisely chose a name that was not common to either the Day or Peake families, this time the choice being Alfred.

They also began to think about baptism, something that had been impossible when Henry was an infant, following his secretive birth in Brighton. All infants were baptised as a matter of course. Baptismal records kept by the parish churches were the only form of recording the existence of a child, formal state registration still being some years in the future. A large new parish church was just being completed nearby at Bryanston Square, to be known as St Mary's. But the building was not fully operational yet and baptisms would not commence for several months to come. Otherwise, the nearest church was the St Marylebone Parish Church which happened to be almost opposite Harley House on the New Road.

Baptismal services were private affairs between the clergy and each individual family and could happen on any day during the week. The clergy would record the baptism in a day book, from which the details were extracted for recording in the main parish register. An appointment was booked for Alfred's baptism to take place on Wednesday 12 January 1825, his baptism being the first of twelve that took place in the busy church that day. A father had to be present and this could obviously not be Charles. He asked Robert Barbrook to stand in, he being the only other male who actually knew the truth. Robert duly assumed the pseudonym of John Price for the course of the service and all went without hitch. Alfred's baptism was recorded in the records of St Marylebone Parish Church, he being stated as the son of John and Sarah Price, 29 Earl Street, and born on 26 December 1824. The father's occupation was merely stated as 'Gentleman'.

With the arrival of Henry and Alfred, it set Charles thinking again about the contents of his Will, especially as his total wealth continued to accumulate at a rapid rate. He had long consultations again with Pinder Simpson who again enlisted the help of Alexander Sidebottom. The result was a lengthy document that was becoming ever more complicated. This concerned Pinder because the more complicated a Will became, the more likely it was to be challenged and become prey to the painfully slow legal processes that had developed in recent years. But Pinder also noted, without making any comment, that the annuity to Susannah Peake had increased by half to £300, but even more surprisingly that the annuity to Sarah Peake had increased fivefold to £100. He also spotted that an annuity to Charles' trusty clerk, Robert Barbrook, had increased from £30 to £100. Charles was clearly wanting to favour those on whom he relied to look after his second and secret family, whilst realising that he could never reveal in a Will the existence of the two natural children.

The remainder of 1825 and 1826 was a time of quiet consolidation for Charles. Day and Martin continued to thrive and expand with John Weston doing an admirable job. Life in Edgware had settled down to a steady routine. If Charles was not there, as was frequently the case, Rebecca only had Caroline for company. But Caroline was now in her late teens and wanting to spread her wings. The social excitement of George IV's London was too tempting to ignore and Caroline's demands were becoming an irritation to Charles. Rebecca was her usual ambivalent self. Her increasing deafness was causing her to retreat even more into herself. With Caroline finding any excuse to disappear for the day, Rebecca's life was becoming increasingly solitary. There was little Charles could do about this apart from keeping her in the luxurious comfort that he could afford.

Meanwhile, there was a far happier state of affairs with Charles's second family in Earl Street. Alfred was a healthy baby and Henry clearly seemed to be developing into a bright young child. Susannah spent most of her time there and Sarah was a very devoted mother. Charles would visit whenever he could but it was decided that the boys should not be brought up knowing that he was their father. They would just be told as they grew up that their father John was always working away in far off foreign lands.

So, the frequent visits from Blind Uncle Charles, who usually came on foot guided by Susannah, became events of great anticipation. He would of course stay for as much of the day as possible and the atmosphere was always very happy and relaxed. In fact, Charles could not recollect a more settled period in his life with overflowing contentment. His relationship with Sarah was as romantic as ever and any past feelings of frustration were entirely forgotten. Consequently, it was no great surprise when Sarah realised, later in in 1826, that she was pregnant again.

Charles and Susannah were agreed that something would have to be done about the family's living accommodation. The house in Earl Street was ideal but small and, with three small children and space required for Susannah to stay most of the time, there simply was not enough room. Something bigger would have to be found.

The Portman Estate was consulted and a vacant property was becoming available at 16 Seymour Place. Charles was attracted to this property for various reasons. It was a house of greater status, being a town house for the expanding middle class that was becoming well-established in English society. It was a step up from the workers' houses of Earl Street and there was considerably more accommodation, allowing for a living-in servant in the future. The added bonus was that it was even closer to Harley House, making access for Charles very straightforward by foot. The lease was taken in Susannah's name as the Earl Street lease was continued in the name of John Price as a precaution and perhaps to increase the necessary smokescreen. The family moved quietly at the beginning of 1827 with Sarah's pregnancy progressing satisfactorily.

Edmund Price, a third son for Sarah and Charles, was born safely on 20 May 1827. Again, it was decided that the infant should be baptised. The new church of St Mary's, Bryanston Square, was now fully functional and conducting baptisms. What is more, it was only a couple of hundred yards from the new family residence at 16 Seymour Place and was therefore the obvious venue for the private ceremony. This was conducted quietly by the curate on Friday 15 June 1827. Again, Robert Barbrook stood in as the father John Price and no questions were asked. The event was recorded in the church's baptismal register and the father's profession was stated as 'Tutor'. Susannah stayed at home and looked after four-year-old Henry and two-year-old Alfred.

Thereafter, for the rest of that year, the new routine of the family of three children living with their mother and aunt at 16 Seymour Place was established. As there was available space, and the cost was insignificant to Charles, a living-in house maid was employed to carry out the domestic tasks. Susannah would walk over to Harley House and accompany Charles on frequent visits which the boys enjoyed. With Susannah's expert organisation, Charles gave her the title 'Superintendent', the whole arrangement went extremely well and, most importantly, everything was kept secret from Rebecca and Caroline in Edgware.

After Charles's father died, his mother went to live with her older son William in Chelsea. William had always been a quieter person than his more ambitious younger brother. He was happy to work beside his father, making some of the products needed for the hairdressing business and was involved with the blacking manufacture in its early days in Tavistock Street. Latterly, he had run more of a retail business and was certainly selling the products of Day and Martin. For his mother to live with him seemed a sensible arrangement as Charles's household was a complicated affair with its split residence between Harley House and Edgware. Charles was also fairly certain that his mother would not be particularly compatible with her daughter-in-law Rebecca who was becoming increasingly reclusive. Besides, Charles's mother was one of the few people who knew of the existence of the second family, having arranged for Sarah to stay with her sister Ann during the first pregnancy. It was best she kept away from Charles's household, in case she let anything slip. Being a lady of advanced years, this was a risk not worth taking. William had a large family and the younger children would be a happy distraction for their grandmother.

After five years of happy living with William and his family, Mrs Susannah Day finally passed away on 26 February 1828 at the grand old age of eighty-three. Hers had been an adventurous but fulfilling life, beginning in Sussex, relocating to London, picking up her brother-in-law after his wife's (her sister's) early death, living with him and having children before eventually marrying him and having more, and supporting him all along in his own business. The success of her younger son Charles had been a source of immense pride, but not without worries about his personal life and early blindness. She had always been a steady rock for him and, on her death, he was resolute to commemorate her in an appropriate way. She would be interred in Edgware in the family vault, beside her late husband, with a suitable inscription being added to the side of the sarcophagus. The funeral and committal took place at St Margaret's, Edgware, on 13 March 1828 and was conducted by the vicar, Rev Nicholas Fiott.

This was obviously a distraction for Charles, who did not like to be torn away from his business or, for that matter, his second and secret family. He could only be thankful for his mother's long and rewarding life and he was generally in a good frame of mind. A feeling of benevolence came over him and he was keen to give something back to his community. This would mean more in the small village of Edgware than in the city, so he had discussions with the parish vicar as to how would be the best way of helping. Bearing in mind the poverty of many of the villagers, the vicar suggested the building of some almshouses and Charles readily consented.

Charles built eight almshouses on a plot measuring 170 feet x 70 feet, fronting on Watling Street at Stone Grove, north of the village of Edgware, which he subsequently bought in 1829 from the Warden and Fellows of All Souls College, Oxford, for a consideration of £31. 4s. 3d.. Initially, Charles selected the almspeople in consultation with the vicar and other respected villagers, one of whom, Richard Loosley, he made treasurer of the private charity. He gave him £100 a year to cover repairs and other costs, the balance being disbursed to the almspeople at the rate of four shillings per week each. In selecting almspeople, Charles decided to give preference to parishioners of Edgware and Little Stanmore, providing that they did not:

sell Ale, Beer, or Spirituous Liquors, or be guilty of swearing, Drinking, Sabbath Breaking, or any other vice.

9. Day's Almshouses, Stonegrove, Edgware, built in 1828 by Charles Day for the poor of the parish, as they appear today.

The almshouses, built with the best of materials, consisted of a long single-storied range in a neo-Gothic style with steep gables, eight pinnacled buttresses and a slate roof. The front was faced with stone ashlar and had Gothic arcading below the eaves and verges. In the central gable, which was flanked by two smaller ones, was a clock and the date 1828.

On 1 January 1830, the original eight almspeople chosen by Charles took up residence. They were William Taylor, Mary Batt, Mary Granger, Sarah Lynes, Elizabeth Harris, Elizabeth Nichols, Fanny Brown and Mary Greig. It is interesting to note that all, apart from William Taylor who was actually accompanied by his wife Elizabeth, are women, this being just one of several examples where Charles was way ahead of his time in acknowledging the need for female emancipation.

The secretive family life in Seymour Place carried on, quietly but happily. The boys were beginning to develop their own personalities. Henry was quiet but studious and was clearly going to develop an intellect which would require nurturing. Alfred was more gregarious and adventurous and seemed to have a facility for drawing. Edmund was still very young but had a bright young personality. Having a living-in domestic servant made a huge difference to the lives of Sarah and Susannah, the latter being able to concentrate more on the needs of the household and on helping Charles at Harley House. Charles would visit regularly and the boys would look forward to such visits without realising that he was their father. But one matter concerned the adults and that was that Henry had never been baptised, which was a social norm for the times. Being nearly six and quite shy, Henry was clearly worried when this subject was raised with him by Sarah. He could not understand why he was different to his brothers. Sarah asked if he would be happier if his brothers accompanied him and he was cheered by this suggestion. Alfred had been baptised in another church but Edmund's christening had been in their new and neighbouring church of St Mary's where the clergy could still remember the event. Sarah discussed the problem with the local curate and he consented to allow Alfred and Edmund to be recorded again in the baptismal register although they had already been baptised. Consequently, all three boys appeared at the church with Sarah on Wednesday, 14 January 1829 and deliberately there were no other baptisms that day. All three boys stood at the font and their foreheads were duly wetted by the curate. Susannah also attended as their godmother. Robert Barbrook was not asked to stand in again as their father because the boys were old enough now to realise that this was simply not the case. But the father, whom Sarah said was working abroad, was still recorded as 'John Price' and his profession was merely stated in the register as 'Esquire'. As was the practice at St Mary's, the boys' birthdays were also clearly stated and their address was given as 'Seymour Place'.

Charles was delighted that this had taken place. He felt that the family now had a status that should be recognised and the best way to do this would be to list them in The Royal Blue Book, a self-styled 'fashionable directory' of the nobility and wealthy classes in London that carried a substantial subscription for each entry. Charles was happy to do this and in the 1830 edition, the occupant of 16 Seymour Place is listed as 'Mrs Peake'. This refers to Susannah, rather than Sarah, as the head of the household. However, people in the neighbourhood noticed the three boys and knew their surname. Consequently, Charles felt it wise to list the entry for 1831 under the name John Price.

By late 1831, Henry was approaching his ninth birthday, Alfred his seventh and Edmund was four. They were being kept under the impression that they had never met their father but, with their increasing age and awareness, this could not be continued much longer. Charles realised that something had to be done. By chance, Susannah noticed that the funeral had taken place on 29 November at the nearby St George's, Hanover Square, of one John Price. The parish burial register stated that the deceased was sixty-four and his abode was stated as St Marylebone. It was a perfect fit and presented an ideal chance to kill off the boys' fictional father. It was decided that Sarah should break the news to them. They accepted it without too much emotion. How could they feel much for a father they had never met? At the time, there was considerable civil unrest throughout the country as a result of the defeat in the House of Lords of the Reform Bill. Riots took place in London on the day of the funeral at St George's, Hanover Square. The boys were told that their father's funeral had taken place during these riots and this would be a story passed down the family for future generations.

It had always been a risky policy to invent a mythical father for the boys because, at some point, he would have to be extinguished. But how? A credible explanation had fallen into the laps of Charles, Susannah and Sarah. They had grasped it in the hope of being able to move on with no questions being asked – and none ever were.

7. The troublesome daughter and making provisions

Charles' daughter Caroline was becoming one of the most eligible heiresses in London. Being an only child of extremely wealthy parents, Caroline always had everything she wanted. But she never really revealed whether she was a truly happy girl. As she became a young woman, she obviously enjoyed the attentions of her many male admirers. This clearly worried Charles, but for once in his life he was fairly powerless. Eventually a young gentleman by the name of Horatio Clagett was introduced to her parents, and he seemed to become a fairly permanent fixture. Charles was clearly sceptical, but perhaps he would never have approved of even the most perfect suitor.

Charles decided to have some detective work done on Clagett, who was ten years older than Caroline. Being blind, Charles could not do this himself. Various pieces of information emerged. It transpired that the Clagett family originally hailed from Kent but in about 1670, one of the ancestors had decided to emigrate to the new colonies in America – Maryland, to be precise. They became firmly established as a leading family in that area, managing estates of considerable size. Horatio's father, also Horatio, was born in Maryland in 1755. On the outbreak of the American Revolutionary Wars in 1776, he enlisted on the American side and soon rose to the rank of Captain, by all accounts serving honourably and leading his men with distinction.

But surprisingly, soon after hostilities ceased in 1783, he emigrated back to London. It would seem that, in a spirit of enterprise, not unlike Charles, he saw an opening in London for a firm trading American goods in Great Britain. What is now the United States of America won its independence and wanted to establish trade with the 'old country'. So, Horatio Snr established the firm of Clagett and Pratt, American merchants, in John Street, Minories, in the City, and things went well. He met a local girl, Mary English, and they were married in St Mary's Lambeth in 1792, setting up home in that parish. Family started to arrive in plentiful number, Horatio Jnr being the third son, born in 1797 in Brighton unexpectedly whilst the family were taking the sea air. The American trading seemed to go well and the business flourished, producing material rewards.

All of this pleased Charles greatly as the Clagett story bore some striking similarities to his own, the notable exception being the large family of ten children. However, it seems that the Clagetts made the same mistake as Charles had done, in allowing their children to enjoy too many fruits of their parents' labours too soon. Young Horatio's name began to appear in the gossip columns of the press as a bit of a dandy, 'the gayest of the gay', who was not afraid to spend liberal amounts of money, perhaps even in excess of what he had. He became one of the founding members of The Garrick Club in 1831 and clearly enjoyed the company of thespian friends. A scurrilous new publication came out in April 1831 called *The Satirist* and in an early edition there appeared a fairly poisonous article about Horatio and Caroline and their extravagant lifestyle:

SIGH NO MORE MAIDENS
Horace Clagett, who has been on the town for many a long day, as the gayest of the gay, and who has made all ladies, single or married, sigh in soft emotion, and wish with Desdemona, 'that heaven had made them

such a man', is to be united shortly in the bonds of wedlock to Miss Day, the beautiful and accomplished daughter of Mr Day, of the firm of Day and Martin.

This hurt Charles greatly, and there was no way of avoiding him knowing about it. He was not pleased.

Nevertheless, Horatio worked his charm on Charles and when he eventually asked Charles for his daughter's hand in marriage, Charles consented, albeit with some reluctance, knowing that those associated with the stage could be somewhat colourful in their social activities.

However, early in 1832, things went drastically wrong. On 16 February, there appeared the following notice in *The Brighton Gazette*:

Mr Horace Claggett [the spelling of both Christian and surname could vary], *long the idol of fashionable coteries, has married Miss Day, daughter of the wealthy blacking manufacturer, with a fortune of £70,000. He has taken the name of his wife.*

Charles's relations living in the Brighton area spotted the notice, and sent it to Edgware. Charles went off in one of his rages that happened from time to time, over which neither he nor anyone else had any control. Caroline and Horatio were summoned, and they insisted that the report was pure fabrication, which it was. They also had no idea from where the press had obtained the figure of £70,000 which was excessively overstated. But the damage was done.

To make matters worse, there began to emerge a story that Horatio, although definitely not married, might be supporting a second family by one Eliza Payne who lived in Maida Hill. The rumours were that Eliza was a person of low morals but who moved in high society circles. When she and Horatio met, probably around 1827, she already had two sons by 'father unknown'. Their first child Emma was born in 1828, followed by Horatio in 1830. The children stayed with her but their father had promised to maintain them until they attained the age of 21. Charles confronted Caroline with this story and she had to admit it was true. But she was convinced the affair was over and that Horatio's loyalties lay with her. She pleaded with her father who accepted, with a certain amount of reservation, that she and Horatio shared a mutual love for one another.

But then word reached Charles that Eliza and Horatio had had another child, a daughter Virginia, in 1832. Horatio was clearly trying to keep all options open and Charles became convinced that Horatio needed the Day money to support his growing family with Eliza Payne.

As an aside, Eliza died at the young age of 36 in April 1843. In her Will, she stated:

I do hereby further declare that, during such time as my said son Horatio Pyne shall be under the age of 21 years, or my said daughters Emma Pyne and Virginia Pyne shall be under the said age and unmarried, and in case Horatio Clagett of Harley House, St Marylebone, Esquire, shall die before all or either of my said last mentioned son and daughters shall have attained his, her or their age or ages of 21 years or been married as the case may be without the said Horatio Clagett having provided for the maintenance, education and support of all such son and daughters during their respective minority...

So, it was all true.

This was more than Charles could tolerate. He went back on his word, refusing to give his consent to the marriage. He even barred Horatio from entering the house. Despite this, the couple continued their romance and were frequently seen out and about, walking and riding.

All through that summer, the young couple made frequent visits to Edgware when Charles was there. But he would not be moved despite their remonstrations. There seemed to be a complete impasse.

The inevitable result was an elopement. Caroline disappeared and married her beau in Marylebone church, virtually opposite Harley House on the New Road, on 27 September 1832 with just some friends attending. On hearing of the elopement, Charles was greatly shaken but realised that withholding his approval would merely alienate his daughter, perhaps for life, and would be extremely bad publicity for his family and ultimately his business. Nevertheless, this extract from a press report two weeks later does not show up the bridegroom in the best of light:

> *Mr Clagett and Miss Day were married in St Marylebone church on Thursday the 27 ult. Mr Clagett eloped with Miss Day the Tuesday previous, but blundered with respect to the church, taking the lady to St George, Hanover Square, where the minister, discovering the license to be drawn out for St Marylebone Church, refused, of course, to unite them. He then drove the lady to All Souls, Langham Place, with as little success – mistaking the latter for the parish church of St Marylebone. The lady became alarmed at these disappointments, and insisted upon being driven to some of her friends, who reside in the neighbourhood of Berkeley Square, where she remained until Thursday; - in the meantime Mr Day consented to the match. Mr Clagett is the third son of Mr Horatio Claggett, of the late well-known firm of Clagett and Pratt, the American merchants, in John Street, Minories. He is now in his thirtieth year, and when of age, he came into possession of a fortune of upwards of*

£20,000. His subsequent acquaintance with Madame Vestris is sufficiently known without any further allusion to it. Miss Day, it is said, is about the same age, and has at her own disposal upwards of £35,000.

In fact, Horatio was thirty-five and Caroline just twenty-five. The happy couple escaped to Hastings for a honeymoon.

To add insult to injury, there appeared the following pearl of the poet's art in the 'Poet's Corner' of the October edition of *Bell's Life*:

MATRIMONIAL STANZAS TO HORATIO CLAGETT, ESQ

And so, Mr Clagett, the fear has passed,
And in Hymen's soft fetters, you're tied up at last;
No longer from duty to wander astray,
But basking in all the enjoyment of DAY.

To charm you, both beauty and fortune combining,
That Day, like her blacking, must surely be shining;
In making her yours, it must doubtless be wondered,
How as to the church you so woefully blundered.

'Tis said, that in rapture you chose to repair
To the church of St George, in Hanover Square;
When the parson found out, by an effort of high sense,
You had made a confounded mistake with your license.

Then off, quick as lightening, your vehicle rolls,
And you wafted her body direct to All Souls;
Where another grave Clergyman cried, with a sneer,
'By my fire-shovel tile, I can't marry you here!'

But the third time, we know, from experience is lucky,
So, to Mary-bonne Parish you flew with your ducky;
Where you led your fair bride to the altar delighted,
And for better for worse you were firmly united.

Such a chance, friend Horatio, was not to be missed;
For charms thirty-thousand what heart could resist?
Tho' with Love's purest flame your heart doubtless did so burn,
For the Maiden of Blacking – the Pride of High Holborn!

And the money you've got, and of course you will bag it,
And gentle Miss Day has become Mrs Clagett:
I hope that no troubles henceforward will visit ye,
And may Hymen bestow matrimonial felicity!

I know you are kind and I wish you would show it,
By sending a slice of bride-cake to the poet;
So, may nothing on earth to your comfort be wanting,
And Providence keep you from all gallivanting!

This was frankly the last straw for Charles, stretching his restricted sense of humour way beyond its limit. He went into a black mood for some time. Charles was persuaded that the wisest move was to allow Caroline and Horatio to live at Harley House, where he might have some degree of control over them. They rarely visited Edgware, their lives being bound up in the social whirl of London.

Charles had been particularly upset by the death of his brother William on 18 January 1831 at the relatively early age of fifty-two, leaving his widow Harriet and at least six of their nine children. William was the only other son of Francis and Susannah Day who had survived so, although Charles was more than five years his junior, they had always been close.

William had married Harriet in 1798 and their family started to arrive soon afterwards. He had carried on working with his father in the shop but had concentrated more on making the products that his father used in the business, such as hair colourants. He also became involved in the initial stages of Day and Martin, when Charles and Benjamin were experimenting in the back of the shop. However, when that separate business started to fly and move out of the restricted premises, William loyally stayed on with his father. This had always given Charles great comfort as it absolved his conscience at deserting the person who had supported him from the start.

By 1809, it had become a sensible idea for William to set up a separate business at 80 Swallow Street in Mayfair where the products that he and his father had been manufacturing in cramped conditions at the back of the hairdressing shop could be made and retailed to a wider public. This left Francis to concentrate on his real trade of pure hairdressing, but using the materials that William was making.

Some time before Francis's retirement in 1818, William decided to move the business again, this time to Chelsea, with Charles's blessing and no doubt enough financial assistance to ensure that any risks in the change of location would be minimised. A business premises was set up in New Manor Street next to St Luke's Church, and a home was established in nearby Lion Place. This was a prosperous time for the family, which delighted Charles.

In 1823, William's and Charles's mother came to live in Chelsea with William and his family, and spent her entire widowhood there until she died in 1828. It was the right place for her to be with a large, young family around her. She was even able to welcome her first great-grandchild before she died. But William's sudden death in 1831 came as a shock to everyone and especially Charles. It made him think of his own mortality and the fact that he should be reviewing his Will again and making some more plans, especially for his second family.

He consulted with Pinder Simpson immediately. Nearly six years had passed since he had reviewed his Will and it needed some updating after events that had taken place in the meantime, culminating in William's death. Caroline was now of mature age and needed to be included as a legatee. He also wanted to give his three sisters a legacy each as well as annuities to William's widow and two more distant relations, Elizabeth Bourn on his father's side and Mary Ann Skegg on his mother's. Elizabeth Bourn was the sister of William Claughton Dey, the estranged husband of Charles's sister Mary. She was married to a Gainsborough rope manufacturer and had fifteen children by him. At the time of her brother's desertion, Elizabeth had been supportive to Mary, an act which Charles wished to repay. Mary Ann Skegg was a spinster living in Brighton who remained close to the family and had been a great help in Sarah Peake's first pregnancy.

But most significantly, he increased the legacies to all his eighteen nephews and nieces from £200 each to £1000 each – a very considerable commitment. These were the children of his late brother William and his two sisters, Mary and Susannah. His intention was to give the youngsters a good start in life whilst being sure that his sisters and sister-in-law were already comfortable. But strangely, he excluded Rebecca and Caroline from the list of annuitants – probably an oversight, albeit a major one, as he subsequently reinstated them.

Pinder Simpson showed the draft to Sidebottom as before, and he approved it on 31 January 1831, only thirteen days after brother William's death, showing that Charles was clearly treating the matter with some urgency. The final document was signed and sealed on 4 February 1831.

Another event that had had a disturbing effect on Charles was the death on 15 September 1830 of the former cabinet minister, William Huskisson. In a state of post-operative infirmity, and against medical advice, he had attended the opening of the new Liverpool and Manchester Railway. In a most unfortunate series of circumstances, he had alighted from the Duke of Wellington's train and had been hit by Stephenson's 'Rocket' coming in the opposite direction. He later died of the injuries he had sustained and thus gained the unenviable distinction of being the first person in Britain to be killed in a railway accident. As a result of his blindness and with the considerable amount of walking he was doing to visit the boys, Charles was concerned that he might meet with some similar accident and fate in crossing the road. Consequently, his mortality gained even more significance in his own mind.

During 1831, Charles increased the allowance he paid Susannah for the maintenance, clothing and education of the boys to £400 per year, which he paid her in quarterly instalments. But Charles wanted to do more in making a provision for the boys after his death. However, this must not be revealed in any Will. Susannah and Sarah agreed with Charles that they should discuss with his clerk Robert Barbrook what could be done. This had to be achieved without publicly revealing the boys' existence or identity. Charles had already taken Barbrook into his confidence about the boys, instructing him to send money to the Virgos in Brighton during Sarah's first pregnancy and asking him to stand in as 'father' at the baptisms.

Barbrook understood the problem and suggested that he consult, in complete confidence, a solicitor named Antonine Dufaur with whom he had worked on Charles's affairs in connection with the leases of the many properties around London that he owned. Charles was willing to consent, never realising that this would ultimately lead to some catastrophic and long-lasting problems after his death. The connection with the Dufaur family actually went back twenty-five years to around 1807 when Charles (then aged only twenty-three, but already a highly successful young businessman) met and became acquainted with Antonine Dufaur's uncle, also Antonine. Antonine Snr was a chief clerk at the Collector's Office of Excise in the Custom House, situated in the City on the banks of the Thames near the Tower of London. Charles had to go there frequently to settle the duty he had to pay on the secret ingredients of the blacking recipe that had to be imported (molasses from the West Indies were almost certainly needed). They struck up a friendship which became quite intimate and lasting, despite the fact that Antonine was the elder by thirteen years. It lasted until November 1815 when at the age of forty-four, Antonine married one Eleanor Smith who was twenty-four years his junior. The wedding took place in Christ Church, Southwark, and 4 days later their first daughter was baptised in the same church, but clearly conceived out of wedlock. Sadly, this caused Charles to drop his acquaintance to a great degree. Antonine and Eleanor went on to have two more daughters, but it seems that all was not well in Antonine's mind. He died on 18 November 1822 from a self-inflicted wound to the lower part of his body. The coroner's report said that he had already attempted suicide once before by throwing himself into the Thames, but had been rescued. Nevertheless, Charles had a very high regard for him and frequently said that, to a great extent, he attributed his subsequent success in life to the good advice and friendship of Antonine Snr. Even after this friendship cooled, Charles still preserved a close acquaintance with the other members of the family, particularly with Antonine Snr's brother, Cyprian, a Chelsea-based moneylender. As such, he had known Cyprian's two sons, Frederick and Antonine Jnr, since their youth.

Dufaur suggested using a legal device called a *post obit* bond, being an agreement that a borrower promises to pay to the lender a lump sum or a debt, when a person whose property the borrower expects to inherit, dies. In this case the lenders would be each of the three boys (Henry, Alfred and Edmund), the borrowers would be Charles' executors and the person who dies would be Charles. In other words, Charles' executors would inherit Charles' wealth on his death and then be honour bound to pay each of the boys a stated sum of money in order to release the obligation of the bond. This seemed to be a perfect solution. Any legacy in a Will would eventually be public information, revealing the fact that Charles had fathered three illegitimate children. The shame associated with this would be highly damaging to Charles's legitimate family, to say nothing of Day and Martin, the profits of which would be the source of welfare for that continuing family in the future. But the attraction of the proposed bonds was that they could remain completely secret within the immediate circle of Charles Day, Susannah and Sarah Peake and Robert Barbrook. The bonds would be held by Susannah on behalf of the boys and she would merely have to present them to Charles's unsuspecting executors, who would have to honour them and pay over the stated sums to Henry, Alfred and Edmund. Effectively, they were a debt of Charles' estate which his executors would have to clear. Only the executors would know and they were bound to secrecy. But there was now one other person who knew about the second family. That was Antonine Dufaur Jnr. who had trained under the tutelage of his older brother Frederick, with whom he still worked. The brothers had no doubt discussed the case, so allowing Frederick also to be aware of Charles Day's secret.

Antonine Dufaur gave Barbrook a form from which to draw up the bonds and Barbrook proceeded with the drafting. On 26 October 1832, Barbrook and Susannah guided Charles by foot from Harley House to 16 Seymour Place, where they were greeted by Sarah and the three boys, then aged nine, seven and five. After the maid had taken the boys off to prepare them for bed, Barbrook produced the three bonds and explained them to Susannah and Sarah who thoroughly approved. Charles then signed all three bonds, with Barbrook attesting the execution of each. Sarah also witnessed Henry's bond but then had to leave the room to settle the boys for bed. Susannah acted as second witness for the remaining two bonds. They were then sealed and Charles left them in Susannah's safe custody until such time in the future when Charles would die. On that event, Charles's instruction to her was to present them to his executors who would then pay the £5,000 stipulated on each bond to each of the three boys. Charles's legitimate family would never find out about the arrangement and the existence of the three bastard children would remain a secret. But the children themselves would be well endowed. This done, all the parties involved relaxed in the knowledge that the boys' futures were secure. Charles promised to provide separately for Susannah and Sarah in his Will.

Following this, the opportunity conveniently presented itself to kill off John Price, but more worrying were all the civil disturbances that were occurring in London and around the country. This made Rebecca very nervous and thus determined her to stay out of the way in Edgware. But with Caroline having just married her Horatio and, with Charles's blessing, being allowed to live together in Harley House, Rebecca became even more of a recluse. What had originally been the company of her mother, two sisters and her daughter, had now been taken away from her either by death or desertion. To make it even worse, she was becoming increasingly deaf and losing what little self-confidence she had. She was cocooned in her own little world, and communication with anyone was a struggle.

Charles gave Caroline and Horatio strict instructions only to leave the environs of Harley House, which had a reasonably substantial garden for central London, if it was absolutely necessary. They paid little heed, taking great advantage of his blindness. The pleasures of post-Georgian London were too attractive. But the threat of revolution was in the air. Forty years had passed since the bloody overthrow of the French royal family. The status of the British monarchy had been dragged down by George IV during his time as regent and then king. He had died in 1830 and left no legitimate issue. He was succeeded by his younger brother William IV, who was little better. No legitimate issue survived from his marriage, but prior to that, he had fathered ten children by his mistress, Mrs Dorothea Jordan. The institution of the monarchy was in a precarious state and who was to know that the young Princess Victoria, waiting in the wings, would transpire to be such an extraordinary queen? There had been bouts of civil unrest – the Peterloo massacre in 1819 and the riots that led up to the 1832 Reform Act finally being passed into law, being the most notable. The scandal surrounding the case of the Tolpuddle Martyrs was about to erupt. These were unsteady times and Charles wisely decided to keep his head down, enjoy his second family and concentrate on the continued prosperity of his business. He could do little else.

But this feeling of insecurity, encroaching all around, made Charles become almost obsessive about the contents of his Will and by early 1834, he had re-opened the issue again of making further revisions.

8. Towards the end

At the beginning of 1834, another factor was beginning to concentrate Charles's mind on the need for urgent future planning. He was experiencing a strange feeling in his legs which was affecting his walking – nothing too disturbing at this stage, but it was not going away and was slowly becoming more noticeable. For the time being, he decided to keep his worries to himself, but realised that he would soon have to tell Susannah Peake, his main guiding companion when walking, especially to and from the second family in Seymour Place.

Over the years, Charles had made a strong friendship in Edgware with the local surgeon and apothecary, William Foote. On a visit to Edgware, Charles decided to confide in Foote with his medical worries. Foote took this on board and felt it wise to confront Charles with his candid thoughts based on considerable local experience. When coupled with his blindness, Foote considered it likely that the beginnings of paralysis in the limbs would tend to indicate the possible onset of tertiary syphilis. Foote strongly advised Charles to discuss this with his doctors in London.

On business matters, he was now seeing more of John Simpson than John's father, Pinder, who was enjoying his semi-retirement as Charles's tenant in Manor Cottage, Caterham. Further revisions to Charles's Will were discussed and drafted, but with some fairly major revisions being proposed by Charles, the Simpsons felt this time that a personal consultation with Alexander Sidebottom was desirable. This duly took place in March 1834 in Sidebottom's chambers at Lincoln's Inn. Pinder and John Simpson accompanied Charles, there being only these four present at the meeting. Barbrook also accompanied Charles but he was instructed to wait in another room whilst the meeting took place. Sidebottom went over all Charles' affairs with him although it was probably questionable whether he established the exact extent of Charles's wealth. Sidebottom noted that Charles was an uneducated but very acute person of perfectly sound mind, memory and understanding of everything explained to him. Charles talked rationally and sensibly and well understood what Sidebottom was saying, giving clear instructions for altering the Will he had previously made. Charles also discussed some charitable gifts that he wished to make through his Will and Sidebottom suggested these should be stated in a separate codicil, to which Charles readily agreed. These were in connection with the Edgware almshouses that were already built and functioning, and with a new charity for providing assistance to poor blind people. Sidebottom made a draft of the new Will by altering a copy of the former Will and drafting the new codicil in his own hand. The meeting was a long one and the Simpsons merely listened whilst Charles and Sidebottom had their discussions. But Sidebottom noticed some weakness in Charles' bodily health. He never saw Charles again.

Given the vast extent of Charles's wealth, Pinder Simpson suggested the appointment of another executor with specific financial knowledge and skills. In addition to Pinder Simpson, the other existing executor was William Underwood who ran a successful draper's shop on the corner of Oxford Street and Vere Street. Charles had known him as a friend and respected businessman for many years. Through him, Charles had met Underwood's brother-in-law Simeon Bull, an architect and surveyor whose services Charles had been using since about 1817 on the administration of his various properties around London. But Charles agreed that a third executor with specific financial skills would be a wise appointment.

The circle of sharp business and financial minds was still relatively small in post-Georgian London and Pinder and John Simpson would be ideally placed to hear of suitable candidates for the third executor. The name of William Croft had come their way and, before approaching him, they floated the idea with Charles and also William Underwood. On the face of it, Croft seemed an ideal candidate. He was the same age as Charles and had spent his whole life in the St Pancras area. His working life had been in the civil service and therefore complete discretion in all business matters had become a natural attribute. This mattered greatly to Charles because he realised that, if he were to die, his executors would become aware of the existence of the three illegitimate children and they must be entirely trustworthy to keep this completely to themselves. None of the executors were privy to that information yet and Charles could see no reason, at this stage, why they should be.

William Croft had risen to be Assistant Accountant General in the HM Paymaster's General Office with the particular responsibility of being Deputy Treasurer of the Ordnance, that is to say a highly responsible position in administering the finances of the country's armed forces. Thinking ahead, this also meant that he would retire not too far hence and would be entitled to a generous superannuation deal, giving him a desirable level of financial security. He lived with his wife and three sons in Upper Gower Street, not too far from Harley House and the site of the new London University which also gave an education to young boys aspiring to be students at its main institution of higher education.

Although Croft's three sons were of an older generation than Charles', this similarity between them seemed to strike a chord with Charles, although he could not refer to it. Of Croft's three sons, the oldest William had followed his father into the office of HM Paymaster General, the middle son Charles was showing great promise in the field of medicine, and the youngest Henry, still only in his early teens, was showing the potential of perhaps being the brightest of the three with an enquiring scientific mind.

It was agreed to approach Croft with a proposal of becoming Charles' executor and he accepted an invitation to attend a meeting at Harley House with Charles, Pinder Simpson and William Underwood. This went very satisfactorily for all concerned and Croft accepted the appointment, having been assured by Charles that he would receive benefits for the resulting duties. But it was made very clear to Croft that these duties could be considerable, bearing in mind the complexity of Charles's Will which was in the process of being revised yet again. However, no one present could possibly have foreseen how extensive these complexities were to become.

This latest revision of Charles's Will (which transpired to be the final revision, except for the addition of further codicils), together with the accompanying codicil containing charitable legacies, was signed and sealed at Pinder Simpson's house in Old Burlington Street on 1 May 1834. Charles's hand was guided to the spots on the relevant papers and he was able to sign despite his blindness. There were three witnesses to these signatures. These had to be trustworthy individuals because they also had to attest to the fact that the Will was read out to Charles due to his blindness. They had to be sure that he was aware of what he was signing and consequently became aware of the contents themselves. The three trusted individuals were William Simpson, Pinder's youngest son, together with John Shaw and Joseph Jopling. Shaw was a young solicitor who had been known to Pinder Simpson through John, his son, for about six or seven years. He had dined at the Simpsons' occasionally during that time. Jopling was an architect in his mid-forties whom Charles had employed professionally on several occasions. Both Shaw and Jopling had received notes from John Simpson, requesting them to attend. John Simpson read the Will which, at approximately 7,500 words in length, took some time. Jopling followed a copy given to him whilst William Simpson looked over his shoulder. Shaw looked over John Simpson's shoulder as he read. Although Charles listened attentively, he displayed no expressions whatsoever. After the reading was over, he observed to the executors, with reference to the timing of the sale of the business which was provided for in the Will: 'That, gentlemen, I must leave to your discretion.' Nevertheless, the three witnesses were left in no doubt that he perfectly understood every word. All this, together with the actual signing of both will and codicil took some considerable time. Charles had to sign all ten sheets of paper. Charles, John Simpson and the three witnesses were the only people in the room, but were joined after the reading and signing by the three executors, William Croft, William Underwood and Pinder Simpson.

The main changes included in this latest revision of the Will were the introduction of William Croft as an additional trustee and the increase of the legacies to the trustees to £500 each. Substantial annuities were reinstated for Rebecca (£2,000) and Caroline (£3,000) and new annuities of £20 each were given to each of Charles's twenty-one cousins on his mother's side, although they were not stated by name. Further annuities of £20 each were given to Charles's five personal servants and annuities to sisters Mary and Susannah and to Robert Barbrook were each increased by £100. However, there were two major increases in legacies. All annuitants were to receive an immediate legacy of half of their individual annuities and the nephews and nieces who had each received a major increase in legacies to £1,000 in the previous revision of the Will were each to receive a further legacy of £2,000 at a time in the future following the death of Charles' widow, Rebecca. Additionally, two of the clerks at Day and Martin were to receive £500 each.

But of course the main change was the introduction by the codicil of charitable legacies, being £3,333 to the charity that Charles had started by building the almshouses in Edgware, but principally the extraordinary legacy of £100,000 earmarked on Charles's death to set up The Blind Man's Friend, a charity to support poor blind people with annual grants of £10 or £20. This was long before the establishment of any welfare state and demonstrates Charles's remarkably benevolent nature. He was only too aware that there had been an element of good luck in the accumulation of his wealth and his conscience told him that he should repay some of this wealth to those in society who needed it most. Being blind himself, he could easily identify with those fellow sufferers who had not been as fortunate as himself. He had discussed this in detail with his three trustees as they would have to be the ones who would administer the charity and to decide who was to receive the benefits on offer. This would be an onerous responsibility. Nevertheless, this demonstrated again that Charles was a man way ahead of his time in social responsibility and philanthropy and that he would be a trailblazer and example for similar figures of enormous wealth for generations to come. And the fact that the donation was being made through his will rather than in his lifetime (with the accompanying plaudits he would have enjoyed) is a further sign of his modesty and desire that the gift should be for those who need it rather than for his own ego.

However, the effect of all this was that the total of the legacies stipulated in the Will came to £178,403 at that time. Also, annuities were being given amounting to a total annual figure of £7,140 at that time that would have to be paid out of interest on investments kept within the estate. To produce this income, the investments would have to be at least £240,000. In other words, the estate would have to be worth in excess of £420,000 to meet the initial commitments of the Will. However, the estate did include the business of 'Day and Martin'. How much was it worth? Would there be someone willing to buy it? Should it be sold or should it be allowed to carry on trading, the return of its future profits being greater than the income from its invested proceeds? These were all questions that the executors would have to address. In addition, the complexities of the Will would probably result in inevitably high costs for the annual administration of the estate. Charles was a man of staggering wealth, but was it as much as this? There was probably no way of knowing.

Of course, the lawyers accepted his instructions.

Ever since Charles could remember, the Day family in Covent Garden had been patients of the medical practice of Matthew Hewson on the north side of Covent Garden at 28 James Street. The Hewsons were a dynasty of medics. Matthew's father William was achieving great things as an academic anatomist but died young in 1774 when he fatally wounded himself while dissecting. Matthew was practicing in James Street at the time of Charles's birth and it was always believed that he had assisted at Charles's delivery. The families became close friends and Charles was always friendly with the Hewson's son who enjoyed the unusual name of Thomas Ansaldo Hewson. The Days believed the strange choice of middle name was something to do with the child's birthday being Christmas Day, but they never enquired further. Matthew and Juliana Hewson were subsequently blessed with the birth of twin daughters in 1796 but sadly only one, Mary, survived.

A bond developed between Charles and the father Matthew which was as strong as that between Charles and Thomas. As time went by, Charles would confide in Matthew any anxieties he was experiencing such as his unhappy marriage and the consequential loose living in which he was indulging. Matthew warned him to be careful but was not surprised when the blindness began to encroach, syphilis being a condition that patients presented to him regularly.

During a subsequent exchange, Matthew admitted to Charles that he and Juliana had never married. Matthew knew his own health was failing and Charles strongly recommended that a marriage be arranged, followed by Matthew making a Will. A quiet wedding in distant Edmonton took place in August 1819 and Matthew's Will was finalised on 9 May 1820 with Charles agreeing to be an executor. By this time Matthew was seriously ill and he died on 15 June 1820.

Thomas had led a varied life before deciding to follow the family into the medical profession. He qualified at the age of 33 in 1820 just before his father died, and decided to continue his father's practice. He subsequently took into partnership a bright young surgeon, George Beaman, who had been attracting attention at London medical schools during his time as a student. They practised at 8 Henrietta Street, Covent Garden, later at 32 King Street, and established a lucrative practice, which realised £3,000 to £4,000 income a year.

Charles was a witness at the wedding in 1822 of Thomas's sister Mary Hewson (the surviving twin) to George D'Almaine, an embroiderer with a business in Chandos Street, Covent Garden, and he arranged for the couple to live in his house at 3 Euston Square, next door but one to his own home at the time.

In 1823, Thomas Ansaldo Hewson surprised Charles and all those around him by marrying for the first time at the age of 36. Even more surprising was that his bride was a wealthy widow, nine years his senior, by the name of Mrs Anne Sherwin. Her late husband, Joseph Sherwin, had accumulated a significant property empire in the environs of Russell Square. Her maiden name was Parkins and she had come from a family of modest circumstances in Berkhampsted, Hertfordshire, where her father had been the sexton in the church. She played an extraordinary role in helping her nephew, William Parkins, who was Berkhamsted born and bred, to establish his highly successful stationery business, Parkins & Gotto, in Oxford Street, London. Thomas had clearly been strategic in marrying Anne, the marriage settlement confirming that the expenses of their 'establishment' should be paid out of her property income whilst he would only have to provide for the charges of horses and carriages. They lived in considerable style in her house at 6 Woburn Place, Russell Square.

As soon as Charles had confided in William Foote that he was experiencing strange feelings in his legs and that Foote advised him to discuss this with his London doctor (as it may be tertiary syphilis), he mentioned it to Thomas Ansaldo Hewson. Given the patient, that he was a personal friend and the consequences if wrong advice was given, Hewson wisely decided to call in a specialist. The obvious person was Dr Henry Clutterbuck, who was one of the most eminent medical practitioners in the City of London at the time. A native of Cornwall, he had been a brilliant student in London and had gone on to gain all the medical qualifications possible. He was also a gifted communicator and had made a considerable fortune from lecturing and writing and publishing medical books and journals. One of his books was on venereal diseases and he had always maintained a special interest in the topic, especially as these diseases were such a common affliction in London in the early-nineteenth- century. However, the most telling reason why he should be consulted was that he had taken a house in Edgware adjacent to Edgware Place in 1831, so knew Charles as a neighbour although he was never an intimate friend.

Charles agreed that Clutterbuck should visit him at Harley House, and having done so, Clutterbuck's assessment of Charles's condition was the same as William Foote's. Charles accepted this stoically. Clutterbuck also suggested that Charles's speech could become slightly affected, but that the main symptom would be complete paralysis in the lower extremities and that this could progress quite quickly. Clutterbuck tactfully referred to the complaint as a disease of the brain and spinal marrow, rather than mentioning the dreaded word 'syphilis', although Charles was left in no doubt that this was the problem and was not surprised, bearing in mind his lifestyle some twenty years earlier.

Another piece of news that weighed heavily on Charles at this time came from Doncaster in Yorkshire. On 9 October 1834, Charles's former business partner Benjamin Martin died at the age of sixty, leaving behind a widow and seven children, the youngest of whom was only twelve. Charles had always been relieved that he and Benjamin hard parted amicably. Benjamin had made the most of his proceeds from the partnership and left a substantial estate, mainly in property. Nevertheless, this was paltry compared to Charles's vast wealth which had resulted from his successful development of the business since Benjamin's departure. It was also a comforting relief to Charles that John Weston had appeared when he did and carried on the day-to-day management of the business with such success. They had had weekly meetings which continued to this time and Charles maintained complete control. His extraordinary ability to retain huge amounts of information which he could recall instantly remained undimmed, even as his illness progressed into its tertiary stage. The business went from strength to strength, moving with the times and diversifying its products. The marketing effort continued to spread over the whole country. Weston made extensive business trips and reported back to Charles on how they had gone. The strict discipline of the weekly meetings meant that Charles was fully aware of the minutest details as they occurred within the business.

It was not long before Charles was confined to a wheelchair. This made his ability to visit Susannah, Sarah and the boys far more difficult. In 1833, he had arranged for them to move again to 5 Wyndham Place, just around the corner from 16 Seymour Place and right next to St Mary's Church, Bryanston Square. Again, this was a step up in status and Charles wanted nothing less for his second family. However, as the cost was immaterial to Charles, the lease on 16 Seymour Place was carried on in the name of 'John Price'. Charles was also careful to continue the entry for that address and name in The Royal Blue Book, just to perpetuate the smokescreen of identity. He realised that, when anyone had to keep a low profile to maintain secrecy, frequent residential moves were desirable.

However, by 1835, being permanently confined to his wheelchair, Charles wanted the family even closer at hand, if at all possible. Also, another factor was coming into play. Henry was now twelve and Alfred ten, and Charles's paramount desire was that the boys should receive the best possible education. But he was concerned about the usual route for the wealthy which was to engage personal tutors or governesses who quite often would be part of the household. Charles felt this would be far too risky whilst trying to keep the boys' origins secret. In fact, on Edmund's first baptism record, his father's profession had been described as 'Tutor', and the father John Price had now been killed off. Charles was intrigued by the relatively new concept of schools where children could attend as day pupils without having to board. And there happened to be a very good one in its infancy right on his doorstep.

In 1826, The London University had been founded in an attempt to establish a centre for higher education that was secular, as opposed to Oxford and Cambridge which were still both firmly seats of learning for Anglicans, with divinity and the classics being the basis of the curriculum. The idea in London was to embrace new subjects and to make the institution open to members of all denominations of Christianity as well as other religions. By 1830, it was decided to establish a school within the premises for younger boys to attend in preparation for becoming future students at the university. The school was original and ground-breaking – it was never a boarding school, it was one of the first schools to teach modern languages and sciences, and it was one of the first to abolish corporal punishment and to build a gymnasium for physical education. Originally, there were no compulsory subjects and no rigid form system. Most boys learnt Latin and French, and many learnt German, a highly unusual subject to teach at that time. Mathematics, Chemistry, Classical Greek and English were also taught. There was no religious teaching.

The London University premises and its school, later to become University College School, were in Gower Street, to the south of the New Road, later Marylebone Road, and east of Harley House. Henry and Alfred Price started there as pupils in 1834 but this involved a problematic commute from Wyndham Place, west of Harley House. Charles wanted them to be living closer to him and the school, and ideally this meant somewhere between the two. A suitable residence was found at 4 Osnaburgh Street and the family moved there in August 1835. At the same time, eight-year-old Edmund started at the school. Susannah made all the arrangements with the school and explained that the boys' father had died a few years earlier. The boys settled well and derived great benefit from their education, to Charles's immense satisfaction.

In the latter part of 1835, there was a great stir everywhere as Halley's Comet appeared in the sky. A contemporary observer later recorded his observations at the time:

When the comet was first seen, it appeared in the western sky, its head toward the north and tail towards the south, about horizontal and considerably above the horizon and quite a distance south of the Sun. It could be plainly seen directly after sunset every day, and was visible for a long time, perhaps a month...

Charles heard all about this and his blindness caused him awful frustration. He wanted those around him to describe the extraordinary sight in every detail. He knew the skies would be clearer out at Edgware and he made frequent visits with his family for them to see the phenomenon. Sadly, he was far more excited than they were. He was, however, delighted that his three natural sons were able to see the comet on early evening walks to Regent's Park before bed time and were desperate to tell Blind Uncle Charles all about it when they next saw him. This gave him great cheer.

And so, the year turned to 1836, but Charles had understandable forebodings that this may be his last.

On 19 March 1836, a happy event occurred in the Day family. Charles' niece Emma (the fifth daughter of his older brother William) was married to John Martin, a Bromsgrove-born master tailor and employer. The service took place at the fashionable St Luke's, Chelsea, a spectacular building of white sandstone, recently completed in the neo-Gothic style and very near where Emma's parents worked and lived. Even in his wheelchair, Charles was anxious to attend the wedding. Being taken there in his own coach, he succeeded in doing so, accompanied by his wife's sister Susannah Peake, his wife Rebecca preferring to stay in Edgware. He enjoyed the day and meeting many of his family after the service.

On the same page of the parish marriage register is another wedding that took place in St Luke's two weeks later on 2 April 1836, between Catherine Thomson Hogarth of that parish and one Charles John Huffam Dickens of Furnivals Inn, bachelor.

Even in his immobile state, Charles would have regular monthly meetings with John Simpson, when John would read over the latest statements relating to the business affairs of Day and Martin. This was in addition to an annual meeting Charles and Pinder had been having for years at Harley House around Christmas, when an inventory was taken of all of Charles's assets, both within the business and also all his personal investments including property.

But the state of Charles's health was causing concern. There were no outward signs of any further deterioration, but if the diagnosis of the various doctors was correct and he was suffering the effects of tertiary syphilis, the next stage of symptoms could present at any time and this would likely be in the form of epileptic fits and a deteriorating mental capacity. It was therefore essential that he should be kept in a calm and stable environment with as little stress as possible. Consequently, it was recommended that he should stay in the peace of Edgware, rather than the bustle of the city, as much as possible. Grudgingly, he had to accept this.

But in June 1836, something happened that pleased Charles enormously. Word was spreading around London about some monthly pamphlets being published by Chapman and Bull under the fictional title *The Posthumous Papers of the Pickwick Club*. As is now well known, these were to become a novel and a publishing sensation under the shortened title of *The Pickwick Papers*. The author was simply known as Boz, but of course his real identity was none other than Charles Dickens, the bridegroom at St Luke's earlier in the year and subsequently recognised as the most popular author of the early Victorian era. This was his first work of fiction. At the time, he was a humble newspaper law reporter, working long hours in the hope of making a modest living. The first pamphlet came out in March 1836 and the sales of the first three issues were modest. However, in the June 1836 instalment he introduced the new character of Sam Weller, the cockney servant of Mr Pickwick, who seems to have had universal appeal. Sales soared in that month and it was particularly noticeable that the story seemed to appeal to all classes. Each pamphlet cost one shilling, but the power of the narrative was so strong that even the poorest became determined to save up for the next issue.

A BRIGHT IDEA.—"Jeames, I was just a polishing 'em when in comes Sir Chawles, Enery' he says 'you've been at my blacking you dog.' 'Beg your pardon Sir Chawles,' says I, 'but oughtn't hevery dog to have his DAY (& MARTIN?')"

10. A BRIGHT IDEA – one of a series of humorous advertising cards for Day and Martin, dating from about 1835.

Susannah Peake had purchased the June issue soon after it came out and she was delighted to be able to report to Charles that Day and Martin had been mentioned in it. Sam Weller had first appeared as a servant at *The White Hart* pub where his chief duty seemed to be to polish the patrons' boots and shoes. To quote that issue:

Mr Samuel brushed away with such hearty good will, that in a few minutes the boots and shoes, with a polish which would have struck envy to the soul of the amiable Mr Warren (for they used Day and Martin at the White Hart), had arrived at the door of number five.

Not only did Charles realise that this was the best form of advertising (apart from anything else, it was free!) but also it showed up Day and Martin as being superior to Warrens, their main competitor. That issue, and all subsequent ones until the final episode in October 1837, sold in its thousands. It later came out that Charles Dickens had worked at Warrens for two years as a child when his father was in the debtors' prison. He loathed the experience which seems to have left him deeply scarred for life.

In July 1836, the summer term finished at University College School and the boys were released for their summer holidays. They had worked hard and done well. But it had taken its toll on them as Susannah and Sarah reported to Charles. Unhesitatingly, Charles arranged for them to go to Margate on the Kent coast and gain the benefit of a change of air. Sarah went with them but he asked Susannah to stay behind in London as he would find it hard to manage without her, although for most of the time now he was confined to Edgware. He needed her in London to be with him on his occasional but essential visits there. However, by early August, he knew little more would be happening in London, and he proposed that she should go down to Margate to join the others. He arranged to meet her again back at Harley House on Monday 29 August and she would go with him to Edgware for a couple of days to discuss some more financial arrangements he had in mind for the boys. In order to ensure privacy over that time, he resolved to recommend to Rebecca, Caroline and Horatio that they should take a summer break with some sea air at Southend in Essex. Being on the north side of the Thames estuary, this was as far away from Margate as possible, saving any unlikely danger of them meeting by accident Susannah and Sarah with three boys, whom they would not recognise. Brighton was also out of the question as there were far too many family and friends there, some of whom were privy to Charles' secret. Charles knew that any recommendation from him to his immediate family would be taken by them as an order, which was entirely his intention.

So, all was well in the summer of 1836. Charles' life had a regular routine and his health seemed to be stable. John Simpson visited him at Edgware on 11 August and was not left with any immediate concerns about Charles' welfare. But then something happened that rocked Charles terribly and the consequences were not good.

Caroline and Horatio seemed to have settled down to their London life, living at Harley House. With Charles busy on other matters, he was rarely in their company. So, he was appalled to find out from a press report on 8 August 1836, and there was no way it could have been kept from him, that Horatio had been applying to the Insolvent Debtors Court from the Kings Bench Prison for release as an insolvent debtor. He had been languishing in the prison since April that year and Charles had not known.

It turned out that the outstanding debts were £32,383 extending from the year 1827, ie long before the marriage to Caroline. The action had been brought by one particular creditor, Mr William Smith, a silversmith in New Bond Street. It was reported that Horatio had already given up some property and there was other property to be sold. It was also reported that since the marriage of Horatio to Caroline, he had received an allowance from 'his friends'. This probably meant that Caroline was giving him money out of her allowance of £3,000 per year from her father. The report went on:

> *It was true that the insolvent had acted with extravagance, but there was no implication that the debt had been incurred by any false representations of his circumstances.*

Miraculously, or so it seemed to Charles, the court had discharged him forthwith, but the debts still had to be cleared.

Charles was devastated by this and he withdrew into himself. Susannah and Sarah were away in Margate with the boys and Rebecca, Caroline and Horatio were in Southend. He was alone at Edgware with just his immediate servants. His doctors, and especially William Foote in Edgware, were concerned about what effect this could have on his health.

It came as no surprise that on the morning of Friday 26 August 1836, Charles suffered an epileptic fit.

He never left Edgware again.

III. Death

The diary of William Foote
Surgeon: Edgware, Middlesex
26 August 1836 – 26 October 1836

Preface

I found this diary in some papers that belonged to my father, William Foote, who had been the local surgeon in Edgware, to the north of London. It covers a period of two months from 26 August 1836 to 26 October 1836, and describes in great detail the events surrounding the final days of Charles Day, the well-known Edgware entrepreneur and philanthropist.

By way of introduction, I am a retired clergyman, spending my final years in London with my spinster niece, Elizabeth Downing. I have never married. Latterly, I was the curate at St Michael and All Angels Church in Beckenham, Kent, having served in various churches around London.

I was born in Edgware in 1827 and the events described in this diary took place when I was nine years old. I certainly have a distant memory of something significant happening in the village, but until I read this account, I had no idea of the details. My father was always totally discrete about his work.

My father died in 1844, soon after writing this diary from the notes he had made at the time. He had been a devoted servant to Edgware. We were given permission to erect a marble plaque in his memory inside the local church. It reads:

IN MEMORY OF
WILLIAM FOOTE, FOR MORE THAN THIRTY YEARS
SURGEON IN THIS VILLAGE; WHO DEPARTED THIS LIFE
ON THE 10TH OF APRIL, 1844, AGED 58 YEARS:
THIS TABLET IS ERECTED

BY HIS BEREAVED & AFFLICTED WIDOW, AND CHILDREN;
IN AFFECTIONATE REMEMBRANCE OF HIS INESTIMABLE WORTH,
AS A HUSBAND, FATHER, FRIEND AND CHRISTIAN.

I left Edgware a few years later and cleared the house, taking all my father's papers with me. My mother lived with me in my various parishes until she passed away in 1866. My sister and I were allowed to add the following to the plaque:

ALSO OF SARAH, WIDOW OF THE ABOVE;
WHO DEPARTED THIS LIFE MAY 29TH 1866, AGED 79.
MAKE THEM TO BE NUMBERED WITH THY SAINTS IN GLORY EVERLASTING

My parents are both buried in the Edgware churchyard and it is my wish that my remains should be laid to rest with theirs when the time comes.

My father's personal papers had been left undisturbed until now, when I have time in my retirement to deal with them. This diary was wrapped in a sealed parcel marked clearly that it must not be read or produced until after my father's demise and even then, to be treated with the discretion it deserves. But now, sixty-four years after the events that are described within and with all the principal characters mentioned long deceased, I feel the diary can be released. Consequently, I intend to donate the diary to the National Records where it can be kept with all the other papers relating the celebrated Chancery Cause that resulted from the disputed Will of Charles Day.

REV JOHN ANDREWS FOOTE
25 Blomfield Road, London, W9
June, 1900

Dramatis Personae

Charles Day — Proprietor of Day & Martin, manufacturers of boot blacking

Rebecca Day (née Peake) — Wife of Charles Day

Caroline Clagett (née Day) — Daughter of Charles and Rebecca Day

Horatio Clagett — Husband of Caroline Day

Mary Dey (née Day) — Sister of Charles Day

Susannah Lockwood (née Day) — Sister of Charles Day

Elizabeth Poole (née Day) — Half-sister of Charles Day

William Metcalfe — Son-in-law of Mary Dey

Thomas Parsons — Cousin of Charles Day through his mother

Elizabeth Weston (née Peake) — Sister of Rebecca Day, married to John Weston

John Weston — Charles Day's brother-in-law, manager of Day and Martin

Susannah Peake — Sister of Rebecca Day

Sarah Peake — Cousin of Susannah Peake, mother of Charles Day's three sons

Henry Price — First illegitimate son of Charles Day

Alfred Price — Second illegitimate son of Charles Day

Edmund Price — Third illegitimate son of Charles Day

Pinder Simpson — Executor and solicitor of Charles

	Day, married to a Peake
William Underwood	Executor of Charles Day
William Croft	Executor of Charles Day
Frederick Dufaur	Solicitor, acting in some commercial matters for Charles Day
John Simpson	Solicitor, son of Pinder Simpson
William Simpson	Younger son of Pinder Simpson
William Foote	Doctor of Charles Day, based in Edgware
Henry Clutterbuck	Doctor, and neighbour of Charles Day in Edgware
George Beaman	Doctor of Charles Day based in London
Thomas Ansaldo Hewson	Doctor of Charles Day based in London
Thomas Brown Hunt	Charles Day's butler and manservant
Frances Barton	Rebecca Day's maid
Simeon Bull	Surveyor, doing property work for Charles Day
Alexander Sidebottom	Counsel for Charles Day through Pinder Simpson
John Shaw	Solicitor and friend of Pinder Simpson
John Jopling	Architect, employed professionally by Charles Day
William Lawrence	Surgeon, occasionally consulted by Charles Day
John Henry Carr	Clerk to Frederick Dufaur
Daniel Hunt Williams	Solicitor for Henry, Alfred and Edmund Price

Introduction

Surgeons and apothecaries, like all professional men, must always observe absolute confidentiality when considering the circumstances of their patients. It is therefore with a certain amount of trepidation that I am writing this account of an extraordinary episode that happened seven years ago, towards the end of my time in serving the good people of Edgware as their local physician.

This narrative concerns the last two months in the life of my dear friend and neighbour, Charles Day, the proprietor of the well-known boot-blacking manufacturer, Day and Martin. His main residence outside London was Edgware Place, the large house in our village and very close to my own home. The circumstances of his actual death were not medically exceptional, but the personal story that emerged from these two months and the subsequent consequences most certainly are.

In my profession, a little knowledge can be a bad thing when it comes to realising my own medical frailties. For various reasons, I feel I have little time left in this world and it is therefore important for me to write this account before it is too late. I intend to leave it in my personal papers and will mark it clearly that it must not be read or produced until after my demise. Even then, I trust my executors will treat it with the discretion it deserves.

I have always kept a log of the daily events that happened throughout my professional life. After this description of the background to the case, I shall merely revert to what I wrote at the time in my log concerning the events in question and expand it into a more readable narrative.

But before embarking on this story, I should give some details of who I am and my own background.

Prior to coming to Edgware, my life had been exciting to say the least. I was born in 1786 in Canada, the fifth child and fourth son of John Foote and Mary (née Baldwyn). At the time, my father was Surgeon-General of His Majesty's Forces in Canada, a post he had taken up on 17 June 1783. He had left my mother behind in the family home in Peterborough, as she was expecting my elder sister Mary Ann. How my parents coped is something I find unimaginable. They had lost one of my elder brothers before he was two. After recovering from childbirth, my mother took my two remaining brothers five-year-old John and two-year-old Henry with the infant Mary Ann out to Canada to join my father. I was born two years later in 1786, followed by my brother Charles in 1788.

After my father's posting came to an end, the family returned to Peterborough (the voyage back is one of my earliest memories) and continued to expand. Another daughter, Charlotte, was born in May 1793, followed by Peter in March 1795. Before Peter's birth, my father had accepted another foreign posting as Purveyor of the Hospitals in the Caribbean island of St Domingo, based in the capital Port-au-Prince. He managed to return home on leave in the summer of 1795 to see his new son, but shortly after arriving, tragedy struck again with the death of little Charlotte just before her second birthday. Father stayed home as long as he could, but had to return to St Domingo in July 1795, not before leaving my mother pregnant again. But on arrival there, he was struck down by a disease from which he tragically died on 26 August 1795.

So, my poor mother was left a widow with six children aged between seventeen and a few months, with another one on the way. In April 1796, my mother gave birth to a baby girl and decided to call her Charlotte after the daughter she had lost the previous year.

Remarkably, of the five surviving sons, four of us decided to follow our father's career in medicine and become surgeons and apothecaries. Charles and Peter both settled in Gibraltar and are partners together in a medical practice there. John had a successful practice in Tavistock Street, Covent Garden, which, following his sad and rather premature death in 1839, has now been taken over by his son, also John. My other brother Henry has become a successful fine art dealer in Marylebone.

Of my two sisters, Mary Ann is married to a law writer in London and Charlotte has stayed in Peterborough where her husband is a cabinet maker.

I was twenty-eight by the time I had completed my training and settled in Edgware, where a professional opportunity presented itself. I found the community very welcoming. Not long after I arrived, the two Overseers appointed by the parish employed me (on an annual salary of five guineas) to attend the poor of the parish, midwifery and venereal cases excepted. This was not a princely sum, but it took me into the community and earned me its respect.

Life was very busy, but luckily, I soon met a local girl, Sarah Andrews, originally from the neighbouring village of Stanmore. We met through a professional connection I had made with her brother Richard, also a surgeon and apothecary in his native village. This resulted in two partnerships, a professional one with Richard and an emotional one with Sarah. Sarah and I were married on 3 June 1817 in St Marylebone Parish Church which had become her church after her parents moved into London.

Edgware had developed as a result of being on the old Roman road of Watling Street, becoming a staging post for much of the traffic on that route. In medieval times, it was an ideal stopping point for pilgrims, being approximately half way between London and St Albans. The parish church of St Margaret of Antioch dates from this time. Sarah and I are regular attenders there.

In our coaching age, Edgware has enjoyed good communications with London. At one point in the last century, there were four alehouses all doing good trade as a result. In 1791 one stage coach and two other coaches passed through Edgware each day to London and back, and another coach passed through on four days a week. There are now nine coaches from London passing through each weekday, and three on Sundays; seven carters go daily, with one extra on Saturdays, together with one wagon each day and two more on three days a week.

Also, in the last century, the Edgware area had become quite a centre for high culture. James Brydges had retired as an MP possessing a huge fortune (made as Paymaster-General during the War of the Spanish Succession) before losing much of it in the South Sea Bubble of 1720. He decided to build a magnificent house at vast expense in the nearby estate of Cannons, just on the west side of Watling Street. He had acquired the estate through his late first wife, Maria Lake. He held court at Cannons, very much in the fashion of the landed gentry in Germany, employing musicians, artists and the like. The king honoured him and, having been Baron Chandos, he took the title of first Duke of Chandos. The great composer Handel was attracted to his court and Chandos became his benefactor, resulting in Handel's well-known Chandos Anthems which were first performed in the nearby parish church of St Lawrence in Whitchurch. After Chandos died in 1744, the family fell on hard times and the house was largely demolished. But phoenix-like, a more modest replacement was built in its place and enlarged by subsequent owners to the elegant house it is today.

At about the time of our marriage, my good friend William Tootall (who is a conveyancer living in the area) wrote his excellent *A Brief Sketch of the Town of Edgware, Middlesex*, which gives a fascinating account of the town some 25 years ago. Tootall states a very good example of the generosity of the townspeople at that time. The great Battle of Waterloo, at which our Duke of Wellington condemned Napoleon Bonaparte to permanent defeat and exile, had happened just two years earlier. Following a collection, the sum of £35 was paid to a fund raised for the widows and orphans of the brave but unfortunate sufferers who fell during that glorious battle. This money was collected after a sermon given by Rev J Proctor in St Margaret's Church, an immense sum for so small a parish chiefly consisting of people paying rent for their ground and much burdened with poverty. The amount collected compared very well with similar collections in Whitchurch and Stanmore, neither of which exceeded it. But it demonstrated yet again that the inhabitants have suitable feelings for the sufferings of others, bad as their own condition may be.

The generosity of the parishioners did not stop there, because soon afterwards the vicar started another appeal for a new organ in the church. In fact, the appeal exceeded all expectations and the church was able to install an organ superior to the one being proposed. This new organ sounded for the first time on Easter Day 1816. Just three months later, there was an influx to the town of 300 poor Irish and other strangers who had left their homes to assist in gathering the hay harvest. They were almost starving as the weather was unfavourable and they had not been able to earn anything for many days. A gentleman living in the town, who is ever ready to assist the distressed by giving liberal donations, immediately started an appeal and within six hours the sum of £39 pounds was collected, part of which was distributed to the sufferers in bacon and bread the next morning, and the remainder used as required for the same purpose.

Another example of the good community spirit in Edgware is the Lammas Fair that is held every year in early August. An agricultural show had been started in 1760 but this had fallen into disrepute with some fairly unsavoury activities being undertaken. But in 1810, when the wish to have some amusement for the inhabitants at the end of the summer induced a few of the principal tradesmen to form themselves into a committee for organising a fair in early August, the event was resurrected with the help of some generous local donations.

It took place in the field called Baker's Croft and for the first event, a large quantity of cattle, shows, booths, stalls and games appeared, that was well beyond expectations. As a result, the peace and quiet of Edgware was shattered for a few days and it was observed that, though the sale of horses and other cattle was extremely dull, there were however a few merry souls present who kept the event alive. Each evening they presented a series of humorous amusements such as wheeling barrows blindfolded for a new hat, jumping in sacks for a smock frock, grinning through horse collars for tobacco, and climbing a lofty pole for a shoulder of mutton.

The very large attendance of respectable families in the neighbourhood was given considerable amusement by this final activity. This was helped by the fact that the poll in question was covered in grease towards the top, preventing them from reaching their prize. But one clever young boy filled his pockets with sand and with each of his numerous attempts increased the friction on the pole. When he claimed the shoulder of mutton, the cheers from the crowd were deafening.

William Tootall also describes many of the larger houses in the town including Edgware Place, which has particular relevance to my story. He describes it as a handsome house and grounds, tastefully laid out, lately being the property of one Thomas Smith. However, as Tootall was writing his account, the property was sold to none other than Charles Day. Tootall continues:

The present house was built about 14 years ago by the Honourable John Lindsay who actually pulled down part of the erections at Bermondsey Spa and had the materials removed here to build this house with. It is pleasantly situate on a hill and from the front door is an agreeable view of the town.

We lived very nearby and consequently Mr Day and his family became our close neighbours. Charles Day built for it a lodge known as the Blacking Bottle Lodge, because its shape represented one of the bottles in which his firm of Day and Martin sold their liquid boot blacking. Further north at Stone Grove are the handsome Almshouses which Charles built at his own expense in 1828 to house eight single poor folk of the parish. The ageing Atkinson's Almshouses beyond them were originally built in 1680.

In 1817, at the time of Tootall's writing, the population of Edgware was 543, just over a third of whom were employed in agriculture and many others working in the local gravel pits.

Such was the happy community that Sarah and I were honoured to serve as we embarked on our marriage.

Early in 1820, we were blessed by the arrival of our first child, a baby daughter whom we named Catherine Mary after her two grandmothers. She was baptised in our parish church on 6 May 1820. In an age where large families seem to be normal, we had expected to have the same. However, this did not happen and we put all our love, care and attention into raising our beloved daughter. And so, it was a considerable surprise and delight when we realised in the late summer of 1826 that Sarah was pregnant again. The result was the birth of our dear son John Andrews on 30 April 1827. Following our earlier precedent, we named him after his two grandfathers. He was baptised in our parish church on 29 May 1827, a most happy occasion for all concerned. In May 1831, we were blessed with another son (a surprise, as Sarah and I were well into our forties) and he was baptised in the church as William on 30 May 1831. But he was tragically taken from us in March the following year, aged only ten months. This was a hard time for us, but something we had to accept, like so many others around us. He was laid to rest in the churchyard, where we opened a family grave, right next to the vault opened by Charles Day for his mother-in-law and his parents.

Soon after our daughter was born, my brother-in-law and I began to accept that a business partnership between the two of us was not very practical. He had taken over his family's practice in Stanmore, but effectively we were continuing alone in our respective bases of Stanmore and Edgware. There were few benefits of being in partnership and many potential pitfalls. So, as of 29 September 1820, we decided to go our separate ways and avoid running the risk of any unpleasant family argument. Looking back, there is no doubt this was the right decision.

The king had eventually died in 1820 and was succeeded by his son who had been Prince Regent and, to all intents and purposes, monarch for many years. His lifestyle had not set a particularly good example to the nation and it was an open secret that he had had many mistresses. In fact, it had become not uncommon for gentlemen of means to indulge in such practices, exposing themselves to the health dangers associated with them in the form of venereal diseases, and in particular, syphilis. We know much more about this disease now and, if it is caught early enough, the chances of a successful cure are greatly increased.

Our current knowledge is that syphilis has three stages known as primary, secondary and tertiary. The primary and secondary stages occur very soon after infection and are mainly presented in the form of lesions. It is at this stage that the disease is infectious but treatment may be successful. However, if nothing is done and the tertiary stage is allowed to develop, the disease becomes particularly sinister. This is partly because it can lie dormant for many years with symptoms appearing over any period of time, from immediate to very long-term. The symptoms can include blindness, paralysis of the limbs, fits and dementia and eventually death.

During my time in Edgware, I have seen these symptoms present in a number of cases. I do what I can to ease the suffering but I am nearly always right in predicting the eventual outcome. I only mention this at this stage because it will have particular relevance in the sad case of Charles Day.

As I have already said, the Day family purchased Edgware Place in 1817 and became frequent visitors at weekends. The family would spend more and more time in Edgware but Charles would just come out when he could. He was obsessive about his business. On occasions, Charles and I found ourselves alone together. I began to develop a greater understanding of the personality of this remarkably successful businessman, still only in his late thirties, who had come from fairly humble origins. He would tell me about his early life and how his business had started and expanded rapidly. He was clearly very proud of his achievements. But the more I got to know him, the more I realised that he was a fairly introverted person who did not wear his heart on his sleeve. I found this endearing. He worked hard and expected the same from those around him. However, he was not ruthless, but clearly fair-minded. He realised that, in many ways, he had been dealt a lucky hand. As our friendship developed, he held me more and more in his confidence and particularly expressed his wish to give something back to the community in which he lived. But all the time, I felt there was something he was hiding. He did not seem to be emotionally at peace with himself, but he never revealed any details or evidence.

At the same time, Sarah did her best to develop a friendship with Charles' wife, Rebecca, but found this a real struggle. She was remote, distant and very bound up in herself. This only worsened after the death of her mother in 1822 who had lived with them for ten years. This also coincided with Rebecca's two sisters leaving the Day household, one marrying Charles' factory manager and the other leading a more independent life in London. Rebecca clearly had no understanding of or interest in her husband's business affairs. When in each other's company, Charles and Rebecca seemed to be strangely detached from each other.

When I first met Charles, he was virtually blind. He had told me that this was an affliction that had come over him shortly before he bought Edgware Place. I thought he probably had some vision but one eye was larger than the other and he suffered from a slight squint. He never complained about his condition and I was always most impressed that he was able to lead a virtually normal life. Although I attended the family for many minor ailments when they were in residence, Charles never indicated that he had any serious health problems and there were no reasons to examine him in these early years.

During the 1820s, Charles lost both his parents in addition to Rebecca's mother dying. Charles opened a vault in the local churchyard, in which all three were laid to rest. A few of us locals supported the Day family on these sombre occasions. We became really intimate friends around 1824, seeing them very regularly thereafter. However, as the years went by, it became more and more obvious that the three remaining members of the Day family were somewhat dysfunctional. Charles was of course completely bound up in his business which kept him in London, staying in his beautiful mansion at Harley House. Rebecca, on the other hand, was quite a timid soul, totally overshadowed by Charles when they were together. She spent most of her time in Edgware but whenever Charles came there, he took over everything, even the domestic arrangements. For visitors like us, this almost became embarrassing. We wondered what could have brought them together in the first place.

On the other hand, their daughter Caroline was becoming one of the most eligible heiresses in London. She had been born in 1807, the year after her parents had married in Stafford. Charles and Rebecca had had no more children which we thought strange. There could have been something medically preventing this, but if there was, I as their local physician certainly did not know about it. The subject was never discussed and we obviously could not raise it. Sarah and I both felt that a more likely explanation was that there had merely been a parting of the ways. Charles always referred to Rebecca as his 'dear wife' but, given the times in which we live, we all know that such a label could have been simply superficial and convenient.

Caroline was inevitably spoilt by her parents but we were never convinced that she was a really happy girl. We knew her from the age of about eleven and saw her suitors coming and going. But her eventual choice of Horatio Clagett, the Regency dandy and playboy who was the subject of the gossip columns in the press, was something which could not gain her father's approval.

The unavoidable result was an elopement and the couple were married in 1832. Charles was forced to accept this. They clearly wanted their lives to be based in the social whirl of London and Charles felt he could maintain an element of control over them if he allowed them to live in Harley House.

About the summer of 1834, I started to become concerned about Charles's health. His mobility seemed to become restricted and within a few months he had lost the use of his limbs. He became confined to a wheelchair. However, his mind was no less diminished and he still talked actively about his business. With his restricted movement, he inevitably was forced to spend more time in Edgware, although his single-minded determination still allowed him frequent visits to London for regular consultations with his business advisers. They were amazed how a blind man confined to a wheelchair still had such a remarkable grasp of his business and financial affairs.

But what had caused this paralysis of the limbs? On examining him soon after the problem began to present itself, I could see no obvious reason, especially as his continuing good health was undiminished. Nevertheless, he had been blind for about eighteen years and was now paralysed. This inevitably led me to only one conclusion – the onset of tertiary syphilis. The dormant period had lasted eighteen years, but perhaps we were now entering the final period of the disease. I discussed this with him and he accepted my diagnosis calmly. There was little I could do in the way of treatment but I did warn him to call me immediately if he felt the possible onset of a fit of an epileptic nature. I also advised him to let his medical advisers in London know and with his permission, I wrote to them stating my concerns. His two most trusted and long-standing servants were his butler Thomas Hunt and his wife's personal maid Frances Barton (known as 'Fanny', who also attended to Charles when he was visiting Edgware). I emphasised to Charles that it would be wise to confide in these two individuals in case they had to act in any emergency.

During this time, I became well acquainted with some of the regular visitors to Edgware Place – London friends and advisers who now had to visit Edgware on account of Charles' greater and enforced attendance there. In particular, there was a gentleman in his late fifties by the name of Pinder Simpson, often accompanied by his son John who was in his mid-thirties. They were both members of the legal profession. I noted how Mr Simpson Snr always greeted Rebecca Day very fondly and I eventually picked up that his wife and Rebecca were first cousins from Stafford.

After a while, Charles did explain to me that Pinder Simpson had been his legal adviser since he had first started in business in his late teens. Indeed, it was through Pinder Simpson and his wife that he had met Rebecca. With the family connection, a very close friendship had resulted. Consequently, Charles had known John since he was a small boy and had always held him in the highest regard. With Pinder's increasing years and encroaching deafness, Charles had been more than happy to rely on John as his closest confidante whenever advice was needed.

All seemed to be stable with Charles' condition until the middle of the summer of 1836. By necessity and confined to a wheelchair, he was now having to spend most of his time out at Edgware. But the calm atmosphere of the country was a tonic for him, especially when added to the good news in the shape of the free publicity coming from the publishing sensation that was *The Pickwick Papers*. The writer was anonymously known then simply as Boz but he later became known as the greatest writer of our time under his real name, Charles Dickens. He had mentioned Day and Martin in one of the early instalments of the story.

But then Charles was shaken to the core by the news, published in the national press for all to see, that his son-in-law had been spending 4 months in a debtors' prison. Although he was now released, the debts of over £30,000 had to be cleared.

I am quite certain that this was a major contributing factor leading to the commencement of the final stages of Charles' illness.

I was called to Edgware Place at 8am on Friday, 26 August 1836 as Charles had just suffered a major epileptic fit. I shall continue my story in the form of my diary from that day.

The Diary

Friday 26 August 1836

I rose early today. There was much to do about the village. The farm workers were tired after the heavy work of the harvest and were complaining of the usual aches and pains. I had many calls to make before the weekend.

Sarah and I were having breakfast with Catherine and John, when there was a loud rap on the door. Our maid came and announced that it was Thomas Hunt, the butler of Charles Day from Edgware Place. I guessed straight away why he might be calling on us so early.

I went to the hall to see him and he informed me breathlessly that Mr Day seemed to be suffering an epileptic fit. I had told him to come to me immediately if such an occurrence ever happened. I immediately collected my bag and set off with him for Edgware Place.

We were there in no time and Thomas took me straight upstairs to Charles's room. There I found him in bed being attended by Rebecca's maid, Fanny Barton. Poor Fanny was clearly worried, but she told me that the symptoms had already calmed somewhat and he was beginning to be responsive to those around him.

I briefly examined him and could tell that the worst was over and that he just needed rest for the time being. However, my general thoughts were very much along the lines of this being the final manifestation of tertiary syphilis and that this could be the beginning of the terminal phase.

I enquired where the rest of the family were and was told by the two servants that Mrs Day, together with Mr and Mrs Clagett, were away in Southend, in Essex, having a short holiday and taking the sea air for their general well-being. Without hesitation, I advised that they should be contacted immediately and asked to return home with all haste.

I knew that Charles had been receiving medical attention in London from the practice of Hewson and Beaman, 32 King Street, Covent Garden, and I asked that a message be sent there immediately. I wrote a short note to advise them of the position.

Charles's coachman left immediately on these two errands.

I sat with Charles as he gradually recovered. He could remember little of what had happened, but it was remarkable how quickly his mental faculties returned and I was reassured to leave him for a while and undertake my planned visits for the day.

I called again in the early afternoon. Charles seemed calm but Hunt considered he had had another mild fit about an hour earlier. I could see no evidence of it and was not concerned. Charles and I chatted for a while and he seemed his normal self.

Later in the afternoon, George Beaman (the junior partner of Hewson and Beaman) arrived at the house – an admirably quick response to my message sent via the coachman. I was surprised to see him as Charles had usually been seen by Thomas Ansaldo Hewson, a man about the same age as Charles who had become a good friend over the years whilst attending to Charles's considerable medical needs. Beaman explained that Mr Hewson was temporarily out of town, but as he himself had met Charles on a few occasions and was acquainted with his medical history, he felt it was important that he should come immediately. He was thanked by all present, including Charles and myself.

I knew George Beaman, a man in his mid-thirties, to be a rising star in the medical firmament. His reputation was gathering considerable momentum following his appearance as a principal witness at the famous 'resurrectionist' trial in December 1831, when Bishop, Williams and May were found guilty of murdering a poor, young Italian boy. Beaman had discovered the real cause of death which the murderers had disguised by further blows to another part of the body. With the Hewson and Beaman practice being in a wealthy part of town, Beaman had come into contact with some eminent consultants who thought highly of him. I was quietly comforted that Beaman, rather than the older Hewson, had made the visit.

At about 5pm, whilst Beaman and I were still present and discussing what form any treatment should take, Charles suddenly started showing signs of another fit. His body stiffened and he was unable to communicate. It was alarming to observe, but I was relieved that Beaman and I were there to witness it. Again, the symptoms subsided gradually and before too long, Charles had regained his normal composure and mental faculty, whilst being unaware of what had happened.

Beaman left shortly afterwards, saying he would return the next day as a matter of course. Rather poignantly, he had a quiet word with me as he departed, explaining that he was studying these exact symptoms in detail at present so that he could treat one of his own children who was suffering from epileptic fits. He prescribed bromide of potassium, and I was relieved that he was not prepared to countenance the out-dated traditional treatments of bloodletting, purging, blistering, and insertion of setons.

After supper, I returned to see Charles a final time to ensure that he was comfortable for the night. I encouraged Thomas and Fanny to contact me immediately during the night if any symptoms should return. They loyally agreed to take it in turns through the night to be present in Charles's antechamber, so that any symptoms could be detected as soon as they occurred.

This has been an eventful day, but I fear it may result in being typical for the days and weeks to come.

Monday 29 August 1836

This was the start of another working week and, with a fairly quiet morning, I had hoped that the usual routine would be re-established after the exertions of the weekend at Edgware Place.

I called on Charles during the morning and he seemed to have had a quiet night. I was not concerned. He told me that he was expecting two visitors that day. He was hoping to see his wife's youngest sister Susannah Peake. He had spoken to me quite often about her and it was clear that he had a far stronger bond with her than with his wife. I had met her occasionally over the years and it was clear that she excelled in many of the qualities lacking from her eldest sister. But her position as the third daughter in the family had been maintained by her parents and as such, she had drifted from them prior to their deaths. Subsequently, her sisters had treated her with a certain amount of contempt, probably borne out of envy, and they did not get on particularly well. If Susannah called on Charles, she would try and arrange it for a time when Rebecca was away.

As an aside, this reminded me of Rossini's popular opera *La Cenerentola* which had hit the London stage in 1820 and had been performed frequently since. It was based on the old story of Cinderella, the attractive servant girl who was dominated by her two ugly, but much older, sisters. The parallels with the Peake sisters were obvious and perhaps Charles had wished over the years to have been her charming prince!

Charles told me that he had arranged some time ago to meet with Susannah that day at Harley House to discuss a family matter of some urgency. This was clearly no longer possible, so he had sent his coachman in to Harley House with instructions to bring Susannah out to Edgware. Charles did not disclose what the urgent family matter was and I did not ask.

Charles also said that he was expecting a visit from William Croft, someone whom I had not met before. Charles explained that he had sent for him, as he was one of the executors named in his Will. Bearing in mind our recent discussions about his mortality, Charles felt it wise that his executors should be well informed. He explained that he had not known Croft long, he had only appointed him in his most recent draft of his Will in 1834, but had been impressed by his abilities. He was a civil servant, being an Assistant Treasurer of the Ordnance, and as such responsible for the administration of the finances of the Army at a very high level. Bearing in mind Charles's vast wealth, he was relieved to have appointed someone with proven ability in the administration of finances. As it transpired, this turned out to be an extremely fortunate appointment.

I called again on Charles in the late afternoon after completing some routine visits around the village. All seemed peaceful, although neither of Charles's expected visitors had arrived. I was just taking my leave of the house at the front door when Thomas rushed down and said that Charles seemed to be starting another fit. I ran back upstairs and this was indeed the case, a fit of perhaps a more violent nature than those that had gone before. It was alarming to observe. His body went stiff and he was unable to talk. All I could do was attempt to calm him in the hope that the fit would pass, which it eventually did. Again, he gradually returned to consciousness but was unable to recall what had happened. I felt I should stay with him and asked one of his staff to go to my house and explain my absence to Sarah.

Shortly afterwards, William Croft arrived on the scheduled coach from London, followed not long after by Susannah Peake in Charles's own coach. I met them downstairs and explained what had just happened. I felt it best that they should see Charles in his room separately and advised Susannah to go first.

She returned shortly afterwards, clearly shocked by the condition in which she had found her brother-in-law. She said that Charles had almost begged her to stay overnight and this she had agreed to do, albeit with some reluctance bearing in mind that the rest of her somewhat estranged family were now unexpectedly back from their holiday, having heard about Charles's condition. There was a room in another wing of the house where she would not have to socialise directly with them. He was clearly anxious to have these urgent discussions with her and hoped that he would be in a better medical condition by the morning.

William Croft then agreed to see Charles but asked me to go with him, in case his condition should deteriorate again. Charles greeted Croft warmly and was clearly relieved to see him. He explained to Croft that his life might be nearing its end and that Croft's duties, as his executor might have to be fulfilled sooner than had been expected. Croft had no problems with this, especially as he had recently retired from the Civil Service following the reorganisation of the Ordnance Treasurer's department under the new post of Paymaster-General. He was still only in his early-fifties and now had time on his hands. Charles was clearly relieved to hear this. I suggested that we should not stay any longer than necessary, as Charles should rest.

Croft decided to stay the night in a local hostelry and return to London the next day. However, as we left Edgware Place, he said to me that he was concerned, as Charles's mental capacity did seem to him to have deteriorated. I tried to reassure him that this wasn't really the case, but to remember that he had observed Charles very soon after a severe fit.

I returned home quite exhausted. What had seemingly started as a day without serious incident had transpired to be anything but that. Sarah greeted me in her usual patient, but resigned, way. I am so lucky that she accepts the burden of being a physician's wife with such grace.

Tuesday 30 August 1836

I am pleased to report that there have been no more medical emergencies today at Edgware Place. In fact, it has been a day of relative calm. Or has it?

Charles had clearly arranged to see Susannah at this time knowing that his wife, daughter and son-in-law would be away in Southend for a short holiday. But because of his illness, they had returned ahead of schedule. I would have expected Charles to postpone Susannah's visit until the coast was clear, so to speak. But he hadn't. This could only mean that the reason he needed to see Susannah was a matter of the utmost urgency and any bad feeling between the siblings would just have to be tolerated.

After the worrying events of the previous evening, I felt it my duty to call on Charles first thing in the morning. He had had a comfortable night and was basically back to his normal self. But there was a certain agitation about him and he told me that he was glad he was feeling well enough to have some important discussions with Susannah on a family matter. He said no more than that.

I now had a considerable backlog of work and was pleased to be able to reduce this through the day, in the knowledge that Charles's condition was stable.

When I returned in the early evening, I passed Susannah at the door. Charles's coach was waiting for her to take her back to London and she duly departed. In the passing, she asked me about Charles's condition. From my silent reaction, she could obviously tell that all was not well. However, I did then speak and reassured her that he was stable for the time being and was in the best possible care.

On seeing Charles, it was clear that he had recovered well from his fit of the previous evening and we were able to have a perfectly lucid conversation. He alluded to the fact that the day had been awkward for him with all the family present and the obvious tensions between Rebecca and Susannah. However, over the years, Rebecca had become conditioned to complying with Charles's wishes and if he told her that he wished to have a confidential discussion with her sister, she would not question the reasons. But she would quietly harbour a grudge to herself. Caroline knew her mother well enough to detect this and as a result, she and Horatio stayed with her most of the day whilst Charles and Susannah talked.

Charles and I had an extensive chat during which he explained the above in partial detail, leaving me to fill in the gaps by intuition. But then he surprised me: 'William, I hope you will forgive me, but I cannot divulge to anyone – even you, my trusted friend and physician – the actual nature of my discussions with Susannah. They have to be kept completely secret for the time being. However, I may have to rely on your confidence once I have thought about the matter further and in the light of how my medical condition develops. I trust you will forgive and understand me.'

'Of course' I said, assuring him of my absolute confidentiality at all times and of my assistance at any time he may desire it. I left it at that. However, I was puzzled and felt completely in the dark as to what may be happening within this troubled family.

Despite Charles's precarious medical condition, his brain was still as active as ever when he wasn't suffering from a fit and its immediate after effects.

I returned home and was able to enjoy the rest of the evening relaxing with my family. But I could not help feeling that there were going to be developments at Edgware Place of a very unexpected nature, although my mind could not work out what on earth they might be.

Wednesday 31 August 1836

I had known for several years that Charles's London physicians, Hewson and Beaman, had felt it wise to consult one of the capital's keenest medical minds, Dr Henry Clutterbuck, concerning Charles's continuing medical problems. They said they would inform him about the onset of the fits and word reached me that he would visit Charles in Edgware at some point today.

Clutterbuck was a man of nearly seventy years of age, but still working every second God gave him with seemingly indefatigable energy. This appealed to Charles, with whom I had discussed the eminent Clutterbuck's involvement on many occasions. In fact, about five years earlier, Clutterbuck had taken a house at Edgware, very close to Edgware Place and our own house. We had all met now and then as neighbours but had never established close friendships. Despite our common professional interests, I found him somewhat aloof whilst respecting his recognised abilities.

Clutterbuck's reputation went before him. He was a gifted student and passed into the College of Surgeons at the age of only twenty-three, after which he settled into practice in the City of London. He continued his academic studies, publishing his own journal and establishing himself as a dynamic lecturer on medical matters, from which he amassed a considerable fortune. By 1810, he was recognised as one of the foremost physicians in the capital. One of his best-known early publications was *Remarks Respecting Venereal Disease* and I suspect, although such a delicate subject had not been discussed with me in the past, his specialist knowledge was the reason that Hewson and Beaman wished to benefit from his opinions concerning Charles and his ailments.

Clutterbuck arrived at Edgware Place with Thomas Hewson around mid-morning and fortunately I happened to be visiting at the time. He greeted me with great courtesy and was clearly pleased to hear my thoughts on Charles's current medical condition. He explained to me that he had been seeing Charles for five or six years. He had attended him at Harley House several times in the early part of this year, at which time Charles exhibited various symptoms of a paralytic nature, his speech being to a certain extent affected and his lower extremities completely paralysed.

Hewson and I left Clutterbuck to visit Charles alone in his chamber. He emerged about fifteen minutes later and he confirmed his opinion that the illness from which Charles was suffering was a continuation of the same disorder and disease of the brain and spinal marrow that he had had all along. I was quite surprised to hear Clutterbuck's opinion that there was a good deal of feverish excitement about Charles. This was not my opinion and I could only assume it was Charles's emotional reaction to the great man's presence. Clutterbuck also said that, although Charles was perfectly clear at the start of the visit, he was beginning to become slightly confused as the consultation ended.

At this point, Rebecca entered the room and Clutterbuck merely repeated to her what he had said to us. She listened but made no comment.

We exchanged pleasantries at the main door and he said he would visit again soon.

Otherwise, everything was quiet today. Charles showed no signs of any further fits and we all did our best to keep him as peaceful and relaxed as possible. I was able to catch up with much other work but deliberately kept the evening free to enjoy with the family.

Friday 2 September 1836

I was woken just after midnight by Charles's manservant Thomas. I immediately assumed that Charles must have had another fit and Thomas confirmed that it was of a particularly severe nature. Without any delay, I accompanied him back to Edgware Place.

Thomas confirmed that Charles's son-in-law Horatio Clagett, on Charles's instructions, had already left for London with the coachman to summon Pinder Simpson, George Beaman and William Lawrence, another surgeon whom Charles had consulted occasionally in the past.

Although I found Charles in a particularly distressed state, the worst had passed. He was able to converse with me and said he was very anxious to make an alteration to his Will. He was worried that he might die before doing so. He needed Pinder there to draft the codicil and thought it was wise to have three medical men, including myself, as witnesses.

When Lawrence and Beaman arrived at about 5.00am, the three of us discussed the situation before going up to Charles's room so that the others could assess his condition. Horatio came with us and Thomas was already with Charles. Pinder, having arrived by his own transport and already having consulted with Charles, appeared from the adjoining room. He requested Lawrence and Beaman to wait and witness the codicil which Pinder was preparing on Charles's instructions.

When Pinder had completed the codicil, we were summoned into Charles's bedroom again and until then I did not know what the purpose of the codicil was. Pinder stood by the bedside close to Charles's head. Pinder explained that he had already read the codicil to Charles but he explained the contents to us in Charles's hearing, telling us that the codicil was made with reference to a substantial house (modestly named Manor Cottage) and thirty acres of land which Charles had recently purchased at Caterham in Surrey, where he already owned estates. The purpose of the codicil was to ensure that this property should pass to his trustees. It was only later that I discovered that Manor Cottage was in fact Pinder's residence, leased from Charles. The codicil also increased annuities given to Charles' sisters and his servants. Pinder spoke loudly and deliberately and in the manner of a man of business. Charles nodded in assent.

I do not recollect that Charles said anything in particular in approbation or satisfaction of the codicil. I recollect that during the time occupied in the execution of it, he said that his servants had had a great deal of trouble with him lately. Charles signed the codicil by making his cross to it, and then delivered and declared it to be his last act and deed in the usual way.

All this took place in the presence of Lawrence, Beaman, Pinder and myself and then Lawrence, Beaman and myself signed our names as witnesses to it, in the presence of Charles and in the presence of each other.

Charles was of perfectly sound mind, memory and understanding at this time. He was rational and sensible in every respect and, I would say with confidence, fully knew and understood what he said and did, and what was said and done in his hearing. He was quite capable of giving instructions and of making and executing his last Will or a codicil to it. There was nothing to raise a doubt as to his capacity at that time. He was quite himself, a man of good common sense and understanding. Beaman and Lawrence were in complete agreement with me on these points. They left soon afterwards, Lawrence being in something of a hurry. They had only been with Charles a matter of twenty minutes or so.

It still wasn't 6.00am and few of us, including Charles, had had much sleep. I did not need to persuade anyone that Charles needed to rest and we left him in his bed to be quiet and alone.

Downstairs, Pinder confided in me that Charles had ideas for a yet further codicil to his Will. Other papers needed to be brought from Harley House and this would involve contacting the keyholders to his strong room there. They were Pinder's son, John, who was presently in Brighton, and another solicitor by the name of Frederick Dufaur who had been undertaking work in recent years in connection with Charles's houses in London and the collection of the rent pertaining to them. Charles asked for a third friend to be present, being John Shaw, a further solicitor and friend and contemporary of John Simpson. Shaw had been a witness to Charles's last Will made in 1834.

Pinder was anxious to alert these three men that they would be required at Edgware Place tomorrow and this meant writing each a letter and arranging them to be delivered immediately. He wrote the letters there and then, was given some breakfast and left straight away for London.

I returned home exhausted and tried to catch up on some sleep before lunchtime.

I went back to Edgware Place in the afternoon just as Dr Henry Clutterbuck was arriving. He had heard about the events of the very early morning and felt it his duty to call on his patient. He only spent fifteen minutes with Charles, was quite satisfied that everything we were doing for Charles was correct, and returned to London without delay.

I made another late call at Edgware Place. Charles was quite relaxed, but in the knowledge that tomorrow could bring some more intense activity, I advised him to have a good night's sleep.

I returned home, and retired immediately for the same reasons.

Saturday 3 September 1836

Mercifully, the night was peaceful and there seemed to be no further emergencies at Edgware Place. However, on the prospect of Charles being visited by another trio of gentlemen from London for the purpose of writing another codicil to his Will, I felt it important to be at Edgware Place before they arrived to check that Charles was up to the task he had set himself. Consequently, I called mid-morning and found Charles relaxed, but looking forward to receiving his visitors. He asked if I could remain present as he valued my friendship and support as well as my medical knowledge.

At about noon, the three gentlemen arrived. I was of course acquainted with John Simpson, but I had not previously met the other two, John Shaw and Frederick Dufaur. The two Johns were clearly contemporaries and close friends and shared a similar warmth of personality. However, Dufaur seemed different in a distant sort of way. There was an awkward formality about him which acted as a barrier to any friendly conversation. I introduced myself but then retired from the room. Charles had in fact asked me to remain discretely in his anti-chamber and to listen to proceedings as they unfolded.

As directed in the letters drafted the previous day by Pinder, the gentlemen had all met at Harley House before coming out to Edgware. John Simpson had come up from Brighton to London the night before. Having first visited his father that morning, John had in fact gone straight to Harley House and, with his keys to the strong room, had collected the copy of Charles's Will. His father went with him. Dufaur seemed irritated that John Simpson had not called for him at his own house first, as suggested by his father

Pinder in his letter. Instead, John had sent one of his father's clerks to collect Dufaur in a post chaise and take him to Harley House where he found the two Simpsons and Shaw in the strong room. They were actually leaving the house as Dufaur arrived, and Dufaur merely joined them in the post chaise to Edgware. Pinder remained in London. He was after all a conveyancer and not particularly skilled in the drafting of Wills, which was far more his son's speciality.

John had sent up word to Charles that they were here, and Thomas presently came down with a message that Charles wished to see John alone first. John went up to the bedroom where Charles was in bed. No doubt John did not realise that I was in earshot.

On his entering, Charles said, 'Oh! John, I want to make a little alteration. I want to double the legacies to the children of my mother's brothers and sisters'.

John said, 'I suppose you mean their annuities. They have £20 a year under your Will each and I suppose you want that doubled'.

'Yes', he said and added, 'I want to give some additional annuities to my sisters and sisters-in-law'.

John replied, 'Why? For you made those additions yesterday', referring to the previous day's codicil drawn up by his father, a copy of which John had with him.

But Charles said, 'Oh! No. I never signed it. How could I? You were at Brighton and we had no witnesses.'

'Oh! Yes, you did', John said, 'I have got the draft in my hand and I'll read it to you'.

John then read the draft codicil over to him, and Charles said, 'Yes, it's right'.

John added, 'Now, Sir, this is the draft of the codicil my father prepared for you yesterday and it has your mark to it'.

Charles still said, 'No', but upon John saying to him, 'Yes it has, and the medical men are witnesses', the recollection of the circumstances then seemed to flash upon his mind, and he said, 'Oh! Yes. I had forgot, so they are'.

Charles then said, 'Well then, increase the annuities to my mother's brothers' and sisters' children, except Jane Virgo'. Apparently Mr Samuel Virgo was an excepted person in Charles' Will.

John said he would have to make a fresh codicil.

Charles made no comment. 'Now, Sir,' said John, ' I have brought the draft of your Will. Had I not better read it to you? My father told me he thought there was some alteration you wished to make and if there is, you can do it all in one codicil. It is better than making so many codicils,'

'Well, John,' said Charles, 'Then give me the heads of it, in your flippant way'.

That was an old expression of his and John knew what he meant. So, John went through the Will briefly stating the heads of it to him. Charles made no remark till John had finished and then said, 'It's alright, now I will sign'.

John told him that before he could do that he must go downstairs and draft the codicil. He said, 'Why can't you do it here?' John's reason was that Charles would talk so much and that he might therefore make mistakes.

So, John went down into the dining room where he drafted the codicil relating to the additional annuities for Charles's mother's siblings' children.

John stated to Shaw and Dufaur downstairs what had just occurred with Charles and consulted with them as to the propriety of making the codicil for Charles under such circumstances.

They all agreed that there could be no harm in John making it as it was merely in furtherance of Charles's Will. John read the draft of the codicil, just written, over to them and then proceeded with it upstairs to Charles's room.

John then sat down at Charles's bedside and read the draft codicil over to him and said to him, 'Now, Sir, is that what you wish?' He replied, 'Exactly. Now I'll sign it'.

But John reminded him that he must make a copy of it and that it must then be read over to him in the presence of witnesses and that then he could sign it. He seemed angry at this and said, 'Why should they know what I do?'

John suggested that he seemed to forget that, owing to his blindness, it was absolutely necessary that the codicil should be read over to him in the presence of the witnesses. So, John went downstairs, taking the draft codicil with him for the purpose of copying it out.

Whilst John was copying it, Hewson arrived from London and John told him how Charles was and the want of recollection Charles had just manifested to him. He requested him to go up and see Charles and report back to him whether the codicil should be executed. On his return downstairs, he said he thought John should proceed and offered to be one of the witnesses to the codicil.

John went upstairs having finished copying it, taking the copy with him and, accompanied by Hewson, Shaw and Dufaur, the proposed witnesses, he told Charles that he brought the witnesses with him and that he would read the codicil to him and that then he could sign it. John then, in the presence of the three witnesses, read the codicil over distinctly to Charles. Shaw had the draft in his hand and was looking at it.

When John had finished reading, he asked Charles if it was

right and he expressed his approval of it. I am quite confident that Charles well knew and understood the contents of the codicil and that he expressed his approval of it in some way.

John then put the codicil before him and guided his hand whilst he made a scratch or mark to it with a pen. He then handed it to the three witnesses who all three subscribed their names to it in the presence of Charles and John.

After Charles had made his scratch, he repeated with some difficulty, owing to a niggly cough, the words, 'I publish and declare this is to be a codicil to be taken as part of my last Will and Testament and I desire you to be witnesses to it'.

After the witnesses had subscribed their names to the codicil, John put it into an envelope and put it into his own pocket with the said draft he had made of it, and the draft of the other codicil of the day before.

All three visitors then took their leave. In anticipation of this, I had gone down by the back stair to the hall to say my farewells.

John questioned me as to whether I thought Charles was then of sound mind, memory and understanding and capable of doing any act requiring thought, judgement and reflection. I reassured him of my opinion that Charles was, and that he understood what he was doing at the time he gave instructions for the making of and the execution of the codicil in question.

But John did not consider that he was of sound memory. Far from it, inasmuch as he did not recollect the fact of his having made the codicil on the preceding day until it was brought to his recollection by other circumstances.

John felt that another strong proof of his failure of memory occurred as follows. Whilst the witnesses were signing the codicil, Charles said to John, 'Now, John, take my keys to the cellar at Harley House, take out my bankers book and get it filled up' and within two or three minutes, whilst they were still standing round his bed, he gave the same directions in the very same words to Dufaur, evidently forgetting altogether that he had given the direction to John just before. As John had not seen Charles since the fits started, he was much struck with this failure of memory.

John, accompanied by Shaw and Dufaur, then left hastily in the post chaise for London.

Hewson remained and we chatted about this latest episode in some detail. We both agreed that Charles was of perfect, sound mind, memory and understanding and were surprised at John Simpson's concerns. Something suggested to me that it was very unfortunate that John had made these expressions in front of Dufaur at the time, such thoughts proving to be horribly grounded in the light of subsequent events.

I went up to see Charles again briefly before leaving. He was in good spirits, if a little tired. I suggested he enjoyed a late lunch followed by an afternoon nap. He thanked me for staying around and I reassured him that I felt everything had gone very smoothly.

I returned home to salvage what remained of the day with my family. But I did go back to Edgware Place late in the evening. Hewson had decided to stay the night, as he often did, and we enjoyed a nightcap together, reflecting on the day's events and in particular the fastidiousness of John Simpson when in 'professional' mode. We merely put it down to youthful exuberance!

Throughout the day, Horatio and Caroline were hardly in evidence. Rebecca did appear occasionally, but appeared completely bemused by everything. Her deafness did not help, but she simply failed to understand anything that had taken place.

I retired exhausted, and looked forward to a quiet and refreshing Sunday.

Tuesday 6 September 1836

Little of significance happened medically today. In fact, Charles had been in the best form he had been for a while. We had had some good chats about the past in recent days, proving at that point that Charles's long-term memory was still absolutely clear.

To my surprise, Charles opened up to me about his marriage with Rebecca and how they had quickly drifted emotionally after the initial excitement of their marriage and the birth of Caroline. Although I had gathered this myself, I was still surprised that Charles spoke to me about it so openly.

When I saw he was becoming tired, I left him to rest. On the way out, I found Rebecca sitting alone, staring into space. As she was my patient too, I felt I should sit and chat with her. To my further surprise, she also seemed unexpectedly forthcoming. She complained about how lonely she was and how she and Charles had floated apart years ago.

As I came away, and in the light of what Charles had told me earlier, I suddenly realised that this was actually their thirtieth wedding anniversary. Had he realised? Had she realised? There were no obvious outward signs that either had. By a strange coincidence, they had both spent the day pouring out their innermost personal thoughts to the same third party. Given the circumstances of both, this was a strange way to celebrate such a milestone.

I returned home in something of a daze. This was noted by Sarah, but she was used to me returning, laden with people's medical problems, which of course I could not reveal to her. Little did she realise what I had heard today.

I spent a restless night.

Thursday 8 September 1836

As usual, I made a very quick visit to Edgware Place before breakfast to confirm that the night had been quiet and that Charles continued to be comfortable. This was indeed the case, as told to me by Thomas Hunt at the door. I began to hope that we had reached a stage of stability, perhaps caused or helped by the mental activity of recalling his reminiscences to me over the last few days.

I let some time elapse after lunch before making another call at Edgware Place, principally to allow Charles to continue his recollections to me. He needed no encouragement, but he did seem to be more agitated than usual and again fiddling about and wanting my assurance that no one else was in the room or could hear our conversation. In particular, he wanted to talk about his wife's sister Susannah.

As I had already deduced from my chat with Rebecca, a strong bond of respect and emotion had developed between Charles and Susannah. This had started soon after Susannah had removed to London with her mother in 1811 after her father's death. Of all the Peakes, Susannah stood out to Charles as the one who understood him most and shared his level of intelligence. There was no point in looking back, but soon after their friendship developed, it became clear to him that he had married the wrong sister. In confiding in me this sensitive information, it was obvious why he was somewhat agitated, whilst at the same time being relieved that he could share his thoughts in strictest confidence with a trusted friend and adviser.

Charles said that he found himself discussing all elements of his life, both business and personal, with Susannah, something he could never contemplate with Rebecca. He was relieved that he had got to know her before being struck by blindness so that her image was always clearly in his mind's eye.

He said that Susannah had been a huge support to him at the onset of his blindness in 1816. She had understood the problems he faced in running the business and the necessity and importance of employing the right person as manager. Consequently, she had been instrumental in the appointment of John Weston.

She had also been influential in the decision to buy Edgware Place in 1817. Charles expanded on this from what he had said the day before. The real reason for buying a second country residence was to remove his wife, her sisters and mother from London so that he could be left alone for significant periods at 1 Euston Square. He would also invent reasons why Susannah could remain there with him. She knew he wanted this, for reasons that were not only to be left in peace to run Day and Martin. He admitted to me that he had been missing, as a result of his blindness, the 'high life' he had secretly been enjoying in the pleasure palaces of London, although he said this with a weight of guilt in his voice. He knew he was unfaithful but temptation had defeated him. His relationship with Rebecca simply could not fulfil his natural desires and resulting frustrations, evil as he knew such feelings were. He was ill at ease with his conscience. Knowing her sister and Charles as she did, Susannah could understand this and was sympathetic.

He admitted that he had inevitably made advances to Susannah when they were alone together in London, but she had wisely resisted. She realised the risks involved with any such liaison, bearing in mind the proximity of her mother and sisters, even if they were in Edgware for much of the time. Charles reluctantly had to accept this. However, Susannah understood his frustrations and agreed to explore ways these could be relieved. Charles gave her some contacts from his former sighted times. This was a very delicate matter but Susannah had the intelligence to know how to approach it whilst maintaining complete secrecy. And this is how such matters were resolved over the next two or three years.

Towards the end of 1820, Charles encouraged Susannah to make a trip back to Stafford. There were business reasons – Day and Martin had developed some outlets in local shops for their products – but Susannah was also keen to see some wider members of her family. Her Aunt Sarah was still trying to operate The Goat Inn. She had buried two husbands, and of her three children by her first marriage to John Peake, William and John had married, leaving only Sarah, who was by then twenty-five, at home. She was a lost soul, never having identified with her half siblings, the children of Sarah's second marriage to the now deceased John Matthews. Susannah had long chats with cousin Sarah, who felt that her life was going nowhere. She had no alternative but to live with her mother but, to get away from the house, she took on some occasional domestic duties elsewhere in the town. Her mother resented this, feeling that she was being disloyal and should be putting all her efforts into the family business. She wanted to get away but just could not break loose. Susannah realised that her cousin was a bright young woman who deserved better in life.

This gave Susannah an idea. With his blindness, Charles needed a permanent attendant, something that Susannah simply could not do, with her other responsibilities. Perhaps Sarah could fulfil this role. With her few worldly possessions, Sarah jumped at the chance of returning to London with Susannah. Susannah proposed her plan to Charles who agreed, always keen to please his close confidante. However, Susannah had some ulterior motives but decided only to indulge them when the opportunity arose.

Sarah had severed her links with her mother and was refreshed with the excitement of starting a new life. She stayed in the servants' quarters at 1 Euston Square. Rebecca, who could hardly remember Sarah from the time she left Stafford fourteen years ago, was aware of her presence but, for convenience to all, failed to acknowledge her on the rare occasions she saw her.

Charles recognised in Sarah the same intelligent family qualities enjoyed by Susannah. Susannah's plans were falling into place and before long Charles was inevitably working his charms on Susannah's, and let it be said his wife's, first cousin. Sarah was flattered beyond her dreams and offered little resistance. The liaison was established, to the benefit of all concerned.

In explaining all this to me, Charles glowed in his admiration of Susannah and his obvious affection for Sarah. This was all very heady stuff and I felt I had certainly heard enough for one day. Charles was becoming quite agitated and excited. I felt my urgent departure was necessary and I left.

After supper that night, because I was slightly concerned, I called briefly at Edgware Place to be re-assured by Thomas Hunt that Mr Day was by then sleeping soundly. I retired to my own bed, my head spinning with the revelations of that day.

Friday 9 September 1836

I made my usual visit to Edgware Place before breakfast, just to be sure that Charles had passed the night quietly. Thomas Hunt told me that, whilst there were no signs of any further fits, Charles did seem to be somewhat on edge. As a result, I went upstairs to see him.

As I had suspected, the revelations of the day before had left him in a state of agitation. I was sure this was the cause of his present state and the cause of Hunt's concern, although Hunt knew nothing of the reasons. As earlier in the week, Charles kept saying that he had a great secret to communicate to me. He kept fidgeting about to be assured that no one else was in the room and yet, when satisfied that we were alone, it came to nothing. He simply could not speak the words to tell me what the 'great secret' was. I tried to make him relax, changing the topic of conversation and then bringing him around to the subject again, but it was no use. He just froze. I could only assume that it was something concerning Susannah and Sarah. It struck me as strange that the events that Charles had described to me yesterday took place at least fifteen years ago but they were clearly vivid in his mind. What could have happened in the intervening time?

There was no use in speculating. If the story was to come out, Charles would no doubt reveal it at the right moment. In the meantime, I felt it was wise to calm Charles down as best I could and leave him to rest for the whole day. I left the usual instructions with Thomas to summon me if he felt there was anything wrong. But, as I was now clearly aware of the reasons for Charles's anxiety (he had revealed much to me, more than anyone else, on what was clearly a sensitive subject), I felt it wise to keep away for the rest of the day.

I tried to carry on with my normal work but, I have to confess, I could not get out of my mind what Charles had told me the previous day. My contacts with Susannah Peake up until now had always been courteous but I did have a subconscious feeling that there might be something going on under the surface.

With absolutely no intention of seeing Charles, I was still tempted to call at Edgware Place late in the evening and was assured by Thomas that Charles had gone to bed at his usual time. Safe in this knowledge, I duly went to mine.

SATURDAY 10 SEPTEMBER 1836

At about 1.00am, a loud wrap on the front door wakened me. It was one of the coachmen from Edgware Place who had been sent by Thomas Hunt to summon me immediately. I went with all haste.

Thomas greeted me at the door. Although it was only thirty minutes since he had given the instruction to summon me, he said that it had seemed like an eternity. He explained to me that Mr Day had been taken very ill shortly after midnight. He had gone to bed at his usual time the night before, but he had woken feeling a sensation coming over him that he was sinking fast and that he was dying. He said that Mr Day did not seem to be having a fit. He had asked for Pinder Simpson to be summoned immediately and this had been done. Thomas himself seemed to be in a state of shock. When I asked him the reason, he said that Mr Day had just told him something that had shaken him terribly. He would not say what it was as he had to remain discrete, but he was sure that Mr Day would tell me anyway. Perhaps this was at last the 'great secret' about to be revealed.

I found Charles in a state of great nervous agitation and irritation. I could not tell whether or not he had had a fit. He might have had, but I could not diagnose it. He was much alarmed and was under the impression that he was going to die. There was no doubt that he was very ill. He was in a precarious state and I thought that, if he should then be attacked with a fit, he would die. Consequently, I asked that his sisters, Mrs Susannah Lockwood and Mrs Mary Dey, whom I knew were visiting at the time, be wakened and called to the room. Thomas asked Fanny, to go and raise them. As I could make a reasoned guess at what the 'great secret' might be, I felt it wise not to summon Rebecca at this stage.

When Charles' sisters entered the room, Mrs Mary Dey went to his bedside and seated herself. Charles at once began by telling her that he had something to disclose and which he wished to disclose before any greater change took place.

With his sisters present, he just revealed the secret itself without any preparatory introduction.

Charles made the disclosure as a declaration, as a dying declaration of his intentions, and called upon myself and his sisters and servants to bear witness to what he said, which was as near as possible as follows: 'I have three children to whom I have given post obit bonds of £5,000 each which will be presented at my death. And I wish them to be doubled and hope Mrs Day will not object'.

Thomas Hunt was also in the room and nodded to me in acquiescence that this was indeed the information that Charles had imparted to him before my arrival.

Then Charles stated the children's ages as thirteen, eleven and nine and that he wished us to witness what were his wishes. I told him that, if such were his wishes, it was no use his merely saying so, but that it must be properly written down and signed. I proposed writing down what he wished. He might not live until Mr Simpson came. A hundred things might prevent him from coming immediately.

The other sister, Mrs Lockwood, said to me: 'Don't put it off' and Charles added, 'Do as my sister wishes you'. Shortly afterwards, Mrs Lockwood left the room, only to return a little later.

I procured some writing materials and wrote down in the best way I could what he had just said, in the form of a further codicil to his Will. During the writing of it, I asked Charles if the children were to have their money when they came of age and he said that that was to be left to the discretion of his trustees. What I wrote was very short and I made no draft or copy of it. But when I had finished it, I read it audibly and distinctly to Charles in the presence of his two sisters and his manservant. He appeared to understand it perfectly and then signed it by making his mark to it in the presence of his sisters, Thomas Hunt and myself. I, his sister Mrs Mary Dey and Thomas Hunt then signed our names to it as witnesses and in the presence of Charles and each other. I put a wafer seal to it and Charles went through the ceremony of placing his fingers to it, and declaring it to be his act and deed. I was particular in having everything done which occurred to me to be necessary to make it a perfect act, for I thought Charles might die before Pinder Simpson arrived.

The actual time occupied in the preparation and execution of this codicil was only about a quarter of an hour. I wrote it without loss of time, thinking he might die. I had been woken at 1.00am and the codicil had been made by 3.00am.

I held onto the codicil until Pinder Simpson arrived so that I could deliver it to him personally. Charles was of perfect sound mind, memory and understanding throughout the whole procedure. He talked rationally and sensibly. He perfectly understood everything that had happened and was fully capable of giving the necessary instructions, or of doing any act requiring thought, judgement or reflection.

After making the codicil, Charles spoke about the three boys to his sisters. They listened attentively and clearly had no previous inkling of the children's existence. They made no comments, but I noted the somewhat shocked expressions on their faces, which of course Charles could not see.

After this, I was never aware again of Charles mentioning the boys to any other parties, although I certainly did discuss the boys with him in private as I shall later describe. It was a painful subject for him and he merely wanted to ensure that there would be adequate resources for their lifelong wellbeing after his death. However, his son-in-law, Horatio Clagett, whilst confirming that no one in the family knew of the existence of the three boys prior to 10 September, said that after this date, Charles spoke of them several times in an unguarded manner and without any apparent cause or necessity for mentioning them. I was never present when this happened.

When Pinder Simpson arrived, the others (Mrs Dey, Mrs Lockwood and Thomas Hunt) left the room. I gave him the codicil which he read in my presence. He said it would do very well. I wanted him to prepare a more formal codicil but he would not do that. The codicil read as follows:

I Charles Day of Edgware and Harley House being of sound mind so desire that the three Post Obit Bonds for £5,000 each which will be presented at my decease may be doubled, that is made £10,000 each and that the same may be invested for the benefit of my three natural sons by my executors as trustees according to their discretion and this shall be their authority.

As Witness my X mark

Charles Day
Signed, sealed and delivered as my act and deed this 10th day of September 1836 in the presence of us and signed by us in the presence of each other.

William Foote, Surgeon, Edgware
Mary Dey, Chelsea
Thomas Hunt, Servant to Charles Day Esq

But then something even more unexpected happened. Pinder Simpson called Charles's attention to the circumstances of there being another bond of which he had heard. Charles was reluctant to admit that there was such a bond. But eventually he did admit to its former existence, saying that it had been destroyed following the child's death. He said no more about the identity or details of that fourth child and this remains a mystery.

Having now revealed their existence and thinking that he was close to death, he expressed a strong desire for the boys to be brought to him with all haste. He revealed that they were in fact in Margate taking the sea air for their general good health. He also revealed that his wife's sister, Susannah Peake, had always known of their existence and was in fact with them. This came as no surprise to me, bearing in mind what Charles had told me earlier in the week. After discussion, we agreed that the best way of summoning them would be through John Weston at the Blacking Manufactory. It would be best if this instruction came to him from a close family member and Caroline Clagett seemed to us to be the obvious candidate.

Although we were both very short of sleep, we were also wide awake. Charles seemed calm, as though a weight was off his mind, and he asked if we could leave him so that he could sleep. Death seemed to have been averted, at least for the time being. Pinder Simpson and I went down to the drawing room and the rest of the night passed quickly as we discussed the extraordinary news that the night had exposed and its consequences.

When Caroline Clagett appeared for breakfast, we asked her

to draft a note to John Weston which Pinder Simpson dictated as follows:

My father has expressed a wish that Susan Peake should be sent for today. Will you have the kindness to send a confidential person to Margate for her? She lives in Cecil Square but I cannot tell what number. My poor father passed a very restless night. Come down tomorrow at all events.

Yours in haste
Caroline Clagett
Edgware
Saturday morng

Caroline was understandably puzzled as to why she was sending such a note but, as she had always been brought up to be in awe of Pinder Simpson, she dutifully obeyed and asked no questions. Her chief concern was of course for her father.

Pinder Simpson then left the house, bound in all haste for London whence he would go direct to 97 High Holborn. He had told me that he intended to take the codicil to the residence of John Weston, Charles' brother-in-law, and inform him of the existence of the three boys and what Charles had done in their favour as stated in the codicil. He would also say to John Weston that Charles wished Susannah Peake to be summoned immediately from Margate where she was on vacation with the three boys, bringing them back with her. He would deliver to John Weston the note from Caroline Clagett confirming this. Pinder Simpson would request that a confidential person be sent to Margate for that purpose. He would ask John Weston to endorse Caroline's note and send one of his clerks on this errand to Margate. He would say to John Weston that it was a matter of importance that the children should be sent for immediately in order that they might be identified.

Pinder Simpson also said that he would send for his son John who was in Brighton. He felt it was important that he should have discussions as soon as possible bearing in mind the new information about the children. The precarious state of Charles' health made this all the more urgent.

I went home for a late breakfast and to explain my absence to my ever-suffering wife. With my head still pulsating following the night's events, I felt it wise to draft a letter to Horatio Clagett, the 'man of the house' with Charles being incapacitated, begging that Charles's family, friends and attendants do all in their power to humour him and otherwise to keep him quiet, as all matters by which he was liable to be excited or irritated added to the disease under which he was labouring.

For the rest of the day, I was really fit for little else. Sarah made a picnic lunch which we enjoyed with Catherine and John in the garden. After that I fell asleep in a chair under the tree, enjoying the late vestiges of summer and dozing intermittently into the evening.

I made the usual late call at Edgware Place to be assured by Thomas Hunt that for the rest of the day the house occupants had said little and that Charles was resting alone and comfortably. We both knew there would be plenty of goings-on the next day, with amongst others the Westons liable to visit, and agreed that it would be wise to retire early. We quietly went our separate ways, but both feeling that life would never be quite the same in the Day family.

Monday 12 September 1836

I wasted no time in going around to Edgware Place after rising in the morning. Thomas told me that Charles had spent a satisfactory night but was still quiet and within himself.

After breakfast, I called again and met Mrs Mary Dey in the hall. She was about to depart and had her travelling clothes on for leaving. She said that she had just come from Charles's room. She said she had asked him, for her own satisfaction, whether he remembered what he had done over the weekend and whether he was satisfied with it. She confirmed to me that he did recollect it and was perfectly satisfied. She also confirmed that this was all he said and no one else was present. She thought that he was of perfectly sound mind, memory and understanding at the time and conversed rationally and sensibly. He was as comfortable as possible. I was relieved to hear this and bade Mary Dey farewell.

I went up to Charles's room and was disappointed to find Charles in a state that did not agree with Mary Dey's description. He recognised me and was pleased to see me but what conversation we had was not particularly coherent on his part. I would even begin to say that his speech was somewhat childish. I was beginning to fear that the effects of Rebecca and Caroline's challenge to him yesterday might be permanent. On hearing of the children's existence, they had demanded that he revoke the codicil and seek a less public method for providing for the children.

A visitor then arrived in the person of John Simpson, who attempted to persuade Charles to provide for the boys by a more discrete method.

John Simpson and I went up to Charles' chamber together. John Simpson did get Charles to speak a little but it was in such an irrational manner that he could achieve very little with him.

John said something to him to this effect: 'So, Sir, you have been making a codicil, I understand, in my absence, for the benefit of your natural children'.

Upon John saying this, he looked at him savagely and said: 'No John, Bonds, and I will have more'.

He then repeated the word Bonds several times and saying: 'I will have more Bonds'.

John then tried again to bring him round to the subject, saying to him something to this effect: 'Now, Sir, can't we make some arrangement and do away with that codicil'.

He gave John no answer to this but began telling him that he had a great deal to say to him and then he went on to ask him several times, in the most childish way, how long he could stay and how long it would take him to walk up to town.

'Now, John,' he kept repeating, 'how long can you really stay'.

After this, John made another attempt to get him round to the subject of the codicil, asking him if he could not invest the money in the funds for the benefit of the children upon which he said quite petulantly: 'Why?'

John told him that he should do it to save the feelings of his wife and daughter.

He made no reply to the observation but addressing John abruptly, he said: 'You shall have the carriage and go to Pine Apple Gate but tell me how long it will take you to walk up to town and what is the latest moment you can stay'.

Whilst he was going on in this way, visiting medical men were announced, and so we left Charles for a while.

I was relieved to see that it was Thomas Ansaldo Hewson on another one of his regular visits. I was even more relieved when Dr Henry Clutterbuck arrived at the same time. For once, he was coming to Edgware Place when he was really needed. They both examined Charles simultaneously to minimise any stress on him. The three of us had a discussion downstairs and were unanimous that there had been a decline in Charles's condition and that, certainly for the time being, he would not be able to discuss or transact any business.

John Simpson had discussions with all three of us medical attendants together and we conveyed to him what we had just concluded about Charles's condition.

Being aware of the various visitors arriving, Rebecca and Caroline then entered the room and heard what we medical attendants had concluded. We advised Rebecca and Caroline and John Simpson that in future it would be wise to humour Charles by complying at once, or at least pretending to comply, with every direction he gave, however absurd. He had always been used to having his way.

After seeing off Hewson and Clutterbuck, John Simpson and I had a discussion as to what to do next. We decided that nothing further should pass on the subject of the codicil or the provision for the natural children either on the part of Charles or John Simpson, finding that in his present state it was hopeless to fix his mind on any rational point for a second.

John Simpson agreed that no further attempt to renew the subject with Charles should be made. The chance had been lost through no fault of ours.

John Simpson departed Edgware Place before lunch, bearing an air of defeat.

Before I left for lunch at home, I managed to have a quiet and discrete chat with Thomas Hunt. He agreed with me that, for the first time, this morning he had noticed a definite deterioration in his master's mind. Charles Day's memory and mental capacity were becoming impaired, but we certainly would have denied this up to this point.

The events of the morning had left me somewhat deflated. I knew that I would be informed immediately if Charles' condition were to deteriorate and I was losing enthusiasm merely to return to Edgware Place to find out for myself. The afternoon visits last week when Charles had given me his recollections of the past had been enjoyable for me and therapeutic for Charles. But now, with his condition having declined, such lucid discussions were no longer possible, for the time being at any rate. Besides, work was beginning to pile up in the village, and I had to devote myself to my other patients.

Thus, it remained through the afternoon and early evening. I enjoyed a relaxed supper with Sarah and the children and was preparing myself to retire for the night just after 10pm, when there was a loud knock on the door. It was the maid Fanny Barton to tell me that Charles may be having another fit. I hurried over to Edgware Place with her.

When I arrived, Thomas Hunt told me that Charles had woken from a sleep and thought he was dying. Thereafter he had said nothing. He could not be induced to move or speak or do anything whatever. I went up to his room and all was exactly as Thomas had described. Charles did not acknowledge my presence but merely stared into a void, remaining fully awake but unresponsive to anything around him. I can only describe this as a sort of silent fit.

We had no option but to take it in turns through the night to sit with him in the hope that he might emerge from this trance.

Midnight came and went and there was no change. Thus ended a somewhat disheartening day.

WEDNESDAY 14 SEPTEMBER 1836

Today has seen the case of Charles Day re-establish itself on two different fronts – the diminished state of his health and the introduction of a completely new personality to the string of visitors to Edgware Place.

I resumed my practice of a pre-breakfast visit to make sure that Charles had spent a satisfactory night – he had, but otherwise there was no change in his condition.

After a few routine visits in the village, I returned to Edgware Place just before noon. As I arrived at the door, I passed a gentleman probably in his mid-thirties leaving with a rather annoyed expression on his face. More than that, there was just something about his physical presence that I found quite repulsive. I cannot put my finger on it – it was just one of those impressions that linger in the memory. He hardly acknowledged me and left by the carriage in which he had clearly come. It was only after he left that I remembered having met him at the house earlier in the month. He was one of the gentlemen from London who came to witness the codicil that Charles drew up last Saturday week.

When I went into the drawing room, I found Rebecca in an agitated state. I enquired what was the matter and whether it was anything concerning the visitor just departed. She confirmed that it most certainly was. She had never met him before but he had given his name as Frederick Dufaur and from his visiting card, he was clearly an attorney. He told her that he had business to conduct with her husband. He had said something about the purpose of his visit being to procure a written authority from Mr Day which was required in order that her husband could receive a pension from the Treasury, upon which her husband had a charge. Not surprisingly this meant absolutely nothing to Rebecca and, I have to confess, to me neither.

Following my discussion with Rebecca and Caroline the previous evening, Rebecca had quite correctly summoned the courage to tell Mr Dufaur that she was under particular orders from her husband's medical attendant to keep Mr Day quiet. She had told him that her husband's head was very bad.

I complimented Rebecca on standing firm and said she had done absolutely the right thing. She confirmed that she had forbidden Mr Dufaur to see Charles and that Mr Dufaur had not hidden his annoyance at her instruction. He said that he had deliberately come back from Brighton, where he had left his family, for this meeting and the inconvenience of not being able to see Mr Day was considerable. However, he did advise her that her own signature, on behalf of her husband, would be sufficient and she had therefore given it in the hope that this would give him some satisfaction. After she had done this, he took his leave without much further discussion. He certainly did not enquire of Charles's welfare or ask her to pass on his kind regards. She quite rightly thought this rather rude.

I admired Rebecca for her actions but, being of such a timid nature, this had clearly had quite an effect on her and she became very emotional. I comforted her and reassured her again that what she had done was entirely correct and justified. Neither she nor I had heard Charles talk of this gentleman and we were perturbed that he had been visited by such an apparently dark stranger. Also, I quietly thought to myself how strange it was that he should ask for Rebecca's signature, as though she was a proxy for Charles, with seemingly no written authority in place from Charles to fulfil such a role.

After sitting with her for a while until she had calmed down, she agreed that I should go up and see Charles. Mercifully, I was sure that he knew nothing of what had been happening downstairs. He was in a reasonably quiet state and I felt it best to leave him, allowing me to continue with my other work.

Little else of note happened today, except a couple more routine calls on Charles. I noted that, whilst he was not incoherent, I could not contemplate any further reminiscences with him. His mental state was still too fragile and I didn't expect much improvement. All he really said to me was that he was anxious that the Simpsons should visit as soon as possible so that he could make a new Will. He was still clearly troubled about his final arrangements and confused, having now written three codicils in little over a week. Something that was already complicated was now even more so. But I was quite sure that his mental state was too poor to enable him to make a fresh Will, or even to add any more codicils.

I retired at night with this as a firm conclusion of the day's visits, but also concerned by the appearance today of the mysterious Mr Dufaur.

Thursday 15 September 1836

Having made some bleak observations about Charles Day's future over the last few days, I have to admit that today's events lead me to believe that I might have been too pessimistic. The silent fit had subsided on Tuesday afternoon and since then he had rested uneventfully. After today, I feel that the decline will not be at a constant rate but there will be 'ups and downs' and during the 'ups', it will be quite possible to have a lucid conversation with him for a limited length of time.

On my mid-morning visit, I was certainly encouraged. Charles was sitting up and was clearly pleased that I had called. He seemed alert and spoke about the events of the previous weekend, expressing pleasure at the drafting of the latest codicil. I deliberately stayed only a short time, wishing to preserve the energy that he clearly had today. He was sorry that I didn't stay longer but said he was hoping this would be the day when his wife's sister Susannah would visit. With this possibility in mind, it made my swift exit all the more justifiable.

Sure enough, as I was about to leave, a carriage drew up at the house and Susannah Peake emerged. We had a discussion in the hall. There was no evidence of Rebecca, Caroline and Horatio being at home and the servants confirmed that they had gone out for the day in the knowledge that Charles was somewhat improved. Perhaps this was just as well. I briefed Susannah in great detail about what had happened since her last visit on 30 August. I said far more than I normally would to a patient's sister-in-law, but now knowing what I did, I was confident this was appropriate. She thanked me. I explained what had happened and in particular about the latest codicil, which I had drafted, revealing that I now knew all about the existence of the three natural children, their parentage and Susannah's pivotal role in the whole arrangement. I also explained how Rebecca's negative reaction had caused Charles to have a relapse although the signs today were better. I certainly advised that for Charles to have a visit from Susannah would likely be beneficial, but asked her to look for warning signs if he tired and maybe not to stay with him too long for each session. She heeded this advice as the sensible person she clearly was. I couldn't help but notice the intellectual differences between her and her sister Rebecca.

When I returned at about 4pm, I found Susannah alone in the drawing room. She was eager to tell me what had happened and I was equally eager to listen. She said that she had been several times alone with him and he had taken the opportunity of enquiring after the children. He did so very tenderly and affectionately. She said that they had conversed much about the children and he had informed her that he had made a codicil and done what he had promised he would when they had met on 30 August. This was clearly the urgent family matter to which he had referred at the time. He had told her, 'I have a codicil and have done that which I promised for them. I have doubled the sum that will yield £1,200 a year. I could put you in the way of making more of it but that would be intricate and troublesome to you. I should wish you to remove to a larger house such as that I lived in in Euston Square and bring up the children according to their expectation in life'. So, she had asked him what his wishes were respecting them, and she asked whether he would wish them to remain at the new school administered by London University in Gower Street. She said she would explain more about this to me later, but that he had said, 'Yes', if she was satisfied with their progress. He had added his wish that, when they were sixteen, he should like them to be placed with a clergyman for two years.

She certainly realised that he was very ill and had declined markedly since she last saw him on 30 August. He appeared very much altered and enfeebled. However, she was quite certain that, during the whole time she was with him, he was of sound mind, memory and understanding. He spoke clearly to her of the plans he wished her to follow after he was dead.

He also confirmed to her that I had drafted the codicil and therefore was fully in the picture as to the existence of the children. She expressed her relief about this, saying that she would like to have an opportunity as soon as possible to give me all the details of what had happened since their births. I said that I would be pleased to listen if she felt that it would help her in this very difficult situation. I emphasised that this would be in strictest confidence. She expressed her relief and pleasure at this.

I felt that there was no time like the present, if Susannah was keen to tell me her full story. However, I also felt it would be unwise if this happened at Edgware Place. By chance, the family had been away for the day. This was just as well, for all concerned. But they would be liable to return soon. I had to think of something quickly. The only possible solution was to ask Susannah if she would like to come to our house, an invitation which she accepted with alacrity. We walked quickly down the drive and next door to our house.

Sarah was naturally surprised but all I had to say in introducing Susannah was that she was Rebecca's sister and wanted to have a confidential chat with me. Being a physician's wife, Sarah fully understood and left us alone in the drawing room, but not before asking Susannah if she would like to join us for supper. She accepted gratefully and Sarah left us alone.

Firstly, I thought I had better let Susannah know what I

already knew. I explained that Charles had told me all about his special relationship with her and how she had introduced him to her cousin Sarah Peake from Stafford, whom I assumed was the mother of the three natural children, but he had said no more, other than admitting to the existence of the children. Susannah confirmed that this was the case, with herself being the 'superintendent' of the whole arrangement and Sarah being the children's guardian.

I was keen to know what had happened in the intervening sixteen years, since the liaison between Charles and Sarah had been established in 1820. At this point, Susannah started an extraordinary narrative, the telling of which will remain clear in my memory to my dying day. It must have been at least two hours that she spoke without interruption and I listened intently.

She commenced by explaining all the details of how Charles's liaison with Sarah had come about and how this had resulted in the birth of Henry and Alfred. Charles had arranged for them to live quietly in their own house at 29 Earl Street. She described how John Price had been invented as the children's father and that, when a third child was expected, they had moved to a bigger house at 16 Seymour Place. Edmund was born soon afterwards. Susannah had lived with them as their 'superintendent', attending to all the household arrangements and leaving Sarah purely to her maternal duties.

Susannah continued: 'We did everything we could to cover our tracks. When we were in Earl Street, we ensured that the man who paid the Land Tax was recorded as John Price. We removed to Seymour Place in 1827 but retained the house in Earl Street which carried on being in the name of John Price until 1829 when the street was redeemed from the Portman family. So, for those years the Land Tax for Seymour Place had to be in someone else's name. Charles and I agreed that it would be best to appear in my name. After the redemption of the Portman estate, this was no longer a problem.

'Thereafter Charles and I decided, for the avoidance of any doubt to the outside world, to pay for entries in The Royal Blue Book. As you may know, this is a fashionable directory containing the town and country residences of the nobility and gentry. Being privately produced, those who appear in it must pay for their own entries. It is therefore not an exhaustive list of every household, but contains those who wish to be traceable and, by inference, have nothing to hide. We certainly wished to give that impression. Consequently, we made an entry in 1830 in my name and for the years to 1834 in the name of John Price.

'We even had someone calling at the house in 1831 doing a census for the population of St Marylebone. This is a new idea which may be adopted on a national basis in the future. I had to think quickly and put myself as the householder, but because I was flustered, probably gave the wrong numbers of people living in the house. No other names were requested'.

All this made me realise the stress under which Susannah and Sarah must have been living. No one could suspect what was actually going on. The consequences of the truth becoming public would be dire, not only for Charles personally but also for his business.

Susannah also explained how Charles paid her increasing amounts for maintenance allowance as the boys grew older. And it was about this time that it was decided the time had come to kill off the boys' fictional father.

The next part of Susannah's account concerned the creation of the £5,000 *post obit* bonds, deliberately done to make provision for the boys, but in the most discrete way. This involved the confidence of only Robert Barbrook, Charles's clerk. Susannah was now so frustrated that Charles had just decided to double these bonds, but by means of a potentially public codicil rather than a simple alteration to the discrete bonds. But she realised that no one was to blame. Sadly, Barbrook had since lost his mind and was now in a lunatic asylum. Other than those people mentioned, Susannah was hopeful that no one else knew about the bonds and therefore the existence of the children. However, she did know that Barbrook had sought advice on the form of the bonds from a solicitor by the name of Antonine Dufaur. I tried not to look startled when I heard that surname, it being fresh in my mind from yesterday.

The reasons that made Charles anxious to conceal the fact that he had fathered the children and also the fact that he had executed the bonds are obvious, bearing in mind the stigma attached to illegitimacy in our society. However, Susannah felt that this anxiety had reduced very marginally when she saw him today, perhaps because he had now revealed the secret to his immediate family, thus relieving his sense of guilt. When speaking to Susannah today, as with the rest of us who had been told, he was particularly anxious to know that no one else was in the room. But it was clearly a load off his mind.

Immediately after making the bonds, according to Susannah, Charles distinctly said that he meant to do something more for them by and by. 'By my Will or in some other way', he said. Afterwards he frequently spoke in the same way to Susannah and Sarah concerning the three boys and his intention to do something more for them. But he said this to no one else prior to making the codicil.

In 1834, with Charles beginning to lose the use of his limbs (a classic symptom of tertiary syphilis), visiting the boys became far more difficult. They moved a short distance from Seymour Place to Wyndham Place. He frequently visited the children whilst they were at these addresses. But late in 1834, he lost the use of his limbs completely and could not walk. From then on, he used to send for Susannah frequently. She would visit him at Harley House so that he could enquire after their welfare. These enquiries were expressed with the utmost regard and affection and he showed on all occasions the anxiety of a father for their welfare.

Henry was eleven and needing formal school education, a new concept for boys that age being offered by a school operated by London University in Gower Street to the east of Harley House. This all pointed to yet another move for Sarah, Susannah and the boys in August 1835 (that is, just over a year ago), this time to 4 Osnaburgh Street, between Harley House and Gower Street. Henry and Alfred had started at the school in 1834 and Edmund followed after the move in 1835. All are enjoying the school and doing well. They are now aged thirteen, eleven and nine.

Susannah then explained what had been happening in the recent past: 'Since he lost the use of his limbs, I visited him frequently, perhaps once a week or once a fortnight, as it suited him. He always took the opportunity of making appointments to see me when Rebecca and the family were away. There were family disagreements which mitigated against Rebecca and I seeing each other.

'Last month, Charles had asked Sarah to take the three boys to Margate during the school summer vacation for the benefit of their health. He and I had made an appointment to meet at Harley House on 29 August, following which I was to go with him to Edgware for a couple of days to plan future arrangements for the boys. This is when Rebecca, Caroline and Horatio should have been away in Southend.

'But he had been taken ill and instead of coming himself, he sent his carriage for me. I went to Edgware and, as you know, I stayed until the following evening. During that time, we discussed in depth his plans for the boys. He spoke of them with his usual affection and regard. When I mentioned that Edmund had had an accident and hurt his arm, he showed great anxiety for his recovery and wanted him to have the best medical advice. It was only a minor accident but Charles was very concerned. Previously Charles had proposed that I should then join the family in Margate but, with him being unwell, I proposed to defer my journey. He would have none of it and insisted that I go at once to ensure that Edmund had the best treatment. So, I went to Margate on 1 September.

'But the day before yesterday (13 September), I received a letter from John Weston, hand delivered by one of his clerks, saying that Charles wished me to return immediately with the boys to London. I had already sent Sarah back to Osnaburgh Street with the injured Edmund, and so I returned yesterday with Henry and Alfred. Charles had also said that he wanted to see me immediately, causing my visit here today'.

And so finished Susannah's extraordinary story. All the gaps in my knowledge were filled and all was explained. She thanked me for listening and said it was a relief to be able to unload all these secrets to a discrete third party whom she knew enjoyed Charles's trust and confidence.

Sarah then entered and said that supper was ready. It was a relief for both of us to cease talking about such an intense subject, the supper conversation almost seeming like small talk in comparison. By the time our repast was finished, the hour was late and the last coach had left for London. We insisted that Susannah stay the night with us. She could catch the first coach in the morning and not be noticed by anyone. Sarah quickly prepared her bed and we all soon retired, reflecting on the extraordinary circumstances of Charles Day and his two families.

Tuesday 20 September 1836

This was another day of little happening at Edgware Place, with the exception of a rather unfortunate occurrence concerning Horatio Clagett.

On my various visits, I observed Charles continuing to drift in and out of periods of lucidity, but Fanny and Thomas said, unless you were with him all the time, it could be difficult for a chance caller to decide what state he was actually in at that precise moment.

Horatio had wisely always kept his distance. Although he was present in the house most of the time, he rarely saw Charles. However, he was happy to act on Charles' orders and fulfil the role of being his scribe.

When I called on Charles in his room in the late forenoon, Thomas told me that Horatio had just left the room having taken down some dictation for Charles, being a letter to Simeon Bull which Horatio said he would dispatch immediately. However, Horatio was clearly unaware that Mr Bull had visited Charles on Sunday when Charles's mind was quite clear, and had discussed some business. In the light of this the letter made little sense, but Horatio was not to know this.

Firstly, it was maintaining that Mr Bull had a debt to clear with Charles. If in the very unlikely event that this was true, Charles would have surely mentioned it on Sunday.

The letter then went on to ask Mr Bull to pass on an invitation to Frederick Dufaur for this coming Thursday, to come out to Edgware for dinner and to stay the night. If that were the case, why didn't Charles send such an invitation to Dufaur direct?

Finally, the letter referred to the matter of the lease, which had been fully resolved on Sunday. Clearly Charles had forgotten all about the Sunday meeting with Mr Bull and was in a confused state when he had dictated the letter to Horatio.

But the letter had now been sent and little could be done about it.

It was a lesson to all of us to confer amongst ourselves at all times before undertaking any orders given by Charles in his current confused state.

Otherwise, as I have said, this was a quiet day when routine work could be attended to. The peace at Edgware Place was almost eerie, as though we were just waiting for something major to happen.

WEDNESDAY 21 SEPTEMBER 1836

Today started very much as before, so far as the happenings at Edgware Place were concerned. I had made two brief calls in the morning and all was stable.

Later in the afternoon, I called again and was pleased to see that Thomas Ansaldo Hewson had recently arrived. I was just apprising him of the latest state of Charles's health when we heard another visitor arriving. I recognised the shrill voice of Frederick Dufaur. I could hear very clearly what he was saying. He had acted on Charles's invitation but had come a day early because, as he explained in his agitated sort of way, he had left his wife and family in Brighton, taking the sea air, and was anxious to return to them as soon as possible. As he said this, he barged past the servants and went straight up to Charles's room, without seeking anyone's permission.

Hewson and I were enraged and were forced to make a quick decision, whether or not to enter Charles's room, so that a medical attendant was on hand in case of an emergency. By not going in, we were leaving Charles at Dufaur's mercy. Conversely, by going in, we could cause a commotion if Dufaur was resentful of our presence, thus potentially upsetting Charles even more. For right or for wrong, we decided to remain downstairs but decided in advance to deliver a stiff admonishment to Dufaur when he emerged.

When Dufaur did come down, we introduced ourselves as two of Mr Day's medical attendants. We made it very clear to him that we had advised the family and the servants that Mr Day's health, and particularly his mental state, was declining fast and as such, we thought it extremely unwise that he should have any visitors and certainly not ones who wished to discuss business matters. I added: 'Consequently we were furious, not to put too fine a point on it, when you arrived and overrode the requests of the staff by proceeding straight upstairs for a business interview with Mr Day'.

Dufaur kept his calm and merely replied, in a particularly repulsive and supercilious manner: 'I am surprised to hear you say that. I actually found him much better and congratulated him on such an improvement in his health. In fact, I expressed a hope that he would cheat the doctors, meaning that he would ultimately recover, to which Mr Day replied that he hoped so too.'

This left both Hewson and me lost for words. The man was both arrogant and a liar, given that we had both seen Charles just before Dufaur arrived and he was clearly in a very confused state of mind. Hewson eventually weighed in with: 'Mr Dufaur – Mr Foote and I accept that you are an experienced solicitor and we would respect your professional opinions. We would appreciate it if you would respect ours as physicians.'

'Gentlemen,' Dufaur replied, 'I came to Edgware in response to a written invitation from Mr Day, conveyed to me by Mr Simeon Bull. As I need to return to my family in Brighton, I came a day early, a fact that did not bother Mr Day. He has invited me to stay the night here. I have had some clear business discussions with him, but Mr Day explained that the real reason he wished to see me was to invite me to be one of his executors. He felt that his existing three executors were getting on in years and he wished to have an extra younger man in the executorship. As with the other executors, I would receive a legacy of £500 and I would continue to receive my commission on his London rents and annuities and mortgages.

'Of course, I am happy to fulfil this role and I said so to Mr Day. I suggested to him that we should wait for the return of John Simpson from Brighton for the drafting of the necessary codicil, but Mr Day insisted we should proceed immediately in his absence as the date and time of Mr Simpson's return was not certain. I suggested that we left this overnight and have another discussion tomorrow after breakfast.'

Needless to say, our reaction to such a bold and brash statement was one of stunned silence. The man had to be lying and inventing a story that was clearly premeditated and to his own benefit. We left him alone in the drawing room with nothing more being said.

Obviously, we considered it essential to see Charles and confirm to ourselves that none of what Dufaur alleged could have happened. We found Charles in a confused state, as we would have expected. Deliberately, so as not to upset him, we did not ask him anything about Dufaur's visit or the extra codicil in Dufaur's favour. Neither did Charles allude to any such matter. We merely stayed long enough to confirm our opinions of Charles's current state of mental health.

We deliberately went down by the back stair to find Rebecca in the parlour. Being quite deaf, she had not heard the arrival of Dufaur and when we told her what had happened even she, of such a timid nature, could not hide her anger. She agreed with us that Dufaur should not be allowed to stay overnight in the house, despite Charles's apparent invitation. We made a plan that, because we were particularly concerned about Charles's health, Hewson and I should both stay in the house overnight, thus using up all available beds. Rebecca concurred.

Hewson and I returned to the drawing room and confronted Dufaur. 'Mr Foote and I have examined Mr Day again,' said

Hewson, 'and we remain very concerned about his state of health. Just so that you can be left in no doubt, we frankly believe that everything you have told us about your interview with Mr Day is pure fabrication. Our immediate concern for Mr Day's wellbeing is so acute that we both feel it is imperative that we stay with him overnight in the house. This will use up available spare beds and you will have to seek alternative accommodation in the village if you wish to stay. We have informed Mrs Day and she agrees.'

Dufaur merely sneered, taking his leave of us and saying we would see him in the morning. Our hope of frightening him away altogether was sadly not achieved.

As it was still reasonably early, both Hewson and I felt it important that we should call upon Dr Clutterbuck to visit immediately, so that he could add his weight to our opinions should there be any disputes in the future. We knew that Clutterbuck would need no encouragement to come out to Edgware, and the later the hour, the greater the fee! Although we both respected his opinions and ability, we shared the same cynicism about his professional practices. We duly sent a message to him.

Clutterbuck arrived late in the evening. He briefly examined Charles and left us in no doubt as to his agreement with our opinions, saying he would be happy to testify accordingly in the event of any dispute. We told him of the difficult time we were having with Dufaur and he found this distressing. He reiterated that the three of us could set aside on medical grounds any actions made by Charles in his present disturbed state. He duly departed back to London, having only been at Edgware Place a matter of fifteen minutes.

In the meantime, I had returned home and explained to Sarah that, for complicated reasons, I would need to stay overnight at

Edgware Place. She understood and helped me pack my essentials for the overnight stay.

Before retiring to our beds, Hewson and I tried to relax with a nightcap in the drawing room. Thomas kindly brought us each a brandy. Whilst he was in the room, we asked him what he thought about Charles's present condition and whether he had had any contact with Dufaur in the house earlier today. We were keen to hear what Thomas had to say, as he was probably closer to Charles than anyone, being in constant attendance.

'I did hear Mr Dufaur say in the dining room, after he had been with Mr Day', said Thomas, 'that he could make nothing of him. I know that we shouldn't have allowed Mr Dufaur in to see Mr Day and I am very sorry about that, gentleman. Please accept my apologies, but there was nothing we could do without causing a considerable commotion which would have upset Mr Day.'

'Do not worry, Thomas,' I replied, 'we quite understand the very difficult situation in which you found yourself and we believe you did the right thing. But what you have just said about Dufaur's remark to you is most interesting. Thank you.'

Hewson and I looked at each other and exchanged a wry grin. We chatted on for a few minutes. We were certain that we were in the right but, at the same time, we were under no illusion that tomorrow was going to be a very difficult day.

Thursday 22 September 1836

A restless night had been spent by all concerned. Hewson and I did not sleep well, both worried about the challenges that tomorrow could bring. It is never particularly enjoyable to have to stand one's ground against anyone, particularly lawyers. Thomas and Fanny had stayed with Charles all night, snatching what sleep they could. They had not found it necessary to call either Hewson or myself but were reassured that we were there. Nevertheless, they said that Charles had been wandering a great deal during the night. Something was troubling him deeply. I began to wonder what really had been said by Dufaur to him at their meeting yesterday.

Through the night, I was beginning to consider my position in what was a seriously intensifying situation. My principal function was that of local physician to Charles Day. I had no locus in any disputes within the family or the executors, especially as any potential disputes would be liable to involve lawyers as the main protagonists. I felt that perhaps I should step back and act as a safety net for the family, rather than running the risk of becoming directly involved myself. I did not see this as a cowardly reaction, but merely my desire to fulfil my principal role as physician to the family. Consequently, after rising and paying Charles an early visit, I decided to leave Edgware Place, safe in the knowledge that Hewson was still there to attend to any medical emergencies. I found Charles to be in a fairly unsatisfactory state after a difficult night. I resolved to continue my usual practice of calling in at the house several times during the day. In any case, my workload in the village was mounting up and I really had to give it my attention.

I left Edgware Place at about 8.00am but not before having an informal gathering in the parlour with Rebecca, Horatio, Caroline and Hewson (who was anxious that everyone should be briefed on tactics). In the knowledge that any actions pushed through by Dufaur could be overturned on the grounds of Charles's mental incapacity (as certified now by Clutterbuck as well as Hewson and myself), Hewson suggested that the prime objective was to have Dufaur leave Edgware as soon as possible. To this end, and with Charles's immediate wellbeing the primary objective, we all agreed that we should allow Dufaur to do what he wished, knowing that it would be subsequently overturned. With no disputes in front of Charles, he would hopefully be kept calm. It was the usual approach of tempering Charles and agreeing to whatever he wished, knowing that he would almost certainly forget about it within minutes. Rebecca, Caroline and Horatio had always been persuaded not to interfere with Charles's affairs, so they readily agreed to this plan.

During our chat, we heard Dufaur arrive and again go straight up to Charles's room, disregarding our request of yesterday. The man certainly seemed to be behaving as we predicted but dreaded.

I didn't call again during the rest of the morning. However, I did pass the house just before noon and I noticed a carriage leaving in the direction of London with two persons inside and one on the box beside the driver. I could not identify who they were.

By mid-afternoon, I had settled many of my local cases and decided, not without a certain amount of trepidation, to call again at Edgware Place. I found Hewson still in attendance. He welcomed me and clearly wanted to tell me what had happened since the early morning. I shall continue in Hewson's own words:

'Dufaur, being alone with me in the breakfast room just before the family assembled for breakfast at about 10.00am, informed me that he had received directions from Charles to prepare a codicil to his Will, thereby appointing himself (Dufaur) an executor to Charles's Will.

'Shortly after this at about 10.00am, the family assembled at the breakfast table, the party consisting of Rebecca, Horatio and Caroline Clagett, Frederick Dufaur, and myself.

'Whilst at breakfast, Dufaur addressing himself primarily to Rebecca, but still making the matter one of general communication, stated that he had seen Charles that morning and that Charles wished that he (Dufaur) should be one of his executors. Dufaur added that Charles's wish was that a younger man should join the existing three executors.

'This is all that Dufaur said on the subject.

'Rebecca's reaction (in line with our agreed plan) was that she would concur, if that was Charles's wish. Horatio and Caroline made no comment.

'A little time afterwards and before we left the breakfast table, Dufaur asked me if I would act as his clerk or amanuensis, or some familiar term of that nature, and fair copy the said codicil which he said he had drawn out in pencil on the back of a letter. I was amazed at his audacity but (again in line with our plan) I duly consented. Dufaur did actually concede that he thought it would be irregular if the codicil was in his own handwriting. Some concession!

'He certainly did not state that it was Charles's wish that I should do the writing. It was apparently his own idea to ask me to do it.

'I then withdrew from the breakfast table to another table at a distant part of the room and was there given pen, ink and paper by Caroline. Dufaur handed me the pencil draft. I copied it verbatim onto a sheet of letter paper which I then handed back to Dufaur.

'Then Horatio, Rebecca, Dufaur and myself adjourned immediately to Charles's room to complete the new codicil. We found Charles sitting in his chair, dressed and supported by pillows. Fanny was with him, as was her usual habit, but she retired immediately into the room adjoining.

'Dufaur handed me the fair copy of the codicil and then in the presence of Dufaur, Rebecca and Horatio, I said to Charles, 'I have prepared a statement in compliance with the request of Mr Dufaur and shall I read it to you, sir?'

'Charles signified his wish that I should read it to him by nodding his head, his usual token of assent. I then read the said codicil to Charles in the presence of the others in the room. I read the document as distinctly and clearly as I could and Charles appeared to pay great attention to it. During my reading of the document, Fanny came back into the room to attend to the fire. Having completed the reading, I asked Charles if the meaning of the codicil was clear to him and he answered 'Yes', firmly and distinctly.

'Then Dufaur said, 'Now Mr Day, you can make your mark to this'. Upon which Charles in rather an irritable tone and manner said, 'Why make my mark? Why should I not sign my name?' I noted Charles' irritation. Other than this, Charles said nothing throughout the whole process.

'Fanny went out of the room to fetch Rebecca who would normally assist Charles in signing documents by guiding his hand. Then Charles himself indicated to Rebecca to bring his laptop writing desk which she did. With the document being placed on it and on Dufaur's instruction, she guided Charles's hand and he signed the said codicil 'Chas. Day'. There was no seal affixed to it. No alteration was made by Dufaur, or myself or anyone else, as a result of Charles actually signing the document instead of making his mark. At this point, Rebecca was relieved to take the opportunity of leaving the room. Fanny had remained in the adjoining room.

'Dufaur recalled Fanny back into the room and myself, Horatio and Fanny signed our names as witnesses. Before Fanny signed, she looked at me to ascertain whether or not she should sign the paper. She just caught my eye and indicated a spot where she should sign and I said, 'Yes, sign it there'.

'I remember that Dufaur asked us three to sign our names as witnesses and that we did so in the presence of Charles, in testimony of our having been present at the execution of the codicil by Charles.

'I do not consider Charles was, at and during the time of the transaction of the reading and executing of this codicil, of sound mind, memory and understanding, that is, not of perfectly sound mind, memory and understanding. He was evidently labouring under a state of irritability. He was not violent, but still different from his natural character. There was also a sullenness about him and, though the distinction is a very fine one, I would say that on balance he did understand what he said and did, and what was said to him and that he knew what he was about. I form that opinion from his reaction to my reading the codicil to him, when I asked him whether or not I should do so, and also from his observation about actually signing his name instead of making his mark. But even that was done in an irritable manner and I know that the nature of his disease was such that his mind was weakened.

'I still do not consider that, at the time of executing this codicil, Charles was capable of making and executing a codicil to his

Will or of doing any serious act requiring thought, judgement and reflection.

'His manner was so entirely distinct from his usual manner. He was on this occasion in a highly irritable state, whereas his natural manner was usually a cool, calm and deliberate mode of transacting any business of similar importance.

'After we had signed the codicil, we all went downstairs, leaving Charles in his room. Dufaur took the codicil and folded it up in an envelope. I did not see him seal or endorse the envelope. He mentioned that he would be passing the document on to John Simpson, although Charles had not directed anything about what should now happen to the codicil.

'Then Dufaur went outside and got into Charles' carriage which was waiting at the door. He remained there for about forty-five minutes, waiting for the Clagetts to join him as they were also going to London'.

Hewson had kept Dufaur's pencil draft of the codicil and showed it to me. The text was as follows:

This is a Codicil to the last Will and Testament of me Charles Day of Edgware in the county of Middlesex, Esquire, which I desire may be considered as annexed to and to be taken as part thereof.

I hereby nominate, constitute and appoint Mr Frederick Dufaur of 23 Queen Ann Street, Cavendish Square, one of my executors jointly with the executors appointed by my said Will and I give and bequeath unto the said Frederick Dufaur the sum of £500 free and clear of legacy duty for the trouble he may have attending the execution of the trust thereof and it is my Will and desire that the said Frederick Dufaur should continue after my decease to receive the rents of my houses in London and also the annuities and a mortgage interest which he now receives for me upon the same terms he now receives the same.

Dated this 22 September 1836.
Charles Day

I had listened intently to Hewson's account and was indeed relieved that I had stepped back and not been in attendance throughout the whole process. Hewson added that, after Dufaur had left to wait in the carriage, Horatio had said to him with deep concern, 'We can hardly have done right'. But Hewson had emphasised that the codicil would stand a challenge, given Charles's mental state as certified by us medical attendants.

Hewson went on to explain that Charles, almost immediately after the codicil was executed, began talking in a very incoherent manner. He asked Horatio to wait and then gave some ridiculous orders. This was the first time he had spoken at any length today and his tongue never stopped for a second. He gave confused orders about game, wildfowl, venison and other items to be bought in London. Fanny was present and told me that Charles lived principally on game and always ordered it himself. Orders arrived once or twice a week. Horatio wrote down all the orders, which included pheasants although, as Horatio pointed out, they were not in season, and then Charles asked how he had written it. On replying, 'In ink', Charles said, 'That's fatal – it must be written half in ink and half in pencil'. So, with Hewson, Thomas and Fanny watching, he made Horatio write it all over again as he desired, causing the delayed departure with Dufaur stranded in the carriage, for which he received no apology!

Fanny made an interesting observation to Hewson soon afterwards, referring to the difference in Charles's manner during the time of giving his shopping list and what he had been like when executing the codicil, 'See how soon he goes off again'.

Hewson and I then had a confidential chat about Horatio's

delicate position in the family. We were sure that Horatio felt disgust at what Dufaur was doing. But, on the other hand, Horatio was not long out of a debtor's prison and had been negotiating with Charles as he to how he could help him clear his debts and not to sully the Day family's reputation. Horatio would have probably refrained from being involved in the whole business of the codicil, had he had a choice. In good times, he knew how his father-in-law could show his temper. He was no doubt given some comfort by our assurance that any of Charles' actions could be overridden on medical grounds.

Charles had continued to be irritable and over-excited all day.

The most telling factor for Hewson was that he knew that Charles had the greatest confidence in the Simpsons. He did not believe that, if he was still of sound mind, Charles would have appointed an executor to his Will without consulting the Simpsons or his other executors first. He was also confident that, assuming Dufaur did deliver the codicil to John Simpson, the latter would disregard it on the grounds of Charles's mental incapacity as certified by the medical attendants.

Almost in a state of mental exhaustion and certainly tiredness, Hewson then decided to take his leave and return to London. He thanked Rebecca for her hospitality but wished that the occasion had been a happier one. In turn, Rebecca thanked him for his attendance which, in the circumstances, she had found reassuring.

I felt it wise to sit with Rebecca for some time, as she was now alone. I had to speak slowly and deliberately bearing in mind her deafness. She was certain that Dufaur was up to no good, although she was probably not capable of understanding the absolute significance of the codicil executed today. There was no doubt in her mind that Charles was in a confused state all the time and could not have had rational conversations about a codicil as Dufaur had maintained. We agreed that it was very clever of Dufaur to be seen to resist drafting the codicil himself and to get Hewson to do it. It gave the whole exercise an air of credibility. She felt it far more likely that Dufaur had seen his chance and come with a premeditated plan which he had then forced on Charles, knowing he would not be capable of resisting, given his mental state. I said that it was crucially reassuring that Dufaur had no witnesses to his conversations with Charles. He was merely asking us to accept his word.

With her deafness, Rebecca had found it difficult to follow all that had been said at the breakfast table. But she asked me to understand that she and Caroline had always been in the habit of agreeing to whatever Charles wanted, given his strong and forceful personality.

We agreed that, by hardly uttering a word during the process of the execution of the codicil and thereafter talking endlessly in giving completely incoherent instructions to Horatio, Charles had demonstrated beyond any doubt that he was not in a fit state to have conducted such business or to have understood its implications.

I stayed with Rebecca for some two hours, for she was alone and I felt she needed support at this difficult time. I did return home for a short time to see the family, but I returned to Edgware Place for my usual evening visit. As it transpired, I am very glad that I did. The carriage returned home with the Clagetts but there was an additional passenger – Charles's sister Mary Dey.

On greeting each other, she explained that she was anxious to see her brother having heard about his deterioration over the last week. She had of course been previously present when the existence of the three natural children had been revealed.

The Clagetts had told her all about the Dufaur episode of the last twenty-four hours. We all sat down in the drawing room and she gave us some more interesting information which was new to us. The Dufaur family had been well known to Charles for some thirty years. She recollected well Antonine Dufaur, Frederick's uncle.

Charles and Antonine were both in the Custom House together and although Antonine was Charles' senior by some years (he was born in 1771), they formed an intimate friendship which lasted until shortly before Antonine's death in 1822. He had married a certain Eleanor Smith in 1815 of whom Charles clearly did not approve.

She knew that Charles had a very good regard for Antonine and she frequently heard him say that, as a result of the good advice and friendship of Antonine Dufaur, he largely attributed his subsequent success in life. Although Charles ceased his close friendship with Antonine, he still preserved an intimate acquaintance with the other members of the family, particularly with Frederick's father, Cyprian. We all noted at this point what colourful names this Dufaur family had, probably as a result of their French ancestry.

Mary was not certain that Charles had known Frederick since the latter's boyhood but from the intimacy which existed between his father and Charles, she would have thought this very likely.

She knew that Frederick was a solicitor who had been employed by Charles professionally for four or five years. But she was not certain of the precise business for which Charles employed him. She knew he frequently came to Charles's house in Edgware when she was also there, and she always understood that such visits were on matters of business. She knew that a great deal of correspondence used to pass between them and she had several times heard Charles say that he had appointments on business with Frederick Dufaur.

She was quite satisfied that Charles must have had great confidence in Frederick Dufaur, for Charles was a man of particular and cautious habits. He would not have engaged anyone in any matters of business unless he had strict confidence in such a person.

This was all most interesting background but, after today's events, it was largely information which the rest of us didn't want to hear.

Before leaving for the night, I went with Mary upstairs to see Charles. He was slightly calmer and certainly recognised his sister's presence. I had advised Mary not to stay too long and to say nothing that might cause Charles to become excited. But he started talking about some bonds that he intended to execute in favour of the members of the family and he then said that Frederick Dufaur should prepare them. This jogged my memory from a week earlier when Susannah Peake had told me that Charles's chief clerk, Robert Barbrook, had sought advice from Antonine Dufaur when drafting the bonds for the natural children. But this was Frederick's brother Antonine rather than his uncle Antonine, who had died in 1822

This begged two questions. Was Frederick Dufaur going to return tomorrow to redraft the bonds in favour of the children? More ominously, did Frederick Dufaur know of the children's existence?

If the answer to the second question was in the affirmative, some very nasty scenarios could be about to present themselves. If the latest codicil was to be overturned on the grounds of Charles's mental incapacity at the time of its drafting, Dufaur would almost certainly dispute this and was in possession of information which could be destructive to the Day family and its business interests. This opened up the real threat of him using blackmail if he did not get his way. I had only met the man briefly, but it was enough to form an impression that he would stop at nothing. Perhaps the plan formulated early in the day, to let Dufaur do as he pleased in the knowledge that we could overturn it, was not the cleverest course of action after all.

I left Edgware Place tonight very worried for what awaited the Day family in the future after Charles' inevitable and imminent demise.

Sunday 25 September 1836

My early visit to Edgware Place revealed that Charles had had a restful night and there was no change in his condition. Thomas and Fanny seemed quite relaxed but promised to call me if anything changed. Rebecca, Caroline and Horatio felt it might be a good idea to get away from the house for the day and take the carriage for a ride out into the surrounding countryside. This was clearly a good idea for all concerned and I advised them to go.

I would have dearly liked to sit with Charles and continue our reminiscences. But his condition had deteriorated since our last series of such chats and there was little prospect of these ever being continued. This was a great shame but I can only be grateful that we talked when we did. It certainly gave me an insight into an extraordinary life, an insight that had only been revealed to a privileged few.

Here was a chance at last to devote a whole Sunday to my family. I told Thomas and Fanny that I would not visit again for the rest of the day, unless they were in any way concerned and they called me. They agreed and understood. I cannot overstate my admiration for these two faithful servants and I am sure Charles, even in his present confused state, realises how lucky he is to have them. With all the recent talk of Wills, codicils and other testamentary writings, I trust they have been included in the instructions that Charles has given.

I left them and returned home for breakfast. We all then worshipped together at St Margaret's. It was Harvest Thanksgiving today, one of the most important Sundays of the year in our agricultural community. The church was packed, many folk attending whom we would not normally see. People proudly brought their own fruits of the harvest and these were displayed around the church. We sang lustily about ploughing the fields, scattering the good seed to the land and bringing the harvest home. Living amongst these people now for nearly twenty years, I realised how much this meant to them after their hours, days and weeks of hard labour on the land and I found their giving of thanks to the Lord, for enabling such labours to be productive, a very moving experience.

I am ashamed to say that, during the vicar's fairly predictable sermon, my thoughts wandered to the wider idea of harvest and to Charles in particular. He and Benjamin Martin had been given an idea, a recipe, by a complete stranger whom they knew they would never see again, and had harvested that idea in an imaginative and brilliant way. Whilst being determined and ambitious, there was always an element of generosity in Charles's activities, particularly towards all those who worked for him. He expected their commitment, and if they gave it, he rewarded them accordingly. The basis of his business success was realising that his staff were his most important asset. This was an enlightened approach in our age when there is such a gulf between the wealthy and working classes. Many frowned upon this policy as socially unacceptable and this probably explains why he had few friends. But in the spirit of a true entrepreneur, he was confident to go his own way and not to conform. Only time will tell whether his business attitudes will become more adopted, but I suspect with a certain amount of confidence that he will be regarded in the future as something of a trailblazer.

The last few weeks had undoubtedly revealed a darker side to his personality, but I favoured a charitable rather than judgmental approach to these revelations. He had found himself, in his personal life, a victim of his own success. Faced with matrimonial decisions, he had made a hasty and wrong choice. He had taken the wrong turning. The times in which we live regard infidelity as normal, but nevertheless unforgivable. The hypocrisy of leading a double life was socially acceptable, but must be kept clandestine if the offender could afford it – and Charles certainly could. The consequential harvest had been three sons to whom he was clearly a doting father. He had kept them a secret from his wife because he would not want to upset her. He was anxious to provide her with every comfort, especially as her roots had been fairly modest.

Charles had demonstrated his generosity and fondness for the community in which he lived by providing the excellent row of almshouses on the north side of the village. Although a very private man, his nature was of natural benevolence. His family origins too were of a modest nature, but he realised that he had been dealt a lucky hand and it was his social responsibility to give something back. It would not surprise me if his Will contained some generous charitable donations.

My thoughts re-emerged into the church service as we were asked to stand for the final hymn. All had been safely gathered in, not only from the fields around our village, but also in a wider sense from the results of all our labours in the lives we had led. This was certainly the case for Charles as he approached his inevitable mortality. The problem in his case was that so much had been gathered in that it was difficult for him to know how it should be distributed after his demise. It was rather sad and pathetic to see him in his present state, trying to leave his final arrangements as he would wish, but with his mind and faculties deteriorating, being unable to give the clear instructions that he intended. It was a simple and obvious lesson to all of us to have everything in place when we are still hale and hearty – but will we heed it? Almost certainly not!

We walked home in the beautiful autumn sunshine. After lunch, we had a lovely family day together, enjoying our garden and our mutual recreation. I was indeed thankful for all I had, and it was a great joy to be able to spend time with all those around me, in whose own creation I had perhaps been a facilitating factor.

This had been a day of necessary and gratefully received refreshment. I felt its effects would be needed in the days and weeks that lay ahead.

Tuesday 27 September 1836

Assuming all was quiet at Edgware Place, I did not make an early call and enjoyed a more relaxed breakfast with Sarah and the children.

I did however go over later in the morning and found John Simpson working at the desk in the drawing room on his own. He had arrived the day before and had stayed overnight. Fanny brought us some refreshments and John started describing to me at length his own relationship with Charles and what intelligence he had on Dufaur. To continue in his own words:

'My father, Pinder Simpson, and Charles have been very close friends throughout my lifetime. My mother and Rebecca are half first cousins. Charles has always expressed the highest regard and esteem for my father.

'From when he made his last Will, I never on any occasion heard Charles suggest that another executor should be added, be that Frederick Dufaur or anyone else.

'I know nothing of any connection between Charles and the Dufaur family or between Charles and Frederick Dufaur himself, other than at Christmas time when we listed his property, Charles would occasionally say that a particular security had been arranged by Frederick Dufaur. These securities were chiefly annuities, securities for sums of money lent on annuities, and I think I remember two or three mortgages also, but they were for a very small amount.

'I am not aware that, until Charles' current illness, I ever met Dufaur at Charles' house or that, other than as just described, I ever heard Charles mention him.

'Dufaur was very far from being the only solicitor whom

Charles employed. I could list the names of nine other solicitors whom Charles used occasionally.

'I know that from the time Charles's poor clerk Barbrook went mad, he used Dufaur to collect the rents of his leasehold houses in London. That was about a year ago. I do not know what led Charles to appoint Dufaur. I cannot now remember if Charles told me what led Barbrook to go mad.

'With reference to the said rents, Charles remarked to me: 'I think Frederick Dufaur might as well collect those rents'. That is all I recollect Charles saying on the subject. I cannot remember Charles saying that Dufaur requested to do this work.

'Of course, I never saw Charles last week when Dufaur was instrumental in writing the latest codicil that particularly favours him. I had seen him on 16 September and I saw him again two days ago. I can say with confidence that, on neither of those days, was he capable of doing any act requiring thought, judgement and reflection, but I did not see him during the interval between these two days.'

With that, he finished his account. I had found it absolutely fascinating and it made even more certain that Dufaur was an imposter who saw a chance to benefit from Charles's sad circumstances. He was also a clever and dangerous man whom we all had to treat with the utmost care. I could see the whole administration of Charles's Will, following his inevitable and imminent demise, likely to become a very messy affair.

John soon departed after he had finished. There were no more callers through the day. We had established a routine to keep Charles in a stable, if confused, condition and that is how it remained for the rest of the day.

But, just as I was leaving after my late and last visit of the day, Thomas came down and asked for a quick word. During the evening, Charles had asked him to take down some dictation. Thomas had tried to find family members, Caroline or Horatio, who would normally have done this, because he was not confident of his own abilities. But none were around and Charles was becoming irritable. So, Thomas had to proceed. Apologetically, he showed me the result. He knew there would be spelling mistakes and there were gaps where he simply could not make out what his master was saying. As it was so late, I asked if I could take it home with me and study it in detail. He gratefully consented.

At home, I puzzled over Thomas's paper. It clearly demonstrated the confused state of Charles's mind – but what did it all mean? What was Charles trying to say? I decided to make my own copy, if for no other reason, for my own studies of mental health. But it made absolutely no sense and trying to decipher it (through the mists of Charles mind and Thomas's admitted poor literacy) was almost impossible.

More importantly, this document could clearly be used in evidence if, perish the thought, such were ever needed to demonstrate the inadequate state of Charles's mind at this time, that is to say roughly contemporary with the writing of the codicil in favour of Dufaur.

Friday 30 September 1836

The pattern of the past few days was repeated this morning – a very gradual decline in Charles' condition but no major events, such as further fits. In my general feeling of inadequacy, I did at least feel that the palliative nature of the care I was prescribing was saving him from any unnecessary distress.

I was relieved to see Susannah Peake return to Edgware Place during the afternoon. I enquired after the boys and she confirmed that they were all doing well and had settled into their new term at school. Otherwise, we both reported relatively quiet weeks at both Edgware Place and Osnaburgh Street.

However, with Susannah being a weekly visitor (as opposed to myself, seeing Charles three or four times a day), I valued her thoughts on any deterioration in Charles's condition. She confirmed that she had certainly noted a further decline in the last week. She had spent thirty minutes or so with Charles this afternoon. He had undoubtedly recognised her and was cheered by her visit. But his conversation was wandering and his concentration span on any one subject was short.

She fully understood that we were probably in the final phase of Charles's illness and all we could do was to make him as comfortable as possible and to avoid any excitement that might disturb his mental balance. She courteously thanked me for all my attention to Charles. She did not linger. She knew that her relations were aware of her visit but they made no effort to see her. The tensions within the Day family were to say the least unfortunate.

With no one else around, I was left alone and my thoughts wandered into the chaos that was going on in Charles's mind.

Here was a man formerly in possession of a fierce organisational intellect and memory. His brain was now being attacked by a cruel disease and had become a battleground. There were still traces of coherence but they were being submerged in an overwhelming fog, obscuring all reasonable thought from any expression. Something in him still knew what he should be doing but the evil disease was gradually winning and suffocating any intellect that remained. In my capacity as a physician, I realised how little we knew about the brain. I may have criticised the family for being helpless, but in my own professional capacity, I was too. It made me determined to try and progress some sort of research into diseases of the brain. It could well be of great benefit to medicine if, once poor Charles had submitted finally to this malady, his brain could be donated for medical research. But it was entirely wrong of me to entertain such albeit unvoiced thoughts whilst he was still alive.

Sarah again noticed her husband returning home, somewhat down in the mouth. The stability of my own home and family was something I now treasured more than ever.

Thursday 6 October 1836

Simeon Bull appeared at the house during the afternoon.

After he came down from Charles's room, I had a chat with him and he told me:

'He did not say to me that he was going to make a new Will. He said he was going to make a codicil to his Will and that he should leave me £300 per annum if that would satisfy me and that he had sent for me to tell me so.

'He certainly had not sent for me. I came down of my own accord.

'He did tell me that there was going to be a consultation as to whether he should have his head cut off. He said that he considered it right to sacrifice one member for the sake of the whole body.

'Then putting his finger to his head, he added 'Here is the seat of my disorder and Tom Hewson is coming tomorrow to have a consultation with the other doctors as to taking off my head'.

'I have no hesitation in saying that today he was not in a situation to do any testamentary act or any other business, for that matter.'

I explained to Simeon Bull that Charles' condition was deteriorating fast and such utterances from him were now quite normal. Not having seen him for a while, he was clearly shocked by the amount Charles had gone down. As he realised that it would be impossible to do any business with Charles today, he did not linger and returned to London.

Later on, Susannah Peake appeared inconspicuously for what was now becoming her regular weekly visit. I warned her before going up to see Charles that his condition had regressed considerably since she last saw him and the pace of this regression was accelerating. She did not stay with him too long. She said he recognised her voice but could not engage in any sustained conversation. She thought her presence had a calming influence on him. But she was now a worried person who realised that a load of responsibility was sitting on her with regard to the welfare of Charles's three dear sons. Although he could not voice it, she knew he was relying on her to defend their wellbeing in the future. She realised the difficulties involved what with the opposition of the direct family, albeit understandable, and now the involvement of the loose cannon Frederick Dufaur, who would clearly stop at nothing.

Again, the family remained at a distance when they knew she was in the house. I sat with her for some time and sympathised with her very difficult position. Looking ahead, she realised that, on Charles's imminent death, the legal disputes would start. Monies would be frozen until probate was granted and, if the disputes escalated, this could be for some very considerable time. She and her household were entirely dependent on Charles's money. They could be at the mercy of the moribund legal system for a long time into the future. How would they live? How could the boys' education continue? I agreed that these worries were entirely realistic and there was little obvious solution.

As she left, it struck me again what a woman of immense common sense Susannah was. I could see how she and Charles had formed such a bond. But he was leaving her with an unimaginable burden.

Friday 7 October 1836

I had expected this to be another routine day of witnessing Charles's gradual decline, much like the rest of this week had been. However, during my visit soon after luncheon, Pinder and John Simpson arrived at the house.

John had not visited Charles since 26 September, the previous Monday week. He told me that, having written to Dufaur, who had rejoined his family in Brighton before returning to London, he had had meetings with him in London on Wednesday and Thursday last week. The meeting on Thursday was as a result of a call made by Dufaur at John's own house.

He did not tell Dufaur at either meeting that he had visited Charles the previous Saturday and found Charles quite mad. However, Dufaur did refer to the codicil drawn up on 22 September in his favour and maintained that, when Charles dictated it, he was 'perfectly sensible'. John had told Dufaur that, in the opinion of Charles's wife, daughter and son-in-law, as well as his medical advisers, this most certainly was not the case.

Knowing about the codicil when he and Dufaur met, John had expressed, in the very strongest of terms, his sense of the impropriety of Dufaur's conduct in respect to the codicil and his surprise that he should have allowed Charles, in the state that he was, to make such a codicil. He was careful to show no sign of any jealousy to Dufaur, as he felt none. He had said to Dufaur that he himself would never have allowed Charles to make such a codicil, as Charles was certainly not in a state to undertake any such action.

With the earlier codicils in mind, John had been careful not to say that Charles had been in such a state since the onset of his illness and a commission of lunacy should have been taken out against him, although John may have thought it.

He had made no comments to Dufaur about the circumstances under which Charles had made his Will and the advice given at the time by Mr Sidebottom. Neither had John commented to Dufaur in any respect that he had received a personal benefit in money from Charles. Also, John certainly did not promise to Dufaur that he would see Underwood, one of the other executors, and discuss Dufaur's appointment in the codicil, and certainly Dufaur did not promise to do the same thing, as he had subsequently maintained.

I went up to Charles's room with John and his father. Caroline was already there. Charles, after a variety of observations all perfectly irrational, said to John, 'Here John, I will make a new Will. You write while I talk'.

In order to humour Charles, John correctly sat down by his bedside and wrote down, word for word, from his dictation, several sheets of paper of the most absurd and irrational trash that can be conceived.

John was occupied in writing while Charles dictated for at least three hours. There is little point in reproducing this here, although the original was kept to be used as evidence of Charles's incapacity, if this was ever needed. Poor Charles just went round and round in circles, repeating himself many times and never even reached the point of mentioning any beneficiaries or amounts involved.

John merely wrote a comment at the end, which spoke for itself:

Instructions for Will and codicil taken down verbatim by John Simpson this day in the presence of Mrs Clagett and my father – Mr Day said he would give me £50 or any sum if I would only do this for him – as he was going to Russia to get a new pair of legs and then instantly to make the tour of Europe.

Caroline and Pinder Simpson were present all the time and Rebecca and the servants came in and out of the room at various points in the proceedings. Fanny later said that Charles had been quite well in the morning but by the time of the Simpsons' visit, he had quite gone off. Being with him constantly, she knew the difference between his rational and irrational moods, and that afternoon, he was definitely in the latter.

During the latter part of the time that John was so occupied in writing, about an hour before he finished, Thomas came into the room and said that Frederick Dufaur was below. This came as a complete surprise to all of us. Quite rightly, to demonstrate there was nothing to hide, John suggested that he might come up to Charles's room, which he presently did.

On entering the room, John motioned to Dufaur that he should sit down, which he did. He remained in the room till Charles, who had gone on all this time dictating as before without taking the least notice of Dufaur being present, had finished. This was at least half an hour or more after Dufaur had come in and sat down.

That part of the paper which was written by John and dictated by Charles in Dufaur's presence, was of the same irrational and unconnected description and without a word of sense in it as had been dictated before Dufaur had arrived.

After John had gone on writing to Charles' dictation for three whole hours, being tired and wishing to get away, he said to Charles, 'Well, Sir, I shall lose Mr Sidebottom if I stop any longer and therefore you had better let me be off now' or something to that effect.

At which point Charles said in an excited kind of way, 'Oh! Well then, I implore you not to lose a moment' and John immediately shook Charles's hand and hastened out of the room, leaving Dufaur still there.

The manner of Charles's dictating and the mere dictation by him of the irrational, unconnected trash John recorded, clearly manifested the impaired state of Charles's mind and his entire incapacity to do any act requiring thought, judgement and reflection.

Pinder Simpson left with John. Charles was by now exhausted and failed to contribute any further conversation. I motioned to Dufaur and Caroline that we should leave him to rest.

Downstairs, much as I would have wished to avoid it, a cursory conversation with Dufaur was inevitable. I sensed that he realised that any claims he was making that Charles was of sound mind on 22 September when he made the codicil in Dufaur's favour, were becoming less credible by the minute. He agreed that John had filled four sides of paper with what had been dictated by Charles and still continued writing having commenced another sheet after Dufaur's arrival. Most significantly, Dufaur admitted that what was dictated by Charles to John Simpson in his presence was absurd and irrational.

Dufaur actually conceded that Charles did, on that day and in his presence and hearing, manifest and give proof that he was not at that time in a state to do any act requiring thought, judgement and reflection. Dufaur further said that Charles had been giving, or trying to give, John Simpson instructions for an entirely new Will.

I noted this immediately and will give my note to John when I next see him.

I had been at Edgware Place for several hours. Much as I

wanted to return home, I had no intention of leaving before seeing Dufaur off the premises. He needed no encouragement to go and swiftly departed with hardly any pleasantries. I sensed he was not capable of such courtesies in any case. I said my farewells to Caroline and her mother and, after my usual final chat of the day with Thomas and Fanny, prepared to make my way home, somewhat exhausted.

But as I left Edgware Place, the heavens opened and Fanny told me to take one of Charles's impressive collection of umbrellas. A few years earlier, he had heard of a young chap called James Smith setting up an umbrella shop at Foubert's Place, just off Regent Street in London's West End. The umbrellas were made in a small workshop in the back of the shop and then sold to customers at the front. He always wanted to support young entrepreneurs, and had been a dedicated customer.

THE FINAL DAYS: 9 TO 26 OCTOBER 1836

I feel there is very little point now in continuing with my daily log of events. Charles's condition had deteriorated to such an extent that there were very few further events to report.

Dr Clutterbuck and Susannah Peake continued their weekly visits. The former's only served the continued lining of his pockets. There was nothing he could do. Charles's life was clearly nearing its end. Palliative care was all that could be offered and he knew that that was far more my speciality than his. His visits continued to be very short and Charles was incapable of even recognising him.

Susannah's calls were very different. She seemed to know when it was appropriate for her to call, that is to say when the rest of the family were out or otherwise engaged. She would always have a chat with me first, to see what the latest developments were, if any. Her concern for Charles's well-being was palpable, unlike many of the other 'vultures' who were gathering around. I would advise her to use her discretion as to how long she should stay with Charles and I trusted her completely. Sometimes I attended too and it was noticeable how, even in these terminal stages of his illness, Charles would pick up noticeably at her presence.

She would then stay with me for some time afterwards, sometimes at Edgware Place, sometimes at my own house, discussing what the future arrangements should be concerning the three boys and hoping that all that had been put in place by Charles would materialise without hitch. The boys were now back at school within the University, but she had kept from them anything that was going on. They had occasionally asked why they had not been visited by Blind Uncle Charles recently and Susannah was always able to make up some plausible story. Sarah continued her motherly regime and was of course kept abreast of developments in Edgware by Susannah, whilst necessarily and wisely keeping well out of the way. Susannah took care of all the administration of the household at 4 Osnaburgh Street, including the finances. But she was naturally concerned about how matters would develop after Charles's inevitable and imminent death. Would the executors have the power to keep the flow of money going and how would the unwanted Frederick Dufaur feature in the proceedings? All I could do was to understand fully her concerns and sympathise.

During this final period, Charles continued to ask family and friends to take dictation for him, most of which was completely incomprehensible. However, following my suggestion, they always acceded to his requests in order to keep him pacified and to avoid any further fits.

On one such occasion, around 11 October, Charles asked his daughter to take down a letter from him to John Weston at the factory. In the letter, Charles asked Weston to pay over to Dufaur all the money he could spare at that time.

I had had some detailed discussions with Weston. He knew that Charles had employed Dufaur professionally for about seven or eight years up to that point and he knew, from his mode of treating him, that Charles was very friendly towards him. Weston could not define the various circumstances but the general term of Charles's conduct towards Dufaur was such as to satisfy Weston that this was the case.

Weston knew that Charles was an extremely cautious man and from the long relationship he had had with him, he was perfectly conversant with his habits and was quite positive that he would not have acted towards any person as he did to Dufaur, in regard to the pecuniary transactions between them, unless he had confidence in him.

For instance, Weston had the entire care and superintendence of Charles's pecuniary concerns until Barbrook's departure, and Charles would frequently send Weston a verbal order to give Dufaur cheques for large sums of money, such as £500 or £1,000, which Weston of course gave him. Consequently, Weston had no hesitation in considering that Charles placed great confidence in Dufaur.

Weston was unable to say whether Charles employed Dufaur in any legal proceedings. Certainly, he did not in connection with the concerns of the business at Holborn or Weston would have known it.

Weston had heard Charles say that he was in the habit of employing Dufaur in the investment of money but in what particular way he could not say, except that Charles used to speak with great satisfaction of the interest Dufaur used to make with his money. He had been discounting bills from about June 1834 following Barbrook's illness and departure from the business.

Charles appointed Dufaur in succession to Barbrook as receiver of his London rents but Weston knew no further details as to the amounts of money involved.

At the time of Barbrook's illness, Charles separated his private pecuniary transactions from those connected with the business, and as a result, Weston knew little of what passed between Charles and Dufaur.

Weston knew that Charles had a strong room at Harley House and that Charles had a book containing references to the boxes in the strong room. He had no doubt that the contents of the room had been regularly arranged and inventoried, for he had been present when Charles had referred to the book when he wanted a particular document. But by whom the contents of the said room were arranged or inventoried, Weston was unable to state, nor did he know whether Dufaur had or had not unrestrained access to the room.

Such was Weston's opinion of Dufaur. I discussed this with the various parties who had met Dufaur at Edgware Place. We all agreed that this was somewhat at variance with the impressions we had gleaned, but we did realise that we had met Dufaur and experienced his conduct under quite different circumstances to those experienced by Weston.

Weston had been Charles' servant for over twenty years and was very much conditioned to working under strict instructions. His wife Elizabeth was Rebecca's sister and only eleven months her junior. She had come under the same family influence as Rebecca, and was therefore very much used to Charles's controlling nature. However, Susannah was blessed with less subservience and, like the rest of us, had tended to form a more independent opinion of Charles, recognizing his many good qualities whilst accepting his foibles.

It even crossed my mind that Dufaur had somehow engineered the downfall of poor Barbrook. It seemed too much of a coincidence that Barbrook's departure coincided with Dufaur's arrival in the administration of Charles' personal affairs. Dufaur had known since the children's bonds were drawn up in 1832 that Barbrook was a crucial figure in Charles's secret life and, if he could be removed and replaced by Dufaur himself, it would potentially put Dufaur in a very powerful position. Barbrook would have been reluctant to obey Weston's orders, that had come direct from Charles, to furnish Dufaur with large amounts of money for investment. He would have been suspicious and, in the knowledge that it was him who had unwittingly leaked the existence of the boys to Dufaur, his feeling of guilt would have given him a very troubled mind which had mistakenly led to a diagnosis of lunacy. But I must emphasise that this is purely my conjecture. I have no evidence to back up this theory. Perhaps I should keep my imagination under better control. However, having been a close observer of the events of these last two months and Dufaur's unscrupulous behaviour, I think I can be excused for thinking such thoughts.

During this final period, my closest confidantes at Edgware Place had been the two trusted servants Fanny Barton and Thomas Hunt, both of whom I will always hold in the highest regard.

Fanny had lived for the last eight years in the service of Charles and Rebecca. For the last four or five years of his life, she was Charles' personal attendant. Her recollection of the events of 22 September, and the execution of the final codicil in favour of Dufaur, was most interesting. Her description of what happened tallied exactly with what Hewson had told me.

Fanny described how she had observed Charles having what she called his silent fits. He would sit in his chair and would not say a word, nor would he take any nourishment, nor let anything be done for him. He just sat, apparently in a childish state. Both fits continued over a whole night. For the first one, she was afraid to move him and just left him sitting, but for the second, she put him to bed.

Throughout the period of the epileptic and silent fits, Fanny noticed a gradual decrease in Charles's mental faculties. Being a loyal and faithful servant, she was reluctant to admit this but, when pressed, she had to concede it was true. Nevertheless, she still maintained he had periods of lucidity, although these became less common as time passed by.

He would sometimes say, 'Well, Fanny, could you manage to London this evening. The carriage shall take you as far as Pine Apple Gate and you can walk the rest of the way and get back as you can'. Fanny would agree to it, leave him for a little time and then return. By then, his orders about going to London would have been completely forgotten.

Sometimes he would not have any recollection of having given such orders. At others, he would be aware that he had given some orders but because some were foolish, they were not obeyed, which made him suspect that none of his orders were ever obeyed. And he would then have two or three different persons up and find out whether or not his orders had or had not been fulfilled. We all learned just to calm his nerves and give ambiguous explanations.

After the first silent fit, Fanny remembered Charles was in the frequent habit of talking about making a new Will, and having John Simpson down to take his instructions. Whilst he was in these moods, and more particularly during the last three weeks of his life, he talked a great deal about giving considerable sums of money to various persons, saying he had got more money than he knew what to do with. Fanny should have £200 per annum, as he should like her to be able to go to a watering place every summer.

And he asked me one day just before he died how much I would like to have and whether £500 would satisfy me. He made similar enquiries and observations to many people.

Fanny said he used sometimes to order his book, in which the bills of exchange were entered, to be brought and read to him and would evidently be confused concerning the time at which some of the bills became due. And during those last three weeks, when he was at his most irrational, she said he used to say he wanted to see Bull and Dufaur about money matters and bonds and such like and that they must not be kept away from him.

Fanny considered that, during this final period, the privacy that Charles always maintained about his financial affairs became more relaxed as he gradually lost his mental faculties.

As I have already said, the other tower of strength through Charles's last days was his manservant Thomas Hunt.

Thomas had been in Charles's service for about fifteen years. He was his personal servant and was with him constantly. As a result of Charles's blindness, Thomas had to attend to everything, much as Sarah had done before her sons were born.

As explained in my entry for 10 September, Thomas was the first person after Sarah and Susannah Peake to know about Charles's three natural sons. Charles was convinced he was dying and, in case I did not arrive in time, he wanted someone to know that he wished to double the provision for each of the boys from £5,000 to £10,000. He also hinted to Thomas that Rebecca knew nothing of the boys' existence. Thomas was sure that Charles was of perfectly sound mind, memory and understanding at the time. He knew him well enough for such a judgement to be sound. He also confirmed that, when I arrived early that morning, Charles repeated the same to me and he was as sensible and rational as any person could be.

Thomas confirmed that, prior to 10 September, he had no inkling of the existence of the three natural sons. He now realised that this secrecy was necessary as Mrs Day knew nothing of the existence of the boys, or the affair Charles was having with her cousin or the separate household he was keeping for the boys' upbringing. Thomas was surprised and astonished when Charles first mentioned the matter to him. Charles made the revelation to Thomas voluntarily, freely and without reserve, but he never talked to Thomas about it again and asked Thomas to keep it secret.

Thomas also confirmed that, during the latter part of Charles' final illness, his memory and mental capacity became very much impaired, but it was not until Monday 12 September that he perceived that his mind was actually deteriorating.

Thomas was a great support to me when, in joint consultation with Clutterbuck and Hewson, I informed the family that, if Charles did any act, we would all set it aside on medical grounds.

Like Fanny, Thomas did witness repeated instances of incoherent, irrational and childish behaviour in Charles from about the middle of September. Charles often talked of his financial and business affairs after the 10 September. He never did talk of them before then – never on any occasion.

Thomas said it was the practice of those about Charles to appear to yield the same obedience to him as before, but when withdrawn from his presence, to pay no attention to what he said or directed. This was very much following my advice to one and all.

It was highly relevant that, on one occasion in the dining room, Thomas maintained that he did hear Dufaur give a clear statement. After he had been with Charles, Dufaur specifically said that he could make nothing of him.

Thomas had been very much in evidence on the morning that Charles made the final codicil in Dufaur's favour. He remembered Charles giving absurd orders to Clagett about purchasing game and venison in the town and keeping the carriage and Dufaur waiting. He was sure that, on that occasion, Charles's conduct clearly showed that he was not of sound mind, memory and understanding. And I have always felt that Thomas's observation that, on leaving Edgware, Dufaur travelled on the box of the carriage, with the Clagetts inside, was highly significant.

These two outstanding people, Fanny Barton and Thomas Hunt, remained loyal servants to Charles until he breathed his last and I was so pleased to learn eventually that he had remembered them in his Will.

The month of October went by with very few further developments. As I have said Clutterbuck and Susannah Peake continued their weekly visits but Charles was in such a poor and worsening state that there was nothing much any of us could do. But his condition was purely mental, his physical faculties being no worse than they were when the fits began.

He continued to dictate gibberish to anyone who was with him at the time. On 22 October, William Croft visited again. He knew that Charles's demise was imminent and needed to be prepared for all that he would need to do as an executor. But Charles merely started dictating instructions to him which he knew he had to write down in order to keep Charles calm. They were actually instructions to George, the coachman, to order game at Leadenhall Market in the City. But he was also to call on Dufaur to tell him there were two carriages in town that day – this was completely irrational. There were also instructions to bring various tradesmen out to Edgware and to call on Charles's tailor about some clothing alterations. The people he spoke about were real but the instructions merely reflected the confused state of his mind. Strangely there was a short final instruction to call at the factory and ask Weston to pass on a message that Charles would be pleased to see him and his wife, Charles's sister-in-law, at church the following Sunday (that is, the next day), followed by lunch.

This was strange bearing in mind what happened on that Sunday. The Westons did not receive the message from George, like all other such missives, it was disregarded by all those at Edgware Place on the instructions of myself and my medical colleagues, and did not go to Edgware that Sunday. Instead, Charles gave a further dictation to Caroline, being a letter to Weston, his trusted factory manager for the last twenty years, dismissing him from his post with immediate effect and telling him to vacate his house at the factory. His successor was to be William Metcalfe, the son-in-law of Charles' sister Mary Dey. The letter was disregarded, in the same way as all others and was never delivered.

However, the next day (Monday 24 October), Weston was visited by Metcalfe who verbally transmitted the message in the letter to Weston. Weston rightly took no notice. He was convinced that Mary Dey was behind this unexpected development. She was not happy that her daughter had married Metcalfe, a druggist who would be taking over his father's business. She felt that this was not a particularly secure living and the blacking business of her dying brother gave far better prospects. The matter was never discussed any further, but Mary's standing in the family was suitably tarnished.

On Wednesday 26 October, I made my usual early call. Charles had slept well but he was completely incoherent in what he was saying. He appeared to be weak and exhausted. Later in the morning, John Simpson arrived for a routine visit and went up to Charles's room. He found him lying on his bed, completely lifeless.

I was called immediately by Thomas Hunt and confirmed that Charles Day had died peacefully some time between my earlier visit and that moment. He was fifty-two – still a relatively young age – but had achieved so much.

We had reached the end. I informed Rebecca, Horatio and

Caroline. They viewed the body but showed little emotion. In contrast, the reaction of the loyal servants, Thomas and Fanny, was completely different, reflecting the devoted service they had given this man over many years and the fact that they knew him to be a kind and benevolent person at heart. I asked them if they required any medical attention and they merely shook their heads.

I returned home feeling deflated but at the same time relieved that Charles's suffering was at an end. I was also quite sure that we were starting a new phase in the Day family story which was guaranteed to be turbulent.

IV. Aftermath

1. The beginnings of legal proceedings

Charles Day died peacefully and alone in his room at Edgware on the morning of Wednesday 26 October 1836.

He had been found by John Simpson on one of his routine visits. The immediate formality was to call the local physician William Foote to confirm the death. Then, after informing and consoling the family, John departed for London with a sense of great urgency. He knew that Dufaur would stop at nothing to progress his cause and consequently the three executors, William Croft, William Underwood and John's father Pinder Simpson, should meet without delay to plan their strategy. By that evening, he had succeeded in getting them all into the same room for discussions. Without hesitation, they decided that counsel should be approached to act and they agreed that Charles Bowdler, a proctor of high repute known to them, should be engaged. John was instructed to make this approach the next day and Bowdler was duly retained.

A few days later, something strange happened at the blacking factory. John Weston mentioned that a person, unknown by him, called at the factory and introduced himself to Weston by saying that he had been referred to him by Frederick Dufaur. Dufaur had said to this person that he was an executor to the estate of Charles Day. The person made enquiries to Weston about the possible purchase of the business. Weston did not enter into any discussions with this person, but merely referred him to the other executors, and Pinder Simpson in particular. Neither Weston nor any of the executors ever heard any more of this.

Given the amount of medical attention that Charles had received, especially in the last few months of his life, the various medical attendants decided to make a unified request to Rebecca and the family that a post mortem examination should be carried out, principally for the purpose of medical research. The family agreed that Charles would have been sympathetic to such a course of action and gave permission for it to proceed. This had the added benefit of delaying the funeral and giving more time to plan the arrangements.

The post mortem was attended by, among others, George Beaman, the partner in practice with Thomas Ansaldo Hewson, who had a particular interest in neurological diseases. The examination concentrated on the brain and Beaman was fully aware of the results. There was considerable disease of the nerves of vision and of all the brain from which the nerves arose. There was also a softening of the brain about that portion which supplies the tongue and ears with nerves. There was general vascularity and thickening of the membranes and there was a small bony substance on the surface of the brain which had formed a depression corresponding to its size in one of its hemispheres. That portion of the brain called the fornix which is situated at the bottom of the lateral ventricles was thinner and softer at its edge than if it had been in a healthy state, and the change appeared to have been recent. This was something that could have affected the state of the mind. It would not justify saying that the state of Charles's brain positively indicated an impaired state of his mental faculties, but with the state of the fornix, the expectation would be that his mental faculties had been affected.

On Thursday 3 November, Dufaur wrote to the Day family (Rebecca, Horatio and Caroline) expressing his condolences on Charles's death. But somewhat inappropriately, he also requested that a bill from a Mr Fitzgerald, for the considerable sum of £1,000 and which was due for payment two days later, should be forwarded to him for settlement. This prompted a reply dated 5 November from Horatio on behalf of the family stating that, the day before, Caroline had passed the bill to John Simpson who happened to be in Edgware at the time. She had requested that he forwarded it Dufaur forthwith. He never did this. He maintained that Caroline had given him the bill with the instruction to forward it to the executors, of whom he firmly believed that Dufaur was not one. Croft, Underwood and Pinder Simpson were clearly suspicious and instructed John Simpson to write to Dufaur 'enclosing letters to the drawer and the endorser of the bill giving them notice of its dishonour'. Not knowing their addresses, he sent the letters to Dufaur with a covering note dated 7 November, asking him to forward them. Dufaur was clearly in league with these individuals and the executors were suspecting that he was trying to extract funds from the estate by devious means.

John Simpson had his first consultation with the appointed counsel on Tuesday 8 November, the day before Charles Day's funeral. It was decided to take immediate action. The main point of contention was whether or not Frederick Dufaur had been appointed a trustee by Charles Day when the latter was fully in control of his mental faculties. After careful consideration, counsel gave the advice that, although only the fifth codicil appointing Dufaur was contentious, it would be advisable to challenge all four codicils that Charles had made during his final illness. It could then be demonstrated how the illness was progressive and that by the time the fifth codicil was made, Charles was beyond a state of mind whereby he could make rational decisions. In other words, it was hoped that, by losing the challenges to the second, third and fourth codicils, the challenge to the fifth codicil would be strengthened. Consequently, and rather strangely, the three original executors would be challenging not specifically Frederick Dufaur, which was their actual intention, but in fact Rebecca Day, her daughter Caroline and all the other numerous beneficiaries of the Will. For this reason, the case would be referred to as 'Croft v Day and Others', although paradoxically, Croft, Day and Others were actually on the same side.

11. The Will of Charles Day – an original copy now kept in the archives of The Clothworkers' Company.

Charles Day's funeral took place at Edgware on Wednesday 9 November 1836. Frederick Dufaur was neither notified nor invited by the family. As stipulated in the Will, the funeral arrangements were at the discretion of Rebecca Day and the immediate family. The service was taken by the Vicar of Edgware, Rev Nicholas Fiott, whom Charles had known well, especially during recent years in connection with the operation of his almshouses at Stonegrove, not far from St Margaret's Church. Those attending included members of the immediate family as well as those who loyally served Charles, both in his houses and his business. The parishioners of Edgware were all welcome and turned out in numbers. Among them was the local apothecary and surgeon, William Foote, with his own very personal memories of what he had observed over the previous two months. He would miss Charles, not only as a patient, but also as a neighbour and friend. The coffin was laid to rest in the Day family vault to the east of the church building, beside those of Charles's mother-in-law and parents. It was a sombre occasion, reflected by the autumnal atmosphere of the season. But there was also a subdued feeling of dread amongst the immediate family members. They had observed what had happened over the previous two months and were quite certain that this would be a precursor to the inevitable legal battles ahead. Susannah Peake stood quietly to one side, deep in thought about how this would affect her and the second family of Sarah and the three boys. They had no legal standing and had been entirely dependent on Charles. Unless the courts could come to a quick decision, which was unlikely to say the least, their financial tap was to be turned off. Although they would be safe in the long term, how were they going to manage until the legal challenges had been resolved? Susannah caught the eye of William Foote at the side of the vault. Nothing needed to be said, they could easily read each other's minds.

The next day, Dufaur sent a letter to Pinder Simpson, informing him that he (Dufaur) had a codicil appointing himself as an executor which he wished to prove at the same time as the Will. The letter went on to name his counsel as Messrs Longden and Barlow. John Simpson merely acknowledged the letter in writing to Dufaur the following day. The battle lines were clearly drawn and lengthy court cases were bound to follow.

It was about this time, back in Osnaburgh Street, that Susannah and Sarah Peake made the inevitable decision to put Henry, Alfred and Edmund fully in the picture. After all, they were now of an age (thirteen, eleven and nine respectively) when they were able to understand such things. Also, with the court case coming up, there would bound to be a certain amount of publicity which they could easily pick up at the school, or anywhere else for that matter. Consequently, the whole story was revealed to them – how Charles Day was their father, how John Price never existed and that their surname 'Price' was merely a convenient invention. They were also told how they could be facing financial uncertainty in the medium term, although their father had made generous provision for each of them. However, these benefits could only be enjoyed once the Will had been proved, which could take a long time bearing in mind the disruptive presence of Frederick Dufaur. It was also felt wise that they should meet John Weston and his wife Elizabeth, the sister of Susannah, and it was arranged that they should call at Osnaburgh Street on their way back from the funeral. It was also agreed that it would have been too uncomfortable for all concerned for the boys to be introduced to Rebecca, Caroline and Horatio. The boys were stunned and confused by these revelations, but at least they were now in the picture and prepared for any consequences.

And so it was, the following week on Tuesday 15 November 1836 and less than 3 weeks since Charles Day's death, that a case was registered at the Prerogative Court of Canterbury in the Common Hall of Doctors Commons, near Paul's Wharf in the parish of St Benedict, London, involving the Will and codicils of Charles Day, late of Edgware and Harley House. On behalf of the three original executors (Croft, Underwood and Simpson), Bowdler prayed a decree against the widow Rebecca Day and others for whom Townsend appeared as counsel. Orme appeared for Thomas Parsons, a cousin of Charles Day, representing the other beneficiaries, Longden appeared for Frederick Dufaur and Addams appeared for Henry, Alfred and Edmund Price.

The legal proceedings concerning the Will of Charles Day had commenced and a vast estate was now fully exposed and prey to the antiquated and expensive legal system that existed in England during the early years of Queen Victoria's reign.

Proceedings in the Prerogative Court of Canterbury went on for nearly two years. The operation of the court was on the basis of written submissions. Witnesses did not give evidence in person, but purely in writing. This meant that voluminous amounts of paperwork were generated in the form of proxies, affidavits, condidits, allegations and personal answers, interrogatories to be asked of witnesses and their testimonies. In addition, there were the exhibits, being the last and all preceding versions of the Will and all the five codicils, *post obit* bonds, letters sent and received as well as handwritten notes that had been retained as evidence. All of these had to be copied by scribes so that the relevant parties were appraised of all the information. One copy of all these papers amounted to a bound volume of 962 pages, all handwritten in copperplate.

Proctors were named, exhibit affidavits assigned, the administration of the estate assigned, allegations submitted, witnesses produced, written answers submitted, additional allegations submitted, certificates continued and eventually a judgement pronounced. All these events happened numerous times, over and over and over again. The court met every time for each event and only on very few occasions was more than one event combined with another. In all the court was convened just for this one case a total of seventy-nine times before the case was concluded. Each time the court met, all the parties (the widow, the original executors, the family beneficiaries, the illegitimate children and the alleged fourth executor) had to be represented by their counsel and subordinates. The courtroom was crowded with people, all of whom would have been claiming costs from the estate in one form or another.

The evidence given during the case concentrated on the events of the last two months of Charles Day's life – from the date of his first epileptic fit 26 August 1836 to the date of his death 26 October 1836. The critical point which the three original executors needed to prove was that Charles Day was in sufficient possession of his mental faculties to write a codicil to his Will up to 10 September, covering the second, third and fourth codicils, but by the time the fifth codicil was written on 22 September, this was no longer the case.

It was decided from the outset by the executors and those who knew, that it should not be admitted at any point that Sarah Peake was the mother of the boys. Consequently, this point was never mentioned throughout the proceedings. Also, although the existence of the case could be reported in the press, the actual details of the evidence had to remain within the court. As a result, the existence of the three illegitimate children, which was of considerable embarrassment to the family, was only disclosed in the press shortly before the case concluded. The family were surprised that this was not raised by Dufaur, but his reasons for remaining quiet at the time became clear after the judgement was announced.

Every occurrence during the two months in question was covered in minute detail by the numerous witnesses. Those with the most to contribute were, on the one side and not surprisingly, Frederick Dufaur, and on the other William Croft on behalf of the executors. However, three other individuals emerged as critical figures in the whole episode, with perhaps a greater grasp of the facts than anyone else, namely Susannah Peake, John Simpson and William Foote. Susannah, in particular, comes across as a determined character who earned the respect of Charles Day and who was clearly central in organising his personal life in the aftermath of his blindness.

Reports appeared in the press. In fact, an article appeared in *Bell's Life in London and Sporting Chronicle* on Sunday 13 November 1836 entitled 'Shining Characters', even before the case had started in the court. It began:

> *When immense wealth has been obtained by individuals, it is a natural propensity on the part of the inhabitants of this prying world to search out, if possible, how they got it, hoping, thereby, we suppose, to profit by the secret. Such is the investigation going on respecting the enormous sum of £450,000, which was left by Mr. Charles Day, of blacking notoriety. From this tide of inquiry, we collect the following facts, which reflect great credit on the deceased parties, who raised themselves from obscurity to wealth and eminence. The firm of Day and Martin will never be forgotten; their escutcheon will shine when thousands have mouldered in their grave, and for this reason they have left lots of shiners behind them, and a never-failing recipe to increase the store. But to the point: Mr. Martin was a native of Doncaster, and served his apprenticeship to a hair-dresser at Gainsborough, which place he*

quitted for the metropolis, where he became a journeyman to the father of Mr. Charles Day, his late partner, and who carried on business at that time (nearly forty years ago) as a perfumer etc, in Tavistock Street, Covent Garden; he being also 'York but honest,' it is imagined was the cause of attraction. Mr. Charles Day was also a friseur, but born in London, and they both cut their way for a few years over the heads of their superiors till the following circumstance happened.

Doncaster races have always been attractive, and Mr. Martin resolved to visit, not only that scene of sport, but his relatives. He accordingly arrived there, and sojourned at the house of his brother-in-law, Mr. Anthony Moore, a stay-maker by trade, but who kept the King's Arms, in Sepulchre Gate. At the same house, a soldier was also quartered, named Thomas Florry, who was servant to Captain Wilson, then on the recruiting service in that town. The beautiful polish of Florry's shoes caused the landlord not only to admire them, but eventually to obtain the blacking recipe for a quart of ale, which was readily granted! This valuable document, as it afterwards proved to be, was presented by young Martin on his return to London, and hence the magnificent edifice, No. 97 High Holborn, and its valuable appurtenances [sic]. The 'black diamond' recipe was proffered to young Mr. Day, he having more of the ready than Martin, and soon afterwards business commenced in a small way.

After a full account of the background to the business, the article finished as follows:

The poor soldier has been dead many years, but his only reward was the quart of ale, whilst Anthony Moore, after the dissolution of the partnership, received a 'douceur' to hold the secret till his death. By the above accidental means it will be seen arose the £450,000.

However, the following week, *Bell's Life* added a further, rather sobering, comment:

> *We... omitted to state that the widow of Florry, the poor soldier with whom the blacking receipt originated, is still living in Doncaster, and in such circumstances as would render a few seeds of comfort extremely acceptable to her. This hint may be useful.*

This cynicism by the press was offset shortly afterwards by the following report:

> *THE WILL OF CHARLES DAY, ESQ.– We understand that this benevolent individual has bequeathed the sum of £100,000 for the purposes of establishing a charity to be called 'The Blind Man's Friend', the interest of which, after allowing for the salary of a clerk and other expenses, is to be applied, under the sole direction of his executors, to the granting of annuities of from £10 to £20 each, to poor blind men and women. It is to be regretted that from proceedings now pending in the Prerogative Court, some delay will occur in carrying the testator's benevolent intentions into effect. The names of the executors and trustees stand thus in the Will:- William Underwood of Vere Street, woollen draper; William Croft of Gower Street, Esq; Pinder Simpson of Old Burlington Street, Gentleman.*

As a result, the following short verse appeared a few days later:

> *Benevolence, with riches joined,*
> *Sometimes do wonders in their way;*
> *Here, their united force we find*
> *Can make the sightless bless the Day.*

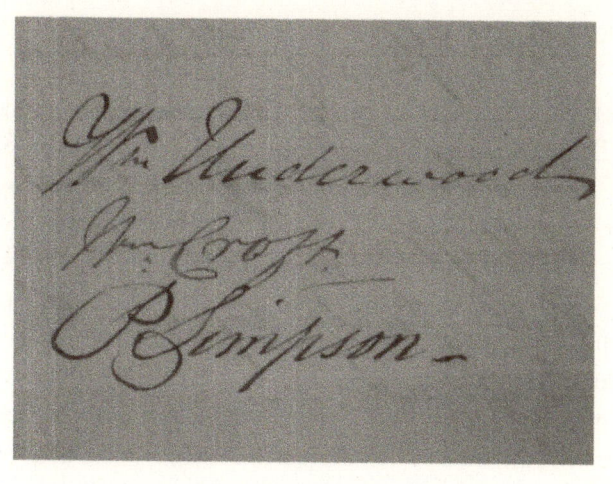

12. The signatures of Charles Day's three executors.

The case ground on with virtually no reporting in the press, which was a relief to all the family and friends of Charles Day. However, on 30 April 1838, there was a short report in *The Globe*, which merely said that the main points of contention were the last two codicils 'giving additional legacies to three natural children, and appointing Mr Dufaur'. This was incorrect as only Dufaur's appointment was in real dispute, but regretfully the existence of the three natural children had been revealed to the public for the first time. A similar press report followed on 3 May.

On 29 June 1838, the Prerogative Court of Canterbury met and Sir Herbert Jenner pronounced 'for the force and validity of the true and original last Will and Testament and of the four codicils thereof of Charles Day, Esquire… and against the force and validity of a pretended codicil to the said Will… bearing date 22 September 1836'. After hearing the arguments in minute detail, the Court had come to its decision after one year and seven months of deliberation. But at least it was a good result for the family and Dufaur had been defeated, despite the fact that costs were having to be paid by Charles's estate.

At this stage, a whiff of blackmail descends over the proceedings. Dufaur was clearly not satisfied with the result. He probably knew that an appeal to the Privy Council, the highest possible court, would not be likely to succeed. However, if he threatened it, the executors would have serious concerns, not least that the case would continue to attract public attention with the accompanying shame to the family of the existence of the three natural children. But there was something even more worrying. Apart from the time it would take for the Privy Council to deliberate, the case would have to be referred to the Court of Chancery to deal with matters relating to the construction and administration of the Will and its four, or perhaps five, codicils. During the case with the ecclesiastical court, John Simpson had been appointed receiver for the estate, principally so that the considerable rental income from all of Charles's properties could be collected in – a function performed by Dufaur during the latter part of Charles's life. However, his receivership ended with the pronouncement of the court's judgement. If an appeal were to take place, the Court of Chancery would have to appoint a new receiver as part of its general administrative function. Knowing the snail's pace at which the Court of Chancery conducted its affairs, any possible involvement it had in the case should be avoided at all costs.

But the executors were determined to resist Dufaur and decided to call his bluff. They failed. On the likely successful gamble that his costs would be covered by the estate, Dufaur decided to appeal to the Privy Council and the appeal was duly lodged on 7 August 1838.

With the appeal lodged, probate could not be granted and the terms of the Will honoured until after the appeal was heard. As a result, the affairs of so many affected by Charles's Will (not least Susannah and Sarah Peake and the three boys) were completely frozen. With so many beneficiaries involved, cracks inevitably began to appear in the unity of the opposition to Dufaur, as no doubt was his intention. By November 1838, newspaper reports were confirming this. Dufaur was claiming that he should be receiving the rents in the interim. Lord Langdale of the Rolls Court was sympathetic to arguments why this should not be allowed but was dismayed to see that the three original executors now all had separate solicitors and counsel acting for them. In referring the matter to the Master of the Rolls, he feared that, if the three executors could not act in concert with each other, this very large estate would not be able to cover its costs whilst honouring all the wishes of the testator, Charles Day.

Eventually, in February 1840, the Privy Council decided to reject Dufaur's appeal, but the estate had to bear the costs. Probate was duly granted on 4 May 1840 on the Will and all the codicils except the last, which would have appointed Dufaur, and the beneficiaries of the Will could finally begin to receive their benefits in the form of legacies and annuities.

But Dufaur's plan had worked, especially as the administration of the Will was now well and truly subsumed into the mire and fog of the dreaded Court of Chancery.

2. Dufaur

Back in 1834 at the blacking factory, there had been a change in personnel working on the administration of the business and more particularly on Charles's personal financial affairs. Towards the end of the year, Charles's trusted servant Robert Barbrook was showing signs of a deterioration in his mental health. At that time, little was known about the treatment of such problems and sadly, it was not long before Barbrook was being admitted to an institution in the Mile End Road, Stepney. It transpired that he would never see the outside world again, dying there on 20 July 1838 at the relatively young age of forty-one, the cause of death being stated as 'apoplexy'.

Barbrook's duties at Day and Martin included collecting the rents of Charles's houses in London, which produced an annual income of around £4,000. This had come up in conversation between Antonine Dufaur and Barbrook in 1832 when the bonds for the boys were being drafted. At the time, Antonine mentioned the matter to his older brother Frederick with whom he worked. Little did he realise it, but this innocuous leak by Robert Barbrook, in whom Charles Day had total confidence, to a professional and supposedly discrete adviser, was to have extraordinary ramifications in the future, not only on Charles's eventual estate but also on the Price family for generations to come.

Frederick Dufaur heard about Robert Barbrook's infirmity and, knowing Barbrook's critical function in Charles's affairs, saw his chance and made an approach to Charles in the most charming way he could manage. He offered his services in collecting the rents, in the knowledge that he would be receiving commission of two-and-a-half percent, and, as this provided an immediate solution to a difficult problem, Charles readily accepted. Sadly, with his blindness and increasing immobility, Charles was perhaps (for once in his life) slightly gullible, because unwittingly he was allowing into his life a person who was obsessed with his own advancement by whatever means it would take. And he knew that, in Charles, he was dealing with someone who was immensely wealthy but increasingly vulnerable.

As he was to become a critical figure in what remained of Charles's life and, more importantly, its aftermath, it is worth looking into the background of Frederick Dufaur in more detail.

The Dufaur family were of French descent, coming from the Haute Garonne department in the south-west of France towards the Pyrenees. The main city is Toulouse and just outside to the west is the town of Pibrac from where the Du Faur family originated. Records of the family go back to the fourteenth century and there are many ancestors of high renown. Perhaps the most famous was Guy du Faur de Pibrac, who was a prominent French statesman in the sixteenth century. Having qualified as a lawyer, he rose to high office, ultimately being the chancellor of Marguerite of France, Queen of Navarre. He was also a noted Latin scholar and poet, and 'left, among other literary remains, elegant and sententious quatraines' (a quatrain is a concise poem of four lines).

In the mid-eighteenth century, one of his descendants John (but probably Jean before he left France) Dufaur arrived in England and found work in Rochester, Kent. One of the clergy on the Cathedral Chapter at the time was Rev William Stubbs who came from an illustrious family of Anglican priests - his father had been Archdeacon of St Albans. He had a daughter Sarah whom the young Frenchman befriended, he being eight years her senior. They were married in 1768 and went to London to find work, establishing their home in Chelsea. Children arrived in quick succession and their third son was given the unusual name of Cyprian – a common name in the old French family. Sarah's father died in 1790 and left her a legacy of £200, a considerable amount at the time.

Cyprian grew up in Chelsea but married a girl from Kent whom he had met on visits home to his mother's family. They set up residence back in Chelsea where their first of nine children, Frederick, was born. Cyprian established himself as a money lender and, as such, was often in need of legal assistance to recover his debts. It was therefore not surprising that he encouraged young Frederick to train as a lawyer which he did with a principal in Hanover Square between 1816 and 1821, but unusually with the articles being transferred to another principal in Lincolns Inn in 1819. However, then comes an event that would soon be seen as typical of the Dufaurs, who would never seem to worry about how to achieve their ambitions, as long as they were achieved. An extraordinary document was signed and witnessed on 3 August 1824 and sworn at the Chambers of Lord Chief Justice Abbott. These were the articles of Antonine Dufaur, son of Cyprian Dufaur, to train as a lawyer, with his principal being his older brother Frederick Dufaur, who was only three years out of training himself. Antonine, another name from the old French family, was the third son of Cyprian and by then only seventeen years old, Frederick being a mere twenty-four years old. It seems strange that this was allowed to happen, but is perhaps typical of the idiosyncratic aspects of the English legal system at the time.

In this document, Frederick Dufaur's address is given as Furnival's Inn, Holborn. This was a building on the site of one of the old Inns of Chancery that bore the same name. The Inn was dissolved as a society in 1817 when Lincoln's Inn did not renew its lease and the medieval building was demolished in 1818. The building was rebuilt as apartments by a new owner who retained the old name. Coincidentally, Charles Dickens rented rooms there between December 1834 and throughout the first year of his marriage, until 1837. He began *The Pickwick Papers* while a tenant there. The character John Westlock in *Martin Chuzzlewit* lives in Furnival's Inn, and describes it as:

> *...a shady, quiet place, echoing to the footsteps of the stragglers who have business there; and rather monotonous and gloomy on summer evenings... there are snug chambers in those Inns where the bachelors live, and, for the desolate fellows they pretend to be, it is quite surprising how well they get on.*

It sounds an ideal residence for Frederick Dufaur in the early days of his professional life before his marriage in 1826. Perhaps he left a reputation there, for Dickens to hear about a few years later and to use in the character of Mr Vholes in *Bleak House*.

Antonine had completed his articles by 1829 and the two brothers set up the practice. They gained some routine work from Charles Day and so became tangentially involved with Robert Barbrook and the drawing up of the bonds for Charles's three bastard sons. They had gained information which could be very valuable in the future.

In 1826, Frederick had married Mary Eliza Harsant of Wickham in Suffolk and the couple lived over Frederick's office at Old Millman Street, Bedford Row, London, to where Frederick had moved from Furnival's Inn. They had three daughters and two sons (both called Frederick). The older son died aged six months, but for the younger, known all his life by his middle name of Eccleston, Frederick could afford an education at Harrow. However, he emigrated to Australia at the age of twenty-one in 1853, a major decision at the early stages of colonisation of that country. Could this imply that he was wanting to build his own life, far away from his difficult father? He returned in 1857 shortly before his father's death, but went out again permanently in 1863 to become a prominent citizen in the early history of that country.

Early in 1833, Frederick Dufaur had featured in the national press as the losing defendant in a highly complicated case involving his father lending money to a young member of the aristocracy, who brought the action. Dufaur's problem was that he was acting for all parties and withheld information from the young nobleman to which he was privy as his father's agent. This defeat does not seem to have affected him and he continued in his work with what was now his apparent overbearing self-confidence. It was just after this that he approached Charles to collect his rents.

Later in his career, Dufaur was once more demonstrating his belief that the best form of defence was attack. It seems he had made a basic error that was causing serious damage to a client's reputation and the client was threatening to have Dufaur struck off. Again, Dufaur lost but not before stating to the court, of his client's actions, 'This is only a dodge of Mr Jones's'.

In another case in the Central Criminal Court, Dufaur prosecuted his footman for having stolen jewellery from Mrs Dufaur but, having brought the prosecution, seemed to have regretted it, asking the court to show mercy to his footman, who had plead guilty and had asked to be deported. Dufaur was admonished by the court for wasting its time, and the footman was sentenced to 6 months in jail – so no one was happy!

But all of this pales into insignificance when compared to Frederick Dufaur's real cause for infamy, being his involvement in the affairs of Charles Day and the eventual estate in administration.

Dufaur died on 27 August 1858, leaving only a modest estate to his widow and a trail of bad practice behind him. His brother Antonine only survived him by a few years. But his son in Australia (who reverted his surname to the original 'Du Faur') had a successful professional career as a land agent and farming adviser, becoming quite involved in the exploration of the outback and founding a national park. His great interest was fine art and he was President of the National Art Gallery of New South Wales. He was also an accomplished Latin scholar. His surviving children were two sons and a daughter, the latter of whom seems to have channelled the family trait of high self-confidence in a more constructive way than her grandfather. Contemporary with the Suffragette movement in England, she was a strong feminist and became the first woman to scale Mt Cook, the highest peak in New Zealand. Even more interestingly and taboo for the times, she led an openly lesbian lifestyle, the criticism of which led to the suicide of her partner. This disturbed her so much that she herself took her own life six years later in 1935.

3. The Price boys and a census

After Charles died on 26 October 1836, life could not stop for the household of Susannah and Sarah Peake, and the three now-fatherless children, Henry, Alfred and Edmund Price. But the tap serving the source of funds that maintained the household had been firmly turned off. Charles would have foreseen this and ensured that Susannah had some funds to keep things going until the provisions of the Will had been brought into effect – hopefully just a matter of months. Thanks to the efforts of Frederick Dufaur, this period had been stretched at least tenfold. Mercifully, Susannah had enough savings (or at least sources of temporary funds from those few who were in the know) to keep things going.

On 24 May 1841, nearly five years after Charles Day's death, Susannah Peake submitted an Affidavit to the Court of Chancery in which she said that the 'infant defendants', Henry, Alfred and Edmund Price, aged by then eighteen, sixteen and fourteen, were placed almost from their birth under her superintendence by their father Charles Day, who had during his lifetime paid her an allowance for the maintenance and education of the children. The children had resided with her ever since, their present residence being 4 Osnaburgh Street, Regent's Park. She said that, in a conversation which she had had with Charles Day on 15 September 1836 during his last illness, he informed her of the provision he had made for the children and that it would yield £1,200 a year. In speaking of the plans that he wished her to follow in case he died, he stated his desire was that she should move into a larger house, such as the one he used to live in at

1 Euston Square, and bring the children up according to their expectations. When they were about sixteen-years-old, he wished them to be placed with a clergyman for two years. She said that when Charles Day died, the children were being educated at the London University School, later University College School, where they continued until the autumn of 1837. The children were then placed at the boarding school of Mr Chapman at Kilburn Priory where they remained until the autumn of 1839. They were then placed with Rev Francis Henry Hutton of 9 St Andrews Place, Regent's Park, with whom they had remained ever since and were still being educated by him. Whilst the children were at the London University School, as well as during the vacations while they were at Mr Chapman's Boarding School and during the time they had been at Rev Hutton's, they continued to reside with her.

She said that ever since Charles Day's death, she had maintained and educated the children and that she had paid for Henry various amounts totalling £546-13s-0d, for Alfred £529-16s-0d and for Edmund £478-4s-5d, the full details being given in schedules attached to the affidavit. She also stated that the fortune of each child consisted of £6,738-15s-2d, Three Percent Annuities, standing in the name of the Accountant General in trust to accounts respectively entitled in each of the children's names. In addition, sums of £5,979-3s-4d, according to a report dated 26 March 1841, were due to each of the children for principal and interest calculated to that date, as per the codicil to Charles Day's Will dated 10 September 1836. No payments from these sources had yet been made, the children having no other sources of funds.

The attached schedules were immaculately detailed, showing all the items of clothing and other supplies, school fees, medical costs, the legal costs of the counsel and solicitor who represented the children in the Will dispute and subsequent appeal, full board and lodging whilst at home and even the costs of annual holidays at the seaside 'for the benefit of their health'.

Shortly after this affidavit was presented to the Court of Chancery, the household at Osnaburgh Street experienced a novel event. The Population Act of 1840 created the roles 'Commissioners for taking account of the population'. It also gave the Registrar General the responsibility for the census for England and Wales in addition to his responsibility for Civil Registration (which had been introduced in 1837). The earliest censuses had been administered by the Overseers of the Poor but the Civil Registration system provided the local administration which could also take on the job of the census. Consequently, the first really comprehensive national census was planned for a date to be arranged as soon as possible. There had been national censuses taking place from 1801, but their reliability was dubious because of the lack of central administration. The idea was to record exactly each living person in the country and their whereabouts on a specific day and to collect the data as quickly as possible. The date chosen was 6 June 1841. Some 35,000 census enumerators were appointed to undertake the data collection, one enumerator per district, covering a population of about sixteen million people, ie about 450 people per enumerator. Census forms were delivered to every household a few days before the day of the census. These were to be completed by the householder and collected by the enumerator on 7 June, the day after the census. Refusing to answer a census question, providing false information or failure to comply with the demand to complete a census form were offences penalised by a fine. The 1841 census recorded people's names, age, gender, occupation, if they were born in the county of their residence, and if they were born anywhere other than in England and Wales. Children under fifteen were to have their age recorded accurately, while those over fifteen were to be rounded down to the nearest five years so, for example, someone aged sixty-three should be recorded as aged sixty. However, not all enumerators followed this instruction and exact ages may have been recorded.

All this provided Susannah and Sarah with several dilemmas. There was little problem with recording the boys. They could only be Henry, Alfred and Edmund Price, aged twenty, fifteen and ten (although their actual ages were eighteen, sixteen and fourteen). One of the occupations available was 'Independent Means' and this was perfectly appropriate for Sarah and Susannah. Sarah's actual age was still forty-five (she would turn forty-six later that month) so to be stated as forty-five in this context was perfectly correct. However, although Susannah was actually fifty-six by this time, the enumerator kindly recorded her age as fifty in the final document. But the real problem was with what surnames were the two ladies to be recorded? With the case stuck in the Court of Chancery and receiving some publicity, to use 'Peake' for both of them would be too revealing. But the using of any other name would be false and could carry a fine. However, if the three Price boys were living with these ladies, one would have to be their mother, as was the actual case, and she would therefore have to be called Price. They had all been baptised as the children of John and Sarah Price and John had been killed off. She therefore had little option but to take the risk of calling herself in the census Sarah Price. But what about Susannah and her wish for anonymity? Her Christian name was often abbreviated to just 'Susan', so that would suffice. But if she used 'Peake' as her surname and state herself as of 'Independent Means', rather than merely F.S. (Female Servant) as the maid Henrietta was being stated, who could she possibly be? Too many questions could be asked. It would just be safer to call herself Price along with the rest of the household. Perhaps she was the surviving sister of the boys' late father, just visiting at the time. That could be a fairly credible, official explanation without much risk of a fine. And just to add to the confusion, the enumerator incorrectly recorded Edmund's name as 'Edward'. So, probably after a certain amount of over-thinking, the 1841 census entry read as follows:

Osnaburgh Street	Sarah Price	45	Ind
	Henry Do.	20	
	Alfred Do.	15	
	Edward Do.	10	
	Susan Do.	50	Ind
	Henrietta Sparshott	25	F.S.

But there was another problem. Susannah had stated to the Prerogative Court that, for a while before Charles's death, they had lived at Wyndham Place, Marylebone. She knew that this property was still in the name of John and Sarah Price with some of the Day servants living there. Before the census date, she visited the property and found the census forms awaiting completion. She ensured that those living there were correctly recorded, but merely added to them John and Sarah Price, aged fifty-five and fifty, of 'Independent Means', as the property was still registered in John Price's name. Hopefully, no further questions would be asked. And as it turned out, they weren't.

13. The three Price boys:
    A. Henry Price aged 25 from an ambrotype made c1848.*
    B. Alfred Price aged 26 from a photograph taken c1851.*
    C. Edmund Price aged 5 from a silhouette made in 1832.
    * Photograph copies by John Glynn Photography

A year after Susannah's affidavit to the Court of Chancery, the solicitor acting for the boys, Daniel Hunt Williams, presented another document to the Court entitled *Statement of facts and charge of the Guardian of the Infants* dated 20 May 1842. Firstly, it calculates the interest due up to that point to each of Henry, Alfred and Edmund Price in addition to the principal sum of £10,000 left to each of them in the 1832 *post obit* bonds, increased by the codicil dated 10 September 1836. This basically takes up the first sixteen of twenty pages. But then it speaks far more personally about each of the boys.

Henry, the oldest, was definitely the most studious of the three and showed considerable academic promise. Ever since their baptism in 1829, Sarah and Susannah, with Charles's blessing, had been keen regularly to attend St Mary's Church, Bryanston Square. While they had been living at Wyndham Place, the church was literally on their doorstep. Even after moving to Osnaburgh Street, they were near enough to continue their connection there. Henry became increasingly involved, and after careful thought, decided to study for the ministry at Cambridge. This would need more financial resources, for which Susannah had to appeal to the Court in the statement of 20 May 1842:

That the said Henry Price, who is now of the age of nineteen years, is desirous of being entered as a Member of the University of Cambridge with a view to preparing for Holy Orders and that an increased annual expenditure will be occasioned by his residence at the University and that an immediate outlay will be required for purchasing books and for fitting up and furnishing rooms for his residence in College and for other necessary expenses.

As a result, Henry's annual allowance was duly increased from £180 to £350. His studies commenced at Gonville and Caius College, Cambridge, on 8 June 1842 when he was 'admitted pensioner' and he graduated four years later with a Bachelor of Arts degree. Interestingly, the College biographical records state that he was the 'son of late Charles Price, Esq., merchant of London'. His father seems to have become a combination of Charles Day and John Price, and his illegitimacy was clearly being kept a secret. The records confirm that he was 'educated for two years by Rev Mr Chapman, at Kilburn; and for two years by Rev Mr Hutton, in London'. It then states that he was curate of Turville, Buckinghamshire, followed by another curacy in St Cadoc's Church, Aberpergwm, Glamorgan, from 1851 to 1854 (which, at the time, was still part of the Church of England, being maintained privately by the Williams Family of Aberpergwm House).

His brother Alfred, on the other hand, seems to have been a very different personality with a particular gift for drawing and painting. With an eye to applying this to a prosperous profession, he was keen to become an architect. On his behalf and in the same document, Susannah made the following appeal:

That the said Alfred Price, who is now of the age of seventeen years, is desirous of following the profession or business of an Architect and that, in order to prosecute the study of Architecture with advantage, it will be necessary for him to have instruction in drawing and designing and to be apprenticed to the business of an Architect and that his yearly expenditure will also be increased by necessary travelling expenses for the purpose of visiting architectural remains and works of art.

14. Watercolour of Amsterdam painted in 1841 by Alfred Price when he was just 16 years old.
(Photograph by John Glynn Photography)

The reference to travel is interesting. Prior to this, Alfred had already travelled far from London despite his young age. No doubt inspired by architecture, he was drawing the medieval St Nicholas Church in Newcastle-upon-Tyne (later Newcastle Cathedral) in 1840 when he was just fifteen-years-old. The following year, he was painting Dover Castle in Kent, followed by a trip across the Channel to Holland where he painted scenes in Rotterdam and Amsterdam. Susannah accompanied him on these trips and became convinced that he had a serious talent. In particular, the buildings were drawn with an instinctive accuracy. And as a result, Alfred's annual allowance was duly increased from £160 to £250.

At this stage, Edmund was too young to be making future plans, with his schooling continuing. Consequently, Susannah's appeal to the court was more modest:

That the maintenance and education of the said Edmund Price, who is now of the age of 15 years, also requires an increased expenditure particularly for his board and lodging.

As a result, Edmund's annual allowance was duly increased from £150 to £250.

And so, the three Price boys advanced into adulthood. Little is known of them until they appear living near each other in 1851 when that year's census was taken, and subsequently when Henry married in 1854 and Alfred in 1858. Edmund never married and died at the age of forty-six in 1874.

4. The Court of Chancery

In order to begin to understand the machinations of the Court of Chancery, it is essential to have a clear grasp of the details of Charles Day's last Will and Testament.

By any standards it is an extraordinary document. With the four codicils for which probate was granted, it extends to over 7,500 words. In all, there are sixty-six legacies specified, sixty-four to individuals and two to charitable trusts created by the Will. Of the sixty-four individuals, thirty-eight are also left annuities of varying amounts, to be paid for the remainder of each annuitant's life. In other words, the administration of the Will would have to continue until the last annuitant died or until an earlier agreement could be reached with the surviving annuitants at the time. The youngest annuitant was Charles's legitimate daughter, Caroline Clagett, who was only twenty-nine when her father died, and her annuity was the largest at £3,000 a year. She could be expected to live for perhaps another forty years, giving the Court of Chancery plenty of time to wallow in its fog.

In fairness, the job was not made any easier by the wording of the Will. Most of the individual legatees were not mentioned by name, but simply as 'each of my nephews and nieces, the sons and daughters of my sisters and of my late brother William Day who shall be living at my decease' and 'each of the sons and daughters of my mother's brothers and sisters, excepting Samuel Virgo now or late of Brighton, as may be alive at my decease'. All these people had to be clearly identified, together with their specific ages. In other words, Charles's family tree had to be constructed meticulously. Those in the former category, his nephews and nieces, were not to receive anything until they were twenty-one years of age and certainly not before the death of Charles's widow, Rebecca. But they could be identified fairly easily through their surviving parents. Also, they were mainly receiving just single legacies.

But the latter category was far more difficult. This related to the Parsons family, the family of Charles' late mother. They originated from the area around Lewes in Sussex and their origins seem to have been humble. John and Elizabeth Parsons had five sons and five daughters between 1742 and 1762. Their third daughter, Elizabeth, married Francis Day, the Covent Garden hairdresser from Yorkshire, but died after giving birth to a daughter, also Elizabeth. Their second daughter then married the widowed Francis, and they proceeded to have seven children, four of whom survived to adulthood, namely William, Mary, Charles and Susannah. Charles was the testator of the Will now being administered by the Court of Chancery, which therefore had to identify the unnamed siblings of Charles's mother and their children who were alive when Charles died on 26 October 1836. They were all to receive a lifetime annuity of £40 from Charles's estate. This was a daunting task, especially as the national registration of births, marriages and deaths had only been introduced in 1837 in England. The Court would therefore have to seek the information from local church records. It would have to ask someone to examine the church record for the relevant information and then give a sworn affidavit to the Court that the information was correct. Alternatively, family members could themselves give a sworn affidavit that certain relations of theirs existed and were still alive.

In all, the Court received forty-eight such affidavits between October and December 1840 to identify the unnamed beneficiaries of Charles's Will. From these, the court was able to construct Charles's family tree on the Parsons' side, the details on the Day side being largely known by Charles's three sisters and sister-in-law. However, it took until 27 June 1843 for this to be ratified by the Court.

The result was that there were eighteen Day nephews and nieces who were each due to receive a legacy of £3,000, complicated by the fact that two, Emma Day and Henry Francis Lockwood, had married each other. In addition, there were twenty-two Parsons cousins who were each due to receive an annuity of £40 for the rest of their lives. Charles had probably done this because, although it was likely that he didn't know them all individually, he knew that they were probably living in straightened circumstances and wished them to benefit from his prosperity. It is uncertain why he omitted by name one of his cousins, Samuel Virgo, from receiving an annuity. The likely reason was that he had disgraced himself in some way. His mother, Ann, and Charles' mother were close and the message had probably come back to Charles through this route. Sarah Peake had boarded with Ann during her first pregnancy which resulted in Henry Price being born in Brighton.

But the bigwigs of the Court of Chancery must have been rubbing their hands in glee at all these glorious complications that were presenting themselves and the prospect of inevitable disputes within such a large number of beneficiaries.

The only beneficiary who had died between Charles's death and the start of the administration of the Will (a gap of nearly four years) was Robert Barbrook, Charles' trusty clerk at the factory who had been instrumental in drawing up the *post obit* bonds for the three boys. Barbrook had died of apoplexy on 20 July 1838 in a mental institution on the Mile End Road in the east end of London. The Court took the 'bolt and braces' approach of determining from the registrar that Barbrook had died when he did, and also of obtaining an affidavit from Barbrook's bother and next of kin, James, that this was one and the same Robert Barbrook. He had been due an annuity of £200 and a legacy of £100 and the Court could now instruct the correct funds to be released to his estate.

Otherwise, the remainder of the beneficiaries were named but still had to be traced and verified.

The other major administrative matter that needed attention was the setting up of the two charities specified by the Will, namely 'Mr Day's Almshouses' and 'The Blind Man's Friend'.

The almshouses had been built in 1828 and in effect, run by Charles Day himself in consultation with the local vicars of Edgware and Little Stanmore. By the time Charles made his Will in May 1834, he had conveyed the land on which the almshouses stood to the trustees of a new charity, being the two church incumbents together with an Edgware resident, Richard Looseley, and the local historian William Smith Tootell, author of *A Brief Sketch of the Town of Edgware, Middlesex*, as already mentioned. But the charity had not been endowed and Charles made provision for this in his Will, directing that a sum of money should be invested that would yield £100 per year to maintain the building and give a weekly allowance to the residents. He had been paying this himself up to his death. A Deed of Trust would need to be drawn up for the administration of the charity, and this would now be the responsibility of the Court. The only record of the trustees meeting after Charles' death was in 1838 when one of the residents died and a replacement needed to be sought.

Recognising that they were still waiting for the Deed of Trust, their minute reads:

> *There being a vacancy in the Almshouse No 7 by reason of the death of Mrs Fanny Brown, this meeting was held to elect her successor but the Trustees, not having the Deed of Trust or any other document in their possession for their guidance, resolved unanimously to admit Mrs Anna Sophie Smith of Little Stanmore, aged 62 years, into such vacant Almshouse and she gave an undertaking that, in the event of her being ineligible by the Deed of Trust on the Will of Mr Day, to quit and wind up the possession of the same within one week after she should be required by the Trustees so to do. And on these conditions only was she elected.*

It would seem that this group of well-meaning individuals were acting in the spirit of their late friend and benefactor but were so intimidated by the legal system of the time that they were anxious to cover their backs as best they could. They could do little else until probate was granted and Mrs Smith should have been very grateful. They did not meet again and record a formal minute until 5 February 1842 when they recorded:

> *That the thanks of the Trustees be presented to Mr Pinder Simpson for his kindness in advancing funds to enable the Almspeople to receive their weekly allowances pending the suit in Chancery respecting Mr Day's Will and that a letter be sent to that effect by the Treasurer.*

It seems that Pinder Simpson, either at his own expense or by some other informal means, had managed to keep the almshouses and their occupants going until the Court had got its act together. In the spirit of Charles Day, he realised that life had to go on and could not go into suspended animation until the

Court had made its decisions. However, the rest of the minute suggested that everything was now in place and the charity could proceed as intended.

Once this had been achieved, the Court seems to have turned its attention to setting up 'The Blind Man's Friend'. The Trustees of this charity were to be the executors to the Will, ie Croft, Underwood and Simpson, with John Simpson being appointed as the first Clerk and Treasurer on a salary of £100 per year and an expenses allowance of £20 per year. The Trustees met for the first time on 15 March 1842 and approved awards of up to £20 each to 235 applicants, quarterly payments commencing on 20 April 1842. The Court had been able to furnish the charity with limited funds in order that the payments could commence and over time would remit to the charity, as and when cash funds were available from the sale of assets, its full £100,000 as stipulated in the Will. But every time funds were released, the Court had to go through all the formalities of issuing the appropriate Order.

In summary, after all the codicils were applied, the Will stipulated legacies totalling a staggering £194,923. With most of the wealth being based on property all over the country together with the value of the goodwill of the highly profitable firm of Day and Martin, a considerable amount of liquidation of assets would be required in order that these legacies could be paid out. However, with the capital required by 'The Blind Man's Friend' not being required in total immediately, and with the £54,000 in legacies of £3,000 to each of Charles Day's nephews and nieces not being due for payment until after the death of Rebecca Day, the Court of Chancery could give itself a certain amount of time. It needed no encouragement to accept this offer.

The more pressing problem was how to start paying out the 38 annuities to the waiting annuitants – a total of £8,080 per year. This would have to rely on the rental income from Charles' various leasehold and freehold properties together a distribution of the profits of Day and Martin.

But what was the value of the estate as a whole and what were the legacy duties likely to be? This never seems to have been quantified. Clearly some sharp financial management of the estate was going to be needed. Could the Court of Chancery, bathed in its contemporary fog and mud of the 1840s, be trusted with this responsibility?

During the original case in the Prerogative Court of Canterbury, the administration of the estate of Charles Day was allowed to be kept with the receiver appointed by the executors, that is to say John Simpson. However, his appointment was not allowed to continue once the appeal to the Privy Council had commenced and a neutral receiver had to be appointed. On 8 February 1839, Samuel Scott, one of the partners in the firm of Sir Claude Scott & Co., Bankers, was appointed receiver of the personal estate of Charles Day, with the exception of matters connected with the trade of Day and Martin. Scott was to prepare accounts for each six-month period ended 15 May and 15 November, the first account being to 15 November 1839.

In appointing Samuel Scott, the Court had gone to the top of the establishment tree. He was in fact Sir Samuel Scott, Bart, MP who had inherited the baronetcy in 1830 on the death of his father, Sir Claude Scott, the First Baronet. His father was a self-made entrepreneur in the corn trade, who had made a huge fortune and had used his money to set up a bank. Perhaps this was an example that Charles Day should have followed.

In his first account to 15 November 1839, he stated that the cash that had accumulated for the estate to that point amounted to £20,281. But much of this represented capital sums rather than income. The Court had allowed Scott a salary of five percent of these funds gathered in, ie £1,014. It was stated that many of the sums received by Scott had been paid into his bank by the parties from whom they were due, and that, generally speaking, Scott had had very little to do for his substantial remuneration. Two of the executors, Croft and Underwood, presented a petition 'praying that it might be referred back to the Master' asking that the receiver should receive only one percent on principal sums from repaid mortgages and redeemed annuities and two percent on rents, interest and other income received, and that certain parties might be asked to pay certain monies forming part of Charles's estate into the Bank of England rather than Scott's bank. After much dithering, the petition was merely referred back for review, but all parties should have their costs except, and here's the rub, 'some annuitants who had filed some irrelevant affidavits'. The dye had been cast and costs were beginning to mount with no progress being made. The Court of Chancery had the potential beneficiaries of the Will, who it should be protecting, in its line of fire. It seemed that the people who should be benefitting from the estate were the only people who weren't.

Meanwhile, the business of Day and Martin carried on unaltered under the continuing management of John Weston. With the profits of the business forming a major part of the income of the estate, the Court saw the obvious wisdom of appointing Weston as the manager of the business which he had managed for twenty-three years up to the time of Charles' death. As the Court was now effectively in charge of the business, it had to go through the formality of making this appointment, with the direction that Weston should produce separate sets of accounts for the business for each successive calendar year – something he had been doing anyway.

John Weston presented the Court with a very interesting document on 7 December 1838 entitled *Affidavit of Mr Weston, the Manager of the Testator's Trade*. In it, he described how he had first met Charles Day in 1806 and had been a close friend for the following 30 years until he died. They were of course married to sisters. In 1813, Charles had persuaded him to give up his business and become the manager of Day and Martin. As his own business had yielded an income of about £1,000 a year, Charles offered him the same as a fixed salary with an annual bonus of one-third of the excess profits over the 1813 profit level. This was always a 'gentleman's agreement' and nothing was put in writing. He was also offered rent-free accommodation in the house attached to the factory in High Holborn. In addition, it was agreed that Charles should withhold £500 a year to accumulate a lump-sum of a maximum of £10,000 for Weston to receive on his retirement. This sum had now fully accrued but none of it had been taken, ie the estate had a liability to John Weston of £10,000. He explained that Charles Day went blind in 1816 but the arrangement continued to their mutual benefit until Charles's death. Since Charles's death, Weston had sent money to John Simpson (the receiver at the time) on a monthly basis equal to the current balance in the account less £2,000, being the necessary funds for the business to continue. In February 1837, a meeting took place between the executors William Croft and William Underwood, John Simpson and John Weston. In his Will, Charles had directed that the business should be sold. But at that point, it was generally realised that, in order to meet the commitments of the Will and its stipulated annuities, it would be best to continue trading just as before, especially if Weston was prepared to remain as manager. With competition since Charles' death becoming particularly keen, there was little doubt that the business could continue as the market leader, but it was crucial that Weston should remain at the helm in order to achieve this.

But what should Weston be paid? In the affidavit, he clearly specifies the bonuses he had received for each of the twenty-three years he had been manager up to Charles's death, ranging from nothing to £4,905. This was interesting in itself as it showed how the business had faired over the years. The most successful period to date was undoubtedly the decade of the 1820s. Weston's bonus of £4,905 was in 1825. This would have represented one-third of the profits over the 1813 level. If a random figure of, say, £10,000 is taken as the 1813 profits, this would imply that the 1825 profits were £24,715, a huge sum for the time. It was also interesting to see how profits had dipped in the years from 1832 to 1834 with Weston receiving no bonus in the latter two years. This was perhaps a reflection of the political situation at the time with the country in a certain amount of turmoil around the time of the 1832 Reform Act. Weston very fairly suggested that his future remuneration should be £1,000 a year plus his average bonus over the twenty-three years being £1,850, ie a total salary of £2,850 payable in half-yearly instalments of £1,425. This was accepted and in fact remained the case until Weston's death in 1863 at the age of eighty-five – he never retired.

In the Trust accounts, a clear pattern emerges as the years go by. A typical example would be for the year ended 15 May 1854 (by then, trust accounts were being prepared annually). The extent of Charles's wealth is clearly revealed. The properties are all identified. There were the leasehold properties in London, including Charles's former home at 1 Euston Square together with four other houses in the same square, various properties in

Marylebone including two in North Bank, one in Vere Street, nine in Crawford Street, one in Wyndham Place (the former residence of Susannah and Sarah Peake and the Price boys), two in Holles Street, six houses in High Holborn next to the blacking factory and one in Cadogan Place (part of the newly-fashionable district to the west of the City known as Knightsbridge). The annual rental income from all these desirable houses was £2,421. Additionally, there were some freehold properties in London near to the blacking factory, one on Holborn Hill and seven in Eagle Street. These brought in a further £314 of rent. The house in Edgware was rented out for £105 and the Caterham Estate, with its large house, several farms and twenty-two small cottages, realised a further £855 of rental income. There were various types of investment income and the manager at Day and Martin sent monthly amounts to the receiver totalling £1,080 for the year. A further source of income was from the fee farm rents in respect of properties all over the country. They are not listed individually but are itemised by county – Buckinghamshire, Dorset, Kent, Monmouthshire, Norfolk, Nottinghamshire, Hampshire, Suffolk, Surrey, Sussex, Glamorgan, Westmoreland and Yorkshire. The greatest concentrations were in the East Midlands and South Wales. The former was probably as a result of the personal connections that Pinder Simpson had there, being from where his family originated. The total rental income was £426.

On what had appeared to be the unresolved question of the receiver's salary calculation, the formula that was used for all future years remained at five percent with the exception of a reduction to two-and-a-half percent for the profits received from the trade of Day and Martin. So, the petition of the original executors (William Croft and William Underwood) seemed to fail completely.

By 1854, the annuities paid out as directed by the Will had reduced to £4,747 (thirteen of the thirty-eight annuitants had died since the administration had started). The estate was generating enough income to meet these commitments (much helped by John Weston's efficient management of Day and Martin and the resulting flow of profits into the estate) in addition to maintaining all the properties it held. So, everything seemed to be running quite smoothly. But what this hid was the turgid way the Court operated.

Any decision relating to the Day estate had to be put to the Court, documents had to be drawn up and a date found for the decision to be made. When the Court sat, all interested parties had to be represented by counsel and solicitors. The issue could have been a number of things; it could be a new lease for one of the properties or a reference for a potential tenant, the establishment of a debt to the estate and its collection, a claim against the estate from a creditor and its payment, accepting the receiver's and manager's accounts, a petition from a beneficiary about their circumstances, the valuation of heritable assets, repairs to heritable assets, the admonishment of misbehaving tenants, the inevitable claiming of costs and many other issues. Affidavits, affidavits, affidavits – boxes and boxes of them. And all the time, the costs mounted up, taking the funds of the estate away from its beneficiaries.

The 1840s turned into the 1850s, the 1850s turned into the 1860s and the 1860s turned into the 1870s. Only in 1875, that is to say thirty-nine years after Charles Day died, did the Court accept that some sort of winding up could be considered. Only three of the original thirty-eight annuitants were still alive, but the estate still had an annual income of £6,114 (£3,400 of which came from the trade of Day and Martin) and the receiver was still taking an annual salary (before expenses) of about £250 for very little work.

Way back, soon after the suit had commenced on 24 April 1841, *The Times* published a Letter to the Editor from William Underwood, one of Charles Day's executors, which is worth quoting in full:

CHANCERY REFORM. – DAY v. CROFT

Sir, - In the discussion which took place last night in the House of Commons on the 'Administration of Justice Bill', two of its honourable members alluded to the above cause, and as there is much misconception relative to this suit in the minds of the public, will you kindly allow me, as one of Mr Day's executors, a space in your journal to offer a short explanation?

Mr Day died in October 1836, disposing of his large property by a Will and codicils, one of the latter, on proving the Will, was opposed in the Prerogative Court by his widow and daughter and three executors, upon being assured that as the matter of opposition was so simple no delay could occur beyond a few months. However, such was the delay that proceedings, which were commenced in November 1836, did not terminate until February 1840, when the probate of the Will was granted to the three originally appointed executors. Pending the suit in the above court and Privy Council, on the 1st of October 1838, the widow and daughter of Mr Day were unhappily prevailed on by a party to file a bill in Chancery which led to all the distress and delay which has since arisen, and the testator's relations are kept from receiving their annuities and the noble bequest to poor blind men and women will not be carried into effect for many months to come.

In the performance of a sacred duty to a deceased friend, I have been thrown into the vortex of a Chancery suit, and I, as an executor, have narrowly watched the proceedings in all their ramifications; I have read the debate of last night in the House of Commons with deep interest on the 'Administration of Justice Bill', upon which occasion the cause of 'Day v. Croft' was alluded to as one of the many distressing cases arising from delay in Chancery suits.

It is intended to appoint two new judges, with a view to expedite the hearing and determining suits more speedily; this may partially prove useful, but my experience convinces me that the cause of delay, and the other serious evils which are subjects of complaint, lie in the system of originating suits and conducting them in the Masters' offices, where, as also in the six clerks' offices, costs are taxed and allowed, numerous warrants are uselessly issued, unnecessary repetitions are made to swell the pleadings, and copies of proceedings are distributed to solicitors which they are compelled to take and pay for, although many of them in a suit represent parties who have the most trivial interest in it. As a practical instance, in the cause of 'Day v. Croft', there are 16 attorneys, most of whom represent the very poor small annuitants, or the parties to whom they have sold their annuities; in consequence of this system, the presentation of a petition by the executors to the Master of the Rolls from the Master's office on a recent occasion cost the estate £1,183.

There is one evil more I shall mention, and that is the great facility at present given to filing bills, whether at all necessary or otherwise; the plaintiff's solicitor, as soon as a suit is snugly lodged in the Master's office, gets the whole control of originating any proceeding, and therefore can delay or forward a suit just as it may subserve his own or the plaintiff's interest, whilst the defendants have no power to take any step, but the expensive one of presenting a petition to the court to remedy any grievance. Such being the present system, I hail with gratitude, on the part of myself as an executor and the public, the effort that is now making in both Houses of Parliament, by noble and able gentlemen, to remedy the abuses which have so long been deplored by every person who has been compelled from various causes to become plaintiff or defendant to a suit in Chancery.

I am, Sir, your most obedient servant,

W. UNDERWOOD
April 24, 1841

That letter was written in 1841. The case was still 'In Chancery' in 1875. Things take a long time to change in the law.

There is one final footnote to add to this sad litany. One of the attorneys representing the 'very poor small annuitants' was, believe it or not, a certain Frederick Dufaur.

5. Caterham

Throughout the Chancery proceedings, much mention is made of Charles Day's estate in Caterham. Numerous affidavits and other documents were written specifically about it. In itself, it forms a sub-plot to the Will case of Charles Day and deserves a detailed description.

With the purchase and partial move to Edgware established in 1817, and Charles Day's wealth continuing to accumulate at an extraordinary pace, Pinder Simpson was determined to divert Charles' attention back to the properties he knew about in Caterham. There was an ulterior motive here. Pinder and his family were still living in Romford, Essex, to the north-east of London, and his work was still in Mayfair where he stayed for most of the working week. Whilst this arrangement seemed to suit the family quite well, he wished to move on from Romford to somewhere more prestigious, commensurate with his own burgeoning success and wealth. The properties around Caterham contained some fairly grand houses which would suit his needs perfectly. If he could persuade Charles that Caterham represented a good real estate investment, he could move his whole family there and act as estate manager. The advantage of having someone on the spot would undoubtedly be attractive to Charles, who was becoming obsessed, especially in his blindness, with knowing all the minutest details of his business affairs. Pinder was still very much involved in Charles's affairs, keeping inventories of all his possessions and advising him on how to invest his expanding wealth. Charles agreed to an initial purchase in Caterham with a view to making further acquisitions if it proved a success.

After the ownership of Henry Rowed and his daughter Katherine, the Caterham estate was purchased by Thomas Clark and on his death in 1816, it passed to his son, also Thomas. In 1818, Thomas Jnr built the spectacular family home in Manor Park on the border with the district of Whyteleafe, deceptively named Manor Cottage. The cost was £5,500. However, by 1819 Charles Day had appeared on the scene, through his agent Pinder Simpson. The Surrey Land Tax Records reveal that initially he bought the Caterham Court Lodge and Farm together with Harestone Farm and some smaller properties, in one of which members of the Rowed family continued to live as tenants into the 1830s. This was followed by Tupwood in 1823, Salmons in 1824, Portley in 1826 and The Manor Farm in 1827. Thomas Clark retired to Manor Cottage by 1827, having by that year sold nearly everything else to Charles, on Pinder's advice. He remained there until his death in May 1833, at which point it was purchased by Charles, who now owned virtually the whole of the parish of Caterham with the exception of the southernmost part of Harestone Valley and a few small plots of land dotted around elsewhere.

Perhaps there was some local resentment to Charles almost monopolising the area, albeit by a very small minority. The following appeared in *The New Monthly Magazine* in December 1830:

> *The extensive farming premises, the property of Charles Day Esq, in the occupation of Pinder Simpson Esq, situate at Caterham, 6 miles south-east of Croydon in Surrey, have been set on fire. In the course of a couple of hours, the whole was nearly destroyed; namely three large barns, filled with corn, two wheat-ricks, and three valuable stacks of hay, together with the stabling and other outbuildings. That this destruction of property was the work of incendiaries, not the slightest doubt is entertained in*

the village where it occurred. It is satisfactory however to know that the labouring people of the neighbourhood evinced every disposition to arrest the progress of the flames.

With his blindness setting in three years before he had purchased any properties in Caterham, it is very unlikely that Charles ever visited the place in person. He clearly looked upon Caterham as an investment and the farms as a commercial venture, and was happy to leave Pinder Simpson in charge.

What indicates that Pinder Simpson had *carte blanche* over everything to do with Charles's Caterham properties, is the fact that he appears as the tenant of the Court Lodge Farm which included Caterham Court itself, this being by far the biggest property on the estate with an annual rent of £364, the next highest rent being for the Manor Farm at £117, whose tenant was a Stephen Gower.

15. Caterham Court, a photograph taken c1910, showing the original Georgian house (the residence of Pinder Simpson c1825) with the Victorian west wing on the left.

From the Land Tax Records between 1819 and 1831, there is no doubt that Pinder Simpson and his family made Caterham Court their home with the blessing of Charles Day, there presumably being some sort of *quid pro quo* between the rent due to Charles and Pinder's professional fees. In 1823 and 1824, Simpson even had his son-in-law as a tenant in one of the properties. In the Surrey Electoral Register of 1832, Simpson is still said to be resident at 'The Court-lodge' in Caterham.

However, with Thomas Clark's death in May 1833, the subsequent sale of his home at Manor Cottage to Charles Day, and a lease existing for the Court Lodge and Farm from Michaelmas 1833 to one Edward Stanford, it seems fairly certain that the Simpsons moved from the Court Lodge to the more desirable Manor Cottage in 1833, remaining there until 25 March 1839, when it was leased to the splendidly named Henry Aglionby Aglionby Esq, who was the MP for Cockermouth in Cumbria, until his death in 1854. The Simpsons then moved to their daughter's residence in Dorking, where Pinder died in 1847.

Pinder Simpson began his Will with the words:

I, Pinder Simpson, formerly of Old Burlington Street in the county of Middlesex and late of Caterham in the county of Surrey, Gentleman, being of sound mind, memory and understanding, do make this my last Will and Testament in manner following:
I desire to be buried at Caterham in the vault wherein the remains of my son Pinder are deposited.

It transpires that his second son, also called Pinder, had died in 1825 and the tender age of just eighteen. The only named vaults are located in the chancel of the church. With regard to other vaults, they were all below the floor of the main part of the church.

It appears that when a major renovation of St Lawrence's was carried out in the 1920s, a workman fell through the floor up to his waist because of the vaults below. For safety's sake the whole floor was cemented over and there are no indications of what lies beneath. It seems strange that the vaults have never been recorded but so far, no such record has been traced. There can be little doubt that the two Pinder Simpsons are below the concrete.

Incidentally, in another act of philanthropy, in 1832 Charles shared with the incumbent priest at St Lawrence's, Rev James Legrew, the cost of the new church porch and vestry.

Pinder's eldest son, John, went on to qualify as a solicitor. Charles had watched him grow up and always had the highest regard for him, allowing him to undertake much of his father's work as Pinder grew older and deafer. After Charles died and during the administration of his Will, John was to state the following:

> *Pinder Simpson of Old Burlington Street, who is one of the Executors of Mr Day's Will, is my father.*
>
> *He and Mr Day were on terms of intimacy and friendship together from the time of my earliest recollection.*
>
> *My father was connected by marriage with Mr Day's wife, now widow, she and my mother being first cousins.*
>
> *Mr Day always expressed the highest regard and esteem for my father.*
>
> *My father was always very much in his confidence and for several, as many as seventeen years back, the same confidence on the part of Mr Day was extended also to myself.*
>
> *He was during the time I have mentioned and, until his mind became impaired, in the habit of entering into his affairs with both of us together and separately, in the most reserved way. The management of his Estate at Caterham, worth probably £1,500 a year, he left almost entirely to our*

management, acting invariably upon any suggestion of ours with regards to all arrangements and expenditure connected with it.

His skill in figures was quite wonderful. He had also an extraordinary memory. As a proof of it, after hearing me once read over to him a long debtor and creditor account relating to his estate at Caterham, the rents of which I received for him and which account extended probably over four sides of a sheet of paper, he would go through it from memory and remember every item contained in it.

After Charles' death in 1836, a complete inventory of all the properties owned by the Estate of Charles Day was drawn up in 1844. This listed all the Caterham properties he owned including the 'Old Manor Court House and Farm Yard' (meaning Caterham Court, being the previous residence of Pinder Simpson), Salmons Farm, Chalk Pit Farm, Manor Cottage and Land, Portley Woods, The Half Moon Inn and Farm, Tupwood Farm, Bottom (or Woods) Farm and numerous cottages. Consequently, it is strange to find evidence that several of these properties were the subject of a proposed public auction sale on 19 July 1833, ie just as Pinder Simpson was moving from Caterham Court to the recently purchased Manor Cottage. The auction notice says that plans and particulars of leases can be seen at the offices of Pinder Simpson in London. It can only be assumed that this sale never happened. Perhaps there was a change of plan, or no interest was shown or that there was a reserve price that was never reached. Certainly, Charles' ownership continued after 1833.

In the 1844 inventory, Caterham Court is described as follows:

A very good substantial Old Manor Court House fit for the residence of a gentleman's family, built with brick, with good hall, drawing room, dining room and breakfast room, good staircase and landing, two best bedrooms and dressing room, two other bedrooms on first floor and four good attics; kitchen, washhouse, bakehouse, mangling room over, (the floor in very bad order), a bedroom and a garret overused as a pigeon loft. Adjoining the house is a lean-to brewhouse, an enclosed domestic yard at the back with poultry houses, all flint and brick and tiled. A capital farmyard with a range of cart stabling for fifteen horses, coach house and chaisehouse, two box stables and nag stabling for three horses, all built with flint and brick and tiled and a harness room. Adjoining the yard is a good bailiff's cottage, occupied by Richard Longhurst, containing three rooms below and three above.

Again, in the 1844 inventory, Manor Cottage is described as follows:

This is a very desirable villa residence, substantially constructed and arranged with every consideration for comfort and accommodation and is respectably tenanted and well adapted for any gentleman's family. It is brick built and slated roof, of handsome elevation, comprising a dining room, breakfast room and drawing-room, another sitting room with library, with excellent cellars, six bedrooms and two dressing rooms and a water closet, excellent kitchen and scullery, dairy and pantry, good supply of water and forcing pump, a washing house, bathroom and laundry over, and a bedroom. A good, well-enclosed court and stable yard with sundry outhouses and poultry houses, a three-stall stable coach house and lofts over, piggery and sheds, a dog kennel, another stable, timber built, with three stalls and loose box. A virandah to the south front of the house and a conservatory or green house at the end. An excellent kitchen garden, most fully stocked and well enclosed with lofty walls, gardeners' rooms and sundry sheds and a capital orchard, also enclosed with walls.

So, it was hardly a 'Cottage' and clearly even more of a desirable residence than Caterham Court, explaining Pinder's wish to move from one to the other.

There is also evidence of a dispute in 1847 between Charles' Trustees and a certain Joseph Chandler who had been listed as a tenant from 1819. He leased Platts Green which included 'The Old Harrow', a public house of which he was the proprietor. The Trustees were clearly trying to get rid of him because he was fencing off a piece of land on which to build a cottage without their permission. In an attempt to discredit him to the court, the Trustees point out that the pub had had its license taken away because it was:

An ill-conducted house and was the common resort of poachers, smugglers and others persons of disrepute.

In addition, there are farm accounts covering the period 1849 to 1853 when receivers on behalf of the Trustees were administering the Caterham Estate. By this time, it was thirteen years since Charles's death and Pinder himself had died in 1847. Clearly, the decision had been made to sell the estate (to help finance the considerable commitments of Charles's Will) and this eventually happened in 1853 when George Drew, a successful solicitor and speculator, acquired it for development on the eventual advent of the railway. Thus, the 37-year ownership of the Caterham Estate by Charles Day and his subsequent Trustees ended.

6. The destination of Charles Day's fortune

After Charles's death, his widow Rebecca, daughter Caroline and son-in-law Horatio had some serious decisions to make about where to live.

Charles' Will, the content being known but probate not being granted until 4 May 1840, stated in connection with Edgware Place:

> *I give and bequeath to my said dear wife all the furniture, pictures, plate, linen, china, wine, horses, carriages, stock and stores of what description soever which may be in or about my Residence at Edgware at the time of my decease to and for her own absolute use and benefit and it is my will that she, my said dear wife, be allowed the free use and occupation of my said house at Edgware together with the garden, pleasure ground, outbuildings and land thereunto belonging for and during the term of her natural life without paying any rent for the same, she keeping the premises in good order and repair and paying all expenses, tithes, taxes, rates and all other outgoings whatsoever during the time she continues to use and occupy the same.*

In other words, Rebecca was being given a liferent of the house in Edgware but the ownership would be retained by Charles's estate. She would be allowed to live in the house for as long as she liked and she would own its contents, but she would have to pay for all the costs associated with the house out of her ample annuity provided by the estate. Presumably Charles did this in the knowledge that Rebecca enjoyed the more peaceful surroundings of Edgware compared to central London.

Concerning Harley House, the Will stated:

I give and bequeath to my daughter Caroline, the wife of Horatio Clagett, Esquire, all the furniture, pictures, plate, linen, china, wine, horses, carriages, stock and stores of what description soever which may be in or about my Residence in the New Road called 'Harley House' at the time of my decease to and for her own sole and separate use and benefit independently of the debts, control and arrangements of her husband and for which her receipt alone shall be a sufficient discharge and it is my will that she, my said daughter, be allowed the free use and occupation of my said house and premises in the New Road for and during the term of her natural life without paying any rent for the same, she keeping the premises in good order and repair and paying all ground rents, tithes, taxes, rates and all other outgoings whatsoever during the time she continues to use and occupy the same.

In the knowledge that Caroline and her husband did not enjoy Edgware and liked the idea of being London socialites, Charles had made a similar arrangement for Caroline and Harley House as he had for Rebecca and Edgware, but emphasising again his distrust for Horatio by making the arrangement entirely independent of him. Harley House would remain in the ownership of Charles's estate whilst Caroline could enjoy a liferent in the property for as long as she liked.

But Charles did not allow for one important thing – the loneliness, introversion and deafness of his wife. Apart from her staff, she would be alone in Edgware. Her daughter would be in London and reluctant to visit, her sister Elizabeth would be supporting her husband John Weston in running the business and living on the premises and she, Rebecca, had become estranged from her other sister Susannah, who was busy looking after her late husband's bastard children.

Nevertheless, with the uncertainty of the continuing Will dispute, Rebecca decided to remain in the solitude of Edgware. John Simpson persuaded her to make her own Will in 1839, leaving several precious items to members of the Simpson family to whom she was related, John's mother being her cousin. Caroline and Horatio clearly felt honour bound to visit her and indeed they were in Edgware when the 1841 census was taken. But after the probate was granted on Charles's Will, and the dust had settled following the public revelations of her late husband's second family, she tended to spend more time at Harley House as she became frailer. She died there on 29 November 1843 at the age of sixty-three, hers having been a comfortable but sad life.

Caroline and Horatio lived on at Harley House for a short while, but soon decided that they should comfortably downsize and let Harley House realise its rental potential. However, this decision was accelerated by a further problem involving Horatio and his debts. Following his bankruptcy in 1836, it had transpired that a further £7,911 of debts had not been in the schedules at the time and now required to be cleared. Horatio signed a petition for this on 27 November 1843, his mother-in-law dying two days later and the notice appearing in the newspapers two days after that, the same day as Rebecca's death notice. Soon afterwards, they moved out of Harley House and into the nearby fashionable but more modestly sized 1 Abbey Road, St John's Wood. They secured a lucrative let for Harley House for £800 per year with the Duke of Brunswick. Horatio's case was finally heard at the Insolvent Debtors' Court on 28 February 1845. With his wife receiving £3,000 per year from Charles Day's estate, and his late mother-in-law £2,000 per year until her death, between them they had given Horatio £2,500 per year with which he had paid interest and costs of between £1,600 and £2,000 per year at a punitive interest rate of sixty percent per annum. With the furniture, horses and carriages at Harley House being entirely in the name of his wife (as stated in the Will of her father), Horatio had no other assets. On Horatio's discharge that day, the newspapers reported:

> *'The Chief Commissioner said there was no case against the insolvent. In his opinion, persons who took sixty percent could not complain to induce the Court to give a remand, although he could not help saying that there had been a degree of carelessness on the part of the insolvent'.*

Clagett was in the Insolvent Debtors Court again in 1849, his debts being about £4,000. His creditors accused him of obtaining money under false pretences and general extravagance, which seemed to have a familiar ring to it. However, the combination of the creditors (who were not trade creditors) not arguing their case very effectively and Clagett having some good lawyers on his side, resulted in a discharge. As the newspaper report stated:

> *'The insolvent was ordered to be discharged, and the learned commissioner hoped he would not repeat his application. There was less excuse for him than persons in humble circumstances, who came to the court through misfortune.'*

Interestingly, and perhaps betraying his extravagant life, the initial notice calling the case had stated Clagett as being:

'*HORATIO CLAGETT, formerly of No 1 Abbey Road, St John's Wood, Middlesex, then of Camperdown Place, Great Yarmouth, Norfolk, afterwards of No 1 Abbey Road, aforesaid, during part of the time at Brussels, in the Kingdom of Belgium, and at Boulogne, and at Paris, both in the Kingdom of France, and late of No 2 Hampstead Square, Heath Street, Hampstead, Middlesex, Gentleman, not in any Trade or Profession, a prisoner in the Queen's prison, in the County of Surrey.*'

No more details of all these geographic wanderings are known, but they must have depleted an already negative purse.

But needless to say, this was not the last of it and the Insolvent Debtors Court was considering Horatio again in January 1851. It is worth quoting the revealing newspaper report in full:

IN THE MATTER OF HORATIO CLAGETT. –

This insolvent, who applied under the Protection Act, was opposed by Mr Lucas, with whom was Mr Sargood, on the part of Sir Wyndham Anstruther, Bart. Mr Cooke supported the application. There was only one debt in the schedule. Sir Wyndham Anstruther was inserted as a creditor for £654, arising out of an annuity transaction, entered into in 1833, when Sir Wyndham became surety for the insolvent, and, respecting a composition on the same, a statement was made on the schedule. It was the only debt he owed.
THE CHIEF COMMISSIONER: Pray, how often have you been in this court, sir?
INSOLVENT: Three times, unfortunately.
MR LUCAS: Three times, and your wife has an income of £3,800 a year.

The insolvent said that, on his first hearing, Mr Day, his father-in-law, was alive. He stated that his first appearance was in 1836, his second in 1846 and his third in 1849. He had filed another petition in this court, and also in the Court of Bankruptcy, but did not proceed on them. He was not now willing to make any arrangement to pay the debt to Sir Wyndham Anstruther. He had received from his wife £300 in the last six months, and had spent about £6 a week in visiting places of amusement. His wife was not in court. She had been summoned to attend, but was too unwell to appear. A discussion arose respecting a letter, which it was said Mrs Clagett had signed to pay the annuity, and Mr Lucas remarked that it should have been paid.

In answer to further questions, the insolvent said that he was living with his wife in Abbey Road, St John's Wood. Mrs Clagett kept four horses and three carriages; he kept none, but rode out in the carriages. Mr Simpson was her trustee. The income of Mrs Clagett, under her father's Will, was £3,000 a year, and she let a house to the Duke of Brunswick for £800 a year.

Mr Lucas asked why he, as a gentleman and a man of honour, did not pay the debt for which Sir Wyndham Anstruther was liable? The insolvent said that he had been excessively ill-treated in the matter. The Chief Commissioner asked the insolvent why he did not pay the debt. It was the only one on the schedule. The insolvent said he had no means of getting the money; and that, about the time of his marriage, Sir Wyndham got £40,000, and went to the continent. Mrs Clagett had lost her fortune through him, as Mr Day was annoyed and altered his Will, by which she would have had £25,000 a year, and cut her off with £3,000 a year.

MR LUCAS: This is what you call losing her fortune?

The insolvent said there was a great difference between £3,000 and £25,000 a year

MR LUCAS: I am afraid it would not have made any difference.

The insolvent said he had been ill-used and, therefore, was not willing to make any arrangement. When Mrs Day died, he was in prison, and the money was obliged to be paid. Mr Lucas said he should ask the court whether this was a case for protection. Was a man whose wife had £3,800 to come to this court and get protection because he would not pay one debt – was he, with £600 a year as pocket money, spending it in places of amusement, a fit person to be protected? It would be a gross libel on the act of Parliament to give a man, with nearly £4,000 a year indulging in every luxury, his protection, when the court was in the habit of making a poor clerk or half-paid officer pay £20 or £30 a year out of their income. It would be monstrous to pass such a case as the present. Mr Cooke rose to reply. The Chief Commissioner told the learned counsel he need not trouble himself. If this case had exhibited the class of debts contained in the schedules referred to, then there would have been some analogy in the cases, but it did not. There was no Tradesman, and only one debt, on an annuity transaction. There was no evidence given before him, no witness called, and he could not, in the absence of evidence, act on the strong observations of the learned counsel. His Honour told the insolvent he ought not to have appeared in this court after his former appearances, and advised him not to come again. The Commissioner named the 29th instant for the final order.'

By this time, Horatio was aged fifty-three and Caroline forty-three. It was clear that they were to have no children and consequently, the many pages of Charles Day's Will devoted to such an occurrence were rendered redundant. For the next twenty-five years or so, they seemed to have lived out their lives in St John's Wood in relative peace and quiet, and certainly not attracting any further adverse publicity. They retained a housemaid, a cook, a butler and a groom and probably enjoyed life, living on the edge of Regent's Park and its Zoological Gardens.

They lacked nothing and her annuity of £3,000 per year from her father's estate was easily covered by the continuing profitability of Day and Martin. John Weston had died in 1853 and the business was now being run by his grandson James Weston Clayton with great success.

However, in 1876, Caroline's health began to fail and there was a danger that she might predecease her husband, despite the fact that he was ten years her senior. He was frail in mind and body but ailing at a slower rate than his wife. She felt it wise to make a Will and this transpired to be a very detailed document. She would no doubt have received advice on the law of the time concerning Wills of married women and the entitlement of their husbands. To put it simply, if a wife did not leave everything to her husband who was still alive, the husband had to give his consent. Caroline would have also been aware that her considerable wealth had arisen from her father's activities and not from anything achieved by her husband. It was also on her conscience that her father never hid his disapproval of Clagett and certainly wished none of his wealth to accrue to him or his family. It was therefore her intention to ensure that he was well endowed in terms of income for the rest of his days, but that the residue of her wealth should revert to the Day family.

At first, she suggested that he should continue to receive the annuity of £3,000 which she had enjoyed for the forty years since her father's death. He wanted more and she was happy to increase this to £5,000 per year. Otherwise, she was clearly under the impression that he had given his consent to the terms of the rest of the Will, the critical point being that the residue of her wealth after covering all stipulated legacies should go to her two cousins, Charles Day Lockwood and Walter Joseph Lockwood equally, following the subsequent death of her husband. Her executors were to be her husband Horatio Clagett, James Weston Clayton and another cousin Henry Francis Lockwood, who was by then a successful and wealthy architect. The Will was executed on 27 November 1876. Caroline Clagett died on 30 March 1877 at 1 Abbey Road, St John's Wood, having apparently put her affairs in order.

Not so. The Clagett family had a reputation to uphold and were not going to take things lying down. Enter Major Thomas William Clagett, Horatio's nephew, who was married to Mary-Eliza, Dowager Countess of Harborough, and residing at her substantial country residence of Stapleford Park, near Melton Mowbray in Leicestershire.

The funeral took place on 6 April 1877. Caroline had left instructions that that she wished to be laid to rest in the family vault in Edgware, and that the only people attending her funeral would be Henry Lockwood, James Weston Clayton and Major Clagett, in place of her frail husband.

But only four days later, Thomas Clagett was issuing a petition to the court that his uncle should be examined under the suspicion that he was a supposed lunatic. The court duly granted the petition on 20 April 1877. The examination took place on 30 April 1877 and the next day, Horatio Clagett was certified as being of 'unsound mind'. Things can move fast when they have to. The tactic was to prove that Horatio was already of unsound mind when Caroline had executed her Will and was therefore not capable of giving his consent. This would nullify at least the assignation of her residue wealth to her two cousins, which would revert to her husband Horatio and his family.

The battle lines were drawn and yet again, the extraordinary aftermath of Charles Day's life would be hitting the courts. With the certification of Horatio, his affairs had to be administered by so-called 'committees' (responsible individuals) and Major

Clagett and his brother-in-law Horatio Kemble were appointed.

Caroline's Will, partially null and void or otherwise, was an interesting document. The first statement, not uncommon for the times, reveals the Victorian preoccupation of being buried alive:

> *I desire my body to be kept above ground until decomposition shall have set in or until such an operation shall be performed as will satisfy a competent medical man that life is actually extinct.*

The next most important instruction was concerning her beloved animals:

> *I direct that my favourite dogs and cats shall be destroyed and their bodies buried in the garden of the house in which I now reside, and as to my favourite horses, I desire that they may be shot at the Zoological Gardens, Regents Park.*

Again, this represented a very Victorian desire for animals to accompany their owners into the afterlife.

In addition to the annuity of £5,000 to Horatio, there followed numerous bequests of mainly paintings together with specific legacies totalling £71,850. The firm of Day and Martin was to be sold to James Weston Clayton, if he wanted it, and the substantial residue, in the order of £120,000, would go to the two cousins. Or would it?

Matters proceeded routinely and on 2 August 1877, special administration of Caroline's estate was granted to James Weston Clayton and Henry Lockwood. Major Clagett and Horatio Kemble gave their consent in writing, although they later maintained that they did not, as they had only been nominated as committees at that stage and not formally appointed.

The dispute escalated with Clagett and Kemble maintaining categorically that Horatio Clagett had been incapable through imbecility of giving his consent to the Will. This was despite the fact that the Will had been executed on 27 November 1876 and he was not certified as being of unsound mind until 30 April 1877. They also maintained that, even if Clagett had been capable of giving his consent at the time, he did not actually know or understand the contents of the Will or their consequences. They said too, even if Horatio was of sound mind in November 1876, between that date and the death of his wife on 30 March 1877, he had become imbecile and incapable of continuing his consent or of revoking a Will. This seemed to betray an uncertainty by Clagett and Kemble as to whether Horatio actually was of unsound mind when Caroline executed her Will, and an assumption that once consent had been given, it could subsequently be revoked.

Thinking that the Day family had a fairly strong case, on 17 May 1878 matters were brought to a head by James Weston Clayton issuing a summons against Thomas William Clagett and Horatio Kemble as committees for the estate of Horatio Clagett. Clayton did this in his sole name because Henry Francis Lockwood was by then seriously ill and in fact died in Richmond, Surrey, on 21 July 1878.

Clagett and Kemble maintained that the amount that was being denied the estate of Horatio Clagett (still alive but a certified imbecile) was £120,000. They asked for the consent of probate given in August 1877 to be revoked, but as a concession were prepared to accept that probate may be granted to James Weston Clayton 'limited to such property as the deceased had at the time of her death for her separate use' which by her Will she had bequeathed or disposed of accordingly.

So, the real question in the case was whether or not Horatio had been imbecile six months before he was actually certified and thus incapable of giving a valid assent to the terms of his wife's Will, dealing with property to the value of £120,000.

Clayton gave evidence to the court that, when Horatio Clagett was told that his wife intended to make a Will, he made no objection and seemed to take little interest in the names of the legatees. He had appeared satisfied when told that his wife (on his request) had increased his annuity from £3,000 to £5,000. In Clayton's opinion, Horatio went out of his mind in March 1877 when told of his wife's death. However, he did admit to noticing a decline in Horatio's mental condition since 1875.

In support of Clagett and Gamble, a doctor gave evidence that, although Horatio's decline was gradual, he was certain that by late 1876 he was incapable of undertaking any matters of business.

The Clagetts' solicitor told the court that he and his clients had only become aware in August 1878 that Caroline Clagett's estate had increased by some £100,000 following the death of a Mr Parsons. This probably referred to Thomas Parsons, a first cousin of Charles Day through his mother, who had in fact died on 4 December 1876, ie a week after Caroline had executed her Will, a fact that does not seem to have been stated to the court.

The complicated terms of Charles Day's Will stated that any residue of his estate should be divided between the survivors of the thirty-eight stated annuitants. By the mid-1870s, only four of these annuitants were still alive – Caroline Clagett (£3,000), Sarah Peake (£100), Mary Ann Skegg (£50) and Thomas Parsons (£40). Settlements had been reached with Sarah Peake and Mary Ann Skegg for them to accept lump sums in exchange for all future payments, but no such settlement had been agreed with

Thomas Parsons before his death. Consequently, in theory when Caroline Clagett executed her Will, she was having to share the residue equally with Thomas Parsons. If this residue was in the region of £200,000, Caroline's share would increase by £100,000 on Parsons's death, which just happened to occur a week later. It is worth noting that Thomas Parsons was eighty-four when he died, the father of six children and that one of his executors was none other than James Weston Clayton. His probate record states that he died with 'effects under £6,000'. The irony of all this is that Thomas Parsons was in fact a man of very humble background, working as a gardener with virtually no means of his own. He was portrayed to the court as a wealthy relative who had died, leaving Caroline £100,000, which was certainly not the case. Clayton's counsel pointed out that when Caroline made her Will, Horatio would have had his annuity of £5,000 (a very substantial figure for the time) but nothing else. This was her intention, knowing the wishes of her father. She intended her residue to go to her two cousins. In fact, the intention of Charles Day's Will would seem to have been that, if Parsons had outlived Caroline, he would have been entitled to the entire residue of £200,000. One wonders whether this was properly explained to Sarah Peake and Mary Ann Skegg when their settlements were negotiated. It also suggests that Charles Day would never have predicted that the figures could have been so great. It seems that the court were not properly informed about the position of 'Mr Parsons' and neither side correctly understood it.

Clayton's counsel's final point was that, although Horatio's memory was very defective by November 1876, it had not been proved that his mind had become enfeebled before his wife's death. Strangely, these arguments seem to have a similar ring to those that were being put forward at the time of Charles Day's death forty years earlier, in relation to whether or not he could have made a rational decision to appoint Frederick Dufaur as an extra executor.

The case dragged on for months but the judge made a final decision on 15 May 1879. The case was fully reported in *The Times* and the judgement stated as follows:

> *His Lordship, in summing up, said the question of Mr Clagett's assent to the making of the Will by his wife involved the further one as to his power of appreciating the nature and meaning of such an act. The evidence showed that before Mrs Clagett's death, he had been in an exceeding feeble condition of mind. Merely because he sought to have his annuity under the Will raised from £3,000 to £5,000, it could not be said that he thoroughly understood the nature of the whole transaction to which it was contended by the plaintiff that he had consented. It did not appear that any attempt had been made to explain its real nature to him, nor did it seem that he had ever contemplated what the effect would have been if he had withheld his consent. He did not, in His Lordship's opinion, give that assent to her execution of the Will which could be considered valid, and therefore the letters of administration granted to the plaintiff must be revoked. No one could have been held to have been in blame for the litigation and therefore all costs would come out of the separate estate of the testatrix.*

James Weston Clayton and the Lockwood cousins were quite entitled to feel aggrieved by this judgement. But the truth is that the self-imposed complexities of Charles Day's Will seem to have left everyone confused and ill-informed, which is hardly surprising considering that the ramifications had ground on in the courts for nearly forty-three years following the events of 1836 and the death of Charles Day. However, the greatest injustice was that his residual wealth, after the payments of legacies and annuities to all his beneficiaries, ended up with the very last person that he intended, that is to say Horatio Clagett, the son-in-law of whom he strongly disapproved.

Horatio Clagett died on 31 January 1880. His Will left everything to his wife – it had not been revised since her death. Consequently, by the rules of intestacy at the time, his estate became divisible amongst his next of kin including, no doubt, Major Thomas William Clagett.

Had justice been seen to be done?

7. The Dickens connection

In December 1839, the occupants of Harley House, that is Caroline and Horatio Clagett together with Caroline's mother, the widowed Mrs Rebecca Day, who stayed with them for much of the time in her silent loneliness, found themselves with new neighbours. Just across the New Road, later Marylebone Road, to the west was the elegant, bow-windowed house of 1 Devonshire Terrace. They were interested to hear that a twelve-year lease had been taken out on it by the exciting new star in the British literary firmament, Charles Dickens. He was the author of *The Pickwick Papers*, which had been the publishing sensation of the time, being brought out in instalments which gathered in popularity as they progressed. This was followed by *Oliver Twist* and *Nicholas Nickleby*, and the public awaited the next book with eager anticipation. He had married Catherine Hogarth in 1836 and they had had a child in each of the following years, Charley in 1837, Mary in 1838 and Kate in 1839. They had been living at 48 Doughty Street for two years, but with the rapidly expanding family and Dickens's new found fame and prosperity (he was still only twenty-seven), a larger and more respectable house needed to be found. What better than this elegant residence on the edge of Regent's Park?

The childless Clagetts were no doubt pleased to hear of a young family moving to the neighbourhood. But more importantly, they would have been excited by the social status of their new resident and the interest that it would engender amongst their circle of friends. After all, Dickens and Clagett shared thespian interests, both becoming members of the Garrick Club soon after its foundation in 1831.

What perhaps the Clagetts didn't know was that Dickens was an inveterate magpie, picking up characters and snippets of stories as they happened around him, and weaving them into his novels in various veiled ways. Sometimes this was very close to home, examples being the characters of Mr Micawber and Mrs Nickleby, mother of Nicholas, based on each of Dickens's parents. The occupants of Harley House would have attracted his interest for a variety of reasons. Dickens would inevitably and quickly discover that Caroline Clagett was the daughter of the late Charles Day, the boot-blacking magnate of Day and Martin whose chief competitor had been Warren. Dickens had worked at Warren's as a twelve-year-old boy, sticking labels on blacking bottles for long shifts in rat-infested conditions, to earn some money for the family whilst his father was in the Marshalsea debtors' prison. The experience had left an indelible impression on him which influenced much of his future thinking on the social conditions of Victorian London and child labour in particular.

Indeed, in *The Pickwick Papers*, as he introduces the memorable Sam Weller of The White Hart Inn, he describes the shine on some boots receiving Sam's attention as 'a polish which would have struck envy to the soul of the amiable Mr Warren (for they used Day and Martin at the White Hart)'. Dickens's use of the word 'amiable' can only have been loaded with sarcasm. And in *Oliver Twist*, as Toby Crackit sits down with Fagin, he points disconsolately to his top-boots and says, 'Not a drop of Day and Martin since you know when – not a bubble of blacking, by Jove!'.

The reference from *The Pickwick Papers* had given Charles Day great cheer just before his death. In addition to this and *Oliver Twist*,

Dickens made numerous other refences to the blacking industry in his works. The fact that he now lived opposite Day's daughter and son-in-law who had a reputation for colourful living would have fired his interest in them and their family story even more.

As a teenager, Dickens had worked as a lowly clerk in a law office and had developed his own strong views on the contemporary state of the law and legal practice. As a freelance law reporter, he had subsequently witnessed the sloth-like progress of cases through the system and the injustices dealt out to both plaintiffs and defendants as a result. And he knew the worst place of all was the Court of Chancery. This had made him an enthusiastic follower of cases in the press, even after he had ceased as a reporter and had become a successful writer. The case of the dispute over Charles Day's Will had been widely reported in the press from the time of Day's death in October 1836 to the pronouncement of the judgement in June 1838 and the subsequent appeal to the Privy Council by Frederick Dufaur. This would have been meat and drink to Dickens, who now found himself living opposite some of the central protagonists in the case. Many of the facts of the case had been revealed in press reports, including the existence of Day's illegitimate family. Dickens's nose would have been twitching and the Clagetts would have been blissfully unaware, but enjoying the social cachet of living opposite the famous author.

The 1840s were a prolific time for Dickens both professionally (five more novels and other writings) and personally (six more children). He also travelled extensively, often taking the family with him and sub-letting the house to others for varying periods. But it remained his home base. Even though the Clagetts moved out of Harley House in early 1844 following Rebecca's death, Dickens would not have lost interest in the Day case as it sank ever more deeply into the mire of the Court of Chancery, and giving him added justification to have a satirical swipe at that institution at some future date. He would have soaked up all the facts of the case.

The lease on 1 Devonshire Terrace was due to expire in December 1851 and alternative accommodation of a suitable nature had to be found. Tavistock House in nearby Tavistock Square fitted the bill well and the Dickens family moved there in October 1851. Almost immediately, Dickens began work on his new novel *Bleak House* which would appear in twenty instalments between March 1852 and September 1853, the last month having a double instalment. This was the great satire on the legal profession that he had been wanting to write for years and now was the time, with his reputation at its height, to release this stinging indictment of everything that went on in the contemporary practice and administration of the law. And the Day case was to give him plenty of ammunition.

However, after having written the first two numbers of *Bleak House* (the first being published on 1 March 1852), something fell into Dickens's lap which gave him further justification for his attack on the Court of Chancery. Dickens's first biographer, John Forster, later stated:

Dickens was encouraged and strengthened in his design of assailing Chancery abuses and delays by receiving, a few days after the appearance of his first number, a striking pamphlet on the subject containing details so apposite that he took from them, without change in any material point, the memorable case related in his fifteenth chapter.

In *Bleak House*, this became the case of Gridley, 'the man from Shropshire'.

The pamphlet in question was *The Court of Chancery: Its Inherent Defects, as exhibited in Its System of Procedure and of Fees; with Suggestions for a Remedy* by William Challinor, a solicitor from Leek in Staffordshire, who had taken up a Chancery case involving the Cook family of Lane End Farm, Onecote, Leek. Thomas Cook left his farm to his wife for life and, after her decease, to his eldest son subject to a legacy of £300 to his second son, Joseph. She died in 1836 and in 1844 Joseph began a Chancery suit to obtain his money, the older brother having claimed that part of the sum had already been paid to Joseph in the form of maintenance.

Continuing Forster's account:

> *The suit, of which all particulars are given, affected a single farm, in value not more than £1,200, but all that its owner possessed in the world, against which a bill had been filed for a £300 legacy left in the Will bequeathing the farm. In reality there was only one defendant, but in the bill, by the rule of the Court, there were seventeen; and, after two years had been occupied over the seventeen answers, everything had to begin over again because an eighteenth had been accidentally omitted.*

In his pamphlet, Challinor states:

> *Now, what a mockery of justice this is - the facts speak for themselves, and I can personally vouch for their accuracy. The costs already incurred in reference to this £300 legacy are not less than from £800 to £900, and the parties are no forwarder. Already near five years have passed by, and the Plaintiff would be glad to give up his chance of the Legacy if he could escape from his liability to costs - while the Defendants who own the little farm left by the testator, have scarce any other prospect before them than ruin.*

16. On 13 March 1852, Charles Dickens thanks Challinor for lending him his pamphlet 'The Court of Chancery; Its Inherent Defects' (1849).

Dickens heard about this pamphlet and requested a copy from Challinor. When he returned it, he added a note in his own handwriting:

Mr Charles Dickens presents his compliments to Mr Challinor, and begs with many thanks to acknowledge the receipt of his pamphlet and obliging notes.

Tavistock House, Tavistock Square, London.
Eleventh March 1852.

Whether it was as a result of Dickens's curiosity aroused by the Challinor pamphlet, or mere coincidence, but the very next month, he found himself making a visit to Staffordshire, visiting the pottery factory of Mr Alderman Copeland and spending a night in the town of Stafford itself. The experience motivated him to write an extended piece for his weekly publication *Household Words* entitled 'A Plated Article' – an extraordinary account of over 4,000 words, describing in damning terms the hotel in which he was staying (the main, and former, coaching hotel of the town, 'The Swan', which he cruelly renamed 'The Dodo') and the town itself and, in a slightly more complimentary way, the processes he had witnessed in the pottery factory. In a typical *tour de force* of descriptive language, the result could be described anywhere between brilliant, biting satire and downright, overblown verbosity. The visit took place on 2 and 3 April 1852, by which time the writing of *Bleak House* was well under way. In fact, soon afterwards he would have been writing the fifth instalment (published at the beginning of July) which describes in detail the case of Gridley.

And in the Preface to *Bleak House*, he states subsequently in August 1853:

The case of Gridley is in no essential altered from one of actual occurrence, made public by a disinterested person who was professionally acquainted with the whole of the monstrous wrong from beginning to end.

Indeed, the facts of his case stated by Gridley in Chapter XV of the novel are exactly the same as those of the Cook case, described by Challinor in his pamphlet, the actual Chancery suit being later revealed as Cook v Fynney (1844 C59).

But something else might have contributed to this interest in Stafford and its county at the time. Dickens goes on to say in the Preface to *Bleak House*:

At the present moment there is a suit before the Court which was commenced nearly twenty years ago; in which from thirty to forty counsel have been known to appear at one time; in which costs have been incurred to the amount of seventy thousand pounds; which is a friendly suit, and which is (I am assured) no nearer its termination now than when it was begun...

Dickens wrote the Preface in August 1853 after completing the book. The letters that Dickens was writing at the time are revealing. On 7 August 1853, he wrote to his assistant editor of *Household Words*, William Wills, from Boulogne where he was staying at the time. He says he was very busy finishing *Bleak House* and in a post script to the letter, he asks Wills:

Will you at once make an enquiry into the Day Chancery Cause, As –
When was it instituted?
How much nearer is it now to its completion?
What has been spent in costs?
How many Counsel appear – about – whenever the Court is moved?

You did ask this for me before, but I made no note of it. I should like to glance at it in the Preface. Of course, I will in no degree whatever, commit your informant; nor shall I ever mention the cause by name. But I wish to be within the facts.

Wills's answers to these questions are written beside them in pencil as follows:

'About 1834 as near as I know.' [in fact, 1838]
'As far off as ever.'
'At least £70,000.'
'Formerly always 17 sometimes 30 or 40 it used to be said the whole bar – the number has been much reduced.'

So, there appears to be little doubt that Dickens was referring to the case of Charles Day's Will in the Preface to *Bleak House* and using it as a major justification for creating the case of 'Jarndyce and Jarndyce'. This forms the backdrop to the novel, although the specific details of the case are never really revealed. The point is that it is complicated and just goes on swallowing up more and more costs over an inordinate length of time. This differs from the case of Gridley and its real counterpart of Cook, where the facts of the case are relatively simple and can be lifted intact straight into the novel. 'Jarndyce and Jarndyce' is not based on 'Croft v. Day' but the latter is used to justify the former, in demonstrating the archaic and constipated practices of the Court of Chancery.

From the letter to Wills, there seems little doubt that Dickens had been following the Day case for some time, especially as it was directly bound up with his former neighbours at Harley House. In studying the case, he would have known that Day's widow's maiden name was Peake and that she came from Stafford. This could have been another factor in his mind when he made the visit to Stafford in April 1852, in the early days of writing *Bleak House*. He had to satisfy his curiosity and perhaps a visit to the town could reveal some more facts. Could it even be that Dickens might collect some ideas from the lives of Day and the Peake family that he could implant into the plot and various sub-plots of his new book? There is an absence of any firm evidence that this might be the case, but there is no harm in looking at some parallels between Dickens's story and some of the facts surrounding the lives of Charles Day and the Peakes.

There is clearly a common strand of illegitimacy in the two stories, and all the stigma attached to it, especially within the social conventions of the time. In Dickens's novel, Esther Summerson is the illegitimate daughter of Lady Dedlock and Captain Hawdon (Nemo), a fact that is stealthily hidden by those few privy to it because of the shame that would be suffered by Esther and Lady Dedlock and anyone connected to them. Charles Day went out of his way to conceal his three illegitimate sons, inventing a surname for them and only revealing their existence unintentionally in his dying days. His wife never knew, just as Sir Leicester Dedlock never knew. The three natural sons of Charles Day (Henry, Alfred and Edmund Price) were all told about their parental background but all the evidence suggests that they kept it strictly to themselves, in the hope that it would be forgotten after any initial stir in the press. Two of the boys married, both below their social status, to two girls much younger than themselves who were probably in their service. If the wives were told at all, they would have been sworn to absolute secrecy. Between them they had eighteen children but, with only four of them marrying, it seems that they were brought up in a fairly enclosed environment. Certainly, none of them or subsequent generations knew of the illegitimacy until it was revealed recently. In *Bleak House*, those who knew of the circumstances of Esther's birth are largely killed off, except for John Jarndyce and Inspector Bucket who are happy to preserve the secret. Esther marries Allan Woodcourt and her background rightly becomes an irrelevance.

In Chapter VIII of Dickens' novel, we are introduced by the scary do-gooder, Mrs Pardiggle, to the brickmaker and his family whom she is trying to convert. The husband is cruel to his wife Jenny and they live in abject poverty. But Jenny has a heart of gold and takes in not only the street boy Jo, but eventually the desperate Lady Dedlock with whom she changes clothes to provide cover. Dickens had just visited Stafford and Stoke when he was writing this part of the book. Although he describes a visit to Copeland's pottery, he would have seen the many brick-making yards in that part of the country, together with the grime and poverty in which the workers lived. Indeed, he describes Stafford and its people in the dreariest possible terms in 'A Plated Article'. In knowing the Clagetts, might he have discovered that Mrs Rebecca Day was the granddaughter of William Peake, a Stafford bricklayer and publican, who passed on his trade to his sons? Certainly, they were bricklayers rather than brickmakers, but were all from the same industrial environment. Indeed, the brick could be seen as a symbol of Charles Day himself – a transformation from a rural origin of clay to the modern prosperity of a construction material.

In *Bleak House*, there is a triangle of characters central to the plot – Esther Summerson, Ada Clare and Richard Carstone. Ada and Richard (distant cousins) are both wards of John Jarndyce and, when they come to live with him at Bleak House, he invites Esther (their contemporary) to join them, nominally as a housekeeper. The three develop a close bond. Ada becomes besotted with Richard and they eventually marry. Esther is the sensible member of the trio and tries to influence both Ada and Richard with prudent advice. Richard becomes obsessed with 'Jarndyce and Jarndyce', an obsession that eventually costs him his life.

The parallels with the triangle of Susannah Peake, Sarah Peake and Charles Day are interesting. Charles is keen to have more children, but not with his wife with whom he has nothing in common. Susannah is respected by the other two and arranges the liaison between Sarah and Charles. But Susannah is the central character, without whose support Charles could not have coped and who managed Charles' second household. Charles became obsessed with his impending death and his Will arrangements, and his death is probably accelerated by these worries.

As an aside, there is a further parallel here with Dickens himself and the triangle of Dickens, his sister-in-law Georgina Howarth and the actress Ellen Ternan. Dickens had married Catherine Hogarth in 1836, but despite producing ten children (an aspect not shared with Charles Day), the marriage was never particularly happy. Almost immediately after the wedding, Catherine's younger sister Mary, with whom Dickens was besotted, moved in with them. Just eight months later, Mary died suddenly. Dickens became distraught, causing him to miss his publishing dates for *The Pickwick Papers* and *Oliver Twist*, something that was never repeated in his subsequent career. Dickens wore Mary's ring for the rest of his life and named his first daughter after her. But even more significantly, when Dickens' marriage finally broke down, another sister-in-law Georgina (who had been part of his household since 1842) decided to continue to live with him as his housekeeper, adviser and close confidante. All of Dickens' children remained with him and Georgina, except for the oldest son Charles Jnr who alone moved out with his mother. Rumours abounded about an even closer relationship between Charles and Georgina but these were very publicly denied. Such a liaison between husband and sister-in-law at the time would have been classified as incest. Nevertheless, Georgina continued to live with Dickens until his death in 1870 and spent the rest of her life until her demise in 1917 promoting his reputation. She certainly knew about his affair with Ellen Ternan and perhaps actively encouraged it. Both Georgina and Ellen were at Dickens' bedside when he died. The similarity with the relationships between Charles Day, his sister-in-law Susannah Peake and the mother of his three illegitimate sons Sarah Peake can be nothing but coincidence, but a strange one at that.

Back in *Bleak House*, Esther Summerson is struck down by smallpox and, although she recovers, she is permanently disfigured with facial scars. Nevertheless, those close to her (Jarndyce, Woodcourt and others) still love her for the person she is. Charles Day contracted syphilis which afflicted him for the last twenty years of his life through blindness, paralysis and epileptic fits. But, like Esther, his faithful family, friends, advisers and servants did not let this affect their relationship with or respect for him. He continued to run his business with great success until just before his death.

There are many fairly unpleasant characters in *Bleak House* who are engaged in the legal profession, but perhaps the most odious is Mr Vholes ('a sallow man with pinched lips that looked as if they were cold' – Chapter XXXVII), who tricks Carstone into thinking that he will be able to triumph on his behalf in 'Jarndyce and Jarndyce'. Of course, this never happens but Vholes gets his fees and Carstone gets nothing. The resemblance to Frederick Dufaur, the solicitor who tricks Day into appointing him as an extra executor with a legacy and indefinite commission on rents, and who eventually blackmails the family on pain of revealing the illegitimate children, is uncanny. And was it a coincidence that Dickens resided at Furnival's Inn just a short time after Dufaur had lived there, perhaps leaving a reputation behind him? Esther's final comment on Vholes is as chilling as the attitude of Day and his followers towards Dufaur:

So slow, so eager, so bloodless and gaunt, I felt as if Richard was wasting away beneath the eyes of this adviser, and there were something of the Vampire in him. – Chapter LX

Although Dickens never precisely identifies the exact location of Bleak House, it is clearly to the north of London. When the street boy Jo heads there in a sickly state (he being the carrier of smallpox), he says: '...she came from Stolbuns, and so I took the Stolbuns Road' – Chapter XXXI. This can only be the St Albans Road which is the old Roman road of Watling Street heading straight north out of London, the same road as taken by the Day family when they were heading out of London to Edgware. This was the medieval pilgrim route to St Albans from London and Edgware was the half-way staging post, the pilgrims praying in the Church of St Margaret of Antioch from the fourteenth century onwards. There is no doubt that, either by accident or design, the fictional Bleak House and the actual Edgware Place are in the same northerly direction out of London, on the same road.

Late one evening at Bleak House, Jarndyce tells Esther that he once received a letter describing a young orphan girl whom the writer had been raising. The writer feared that if she died, the child would be alone, and so she wrote to Mr. Jarndyce enquiring if he would serve as guardian in such circumstances. He replied saying he would. He had to agree never to see the writer but to send a confidential agent, so Mr. Jarndyce appointed Mr. Kenge, a lawyer. The writer said she was the child's aunt, but not revealing that she was in fact the sister of Lady Dedlock. In Chapter XVII, Jarndyce confirms to Esther that she was that child. Similarly, the Price boys had been raised under the superintendence of Susannah Peake, not their actual aunt, but the cousin of their mother. Their father, Charles Day, left clear instructions as to what should happen to them on his demise and he allowed for them generously in a codicil to his Will.

There are two references in *Bleak House* which seem to be too much of a coincidence in relation to the Charles Day story. When approaching Bleak House for the first time, Esther describes it in her narrative as 'an old-fashioned house, with three peaks in the roof in front' – Chapter VI. Later, Esther quotes John Jarndyce, when talking about his great-uncle Tom Jarndyce, 'I was his heir, and this was his house, Esther. When I came here, it was bleak, indeed. He had left the signs of his misery upon it. It had been called, before his time, the Peaks…' – Chapter VIII. In Day's life story, the Peakes were the Stafford family into which he married and by whom he had his children, both legitimate and illegitimate.

The other reference in *Bleak House*, and perhaps the most telling, appears during the visit by George Rouncewell to Grandfather Smallweed. George is the son of Sir Leicester Dedlock's housekeeper and, in his retirement from his army trooper career, has set up a shooting gallery. This he did by means of a loan from Smallweed's 'friend in the city', who employs Smallweed to collect the interest from George. Smallweed constantly reminds

George that his money-lender friend stands no nonsense. 'So, you think he might be hard upon me, eh?' asks George. 'I think he might – I am afraid he would. I have known him do it' says Grandfather Smallweed, incautiously, 'twenty times'. Thereafter, George 'falls to smoking in long puffs', consoling himself with the philosophical reflection, 'The name of your friend in the city begins with a D, comrade, and you're about right respecting the bond' – Chapter XXI. Could this be a reference to Charles Day? Charles' business was in the city and, as his wealth accumulated, he fulfilled the role of a private bank conducting transactions in the same way as a more formal financial institution. He certainly lent money to private individuals, and all these transactions were controlled and recorded by Pinder Simpson and his son John.

It is generally agreed that Dickens envisaged the events described in *Bleak House* to have taken place in the 1830s. In the second paragraph of Chapter LV, the advent of the railways is described. This was at its height in the 1830s. This also fits exactly with the last years of the life of Charles Day, who died on 26 October 1836.

Bleak House is recognized as one of Dickens's greatest novels. At the height of its publication period, it was selling 35,000 copies per monthly instalment. It appealed and was available to all classes. The wheels were already in motion for legal reform, a cause that could only have benefitted from the publication of *Bleak House* and that finally came to fruition in 1875. *Bleak House* allowed that cause to be known to the masses as a worthy one. Decades later, a leading counsel, Sir George Hurst QC, said the novel 'was sufficiently biting to stir even the complacency of vested interests'. If the events and injustices following the death of Charles Day are in any way part of that influence, a crumb of comfort will have been gained by all those who suffered the consequences. Charles Dickens, who died in 1870, would have been greatly satisfied.

The Supreme Court of Justice Act was passed 1875 and the Court of Chancery ceased to exist. The Chancery Division remains to this day part of the High Court of Justice of England and Wales.

V. Epilogue

The Unmasking of John (or Charles) Price

In researching the events recounted in this story, I feel I ought to confess how the actual facts of Charles Day fell into my lap by a fluke discovery in 2015.

My father, Hugh Price, and I had always puzzled over the identity of his great-grandfather. I remember sitting on his knee aged about eight and him telling me all he knew about the Prices but grinding to a halt when it got to his great-grandfather. All he knew was that he was supposedly called John Price. Word had been passed down that he was a merchant in London and that he died in the 'year of repeal of Reform Bill – riots during funeral'.

My father died in 1986 and had spent much fruitless time researching the problem. The task was laborious and rather depressing, being before the instant access era of computers that we now enjoy. However, he did establish that his grandfather Alfred Price was the middle of three brothers, the older being Henry and the younger Edmund. My father had a few watercolours painted by Alfred and I have collected more as elderly relatives have died off. There are also two portraits of the adult Henry and silhouettes of Alfred and Edmund as young boys. In addition, there are photographs of Henry and Alfred going back to the very early days of photography in the 1850s. He also established that Henry had married a Roman Catholic and had seven children, living around Fulham, and that Edmund had remained a bachelor and had died quite young. He knew Alfred was born in 1824 and was amazed that his grandfather had been born only nine years after the Battle of Waterloo. He also knew that Henry's seven children had produced no descendants and that my brother and I and our second cousin were all that remained in our generation from Alfred's 11 children. With the other two both childless, my three children are all that remain of the descendants of John Price, and this made me all the more determined to discover who he was.

17. The headstone of the Price grave in the Dean Cemetery, Edinburgh, the first named being 'Sarah Price, born 26 June 1795, died 7 December 1877'.

In 1975, my father took me to the Price family grave in the Dean Cemetery in Edinburgh, a large public cemetery where the wealthy Victorian middle class of Edinburgh repose (monuments of wailing widows and veiled urns). There are five in the grave, headed by Alfred's mother Sarah Price with her precise dates (26 June 1795 – 7 December 1877). At the same time, I traced Sarah's Scottish death certificate, which stated that she was the widow of John Price (fundholder), that her maiden name was Peake, that her father was an architect and that the informant was her son Alfred.

18. The 1877 Scottish death certificate of Sarah Price, stating she was the 'Widow of John Price, Fundholder' and that her father was ' – Peake, Architect' ('bricklayer' having morphed to 'architect'). Informant: 'Alfred Price, son'.

In the last fifteen years or so, I had become confident of solving the problem now that the internet provides comprehensive genealogy websites. One point became clear early on with initial searches on census returns and that was that Henry, Alfred and Edmund all lived in very respectable houses and appeared to be comfortably well-off to the extent that they didn't need to work. Their profession was usually described as 'Fundholder'. From where had this money come?

The censuses revealed that Alfred was born in Marylebone, London, whilst Henry's birthplace was mysteriously always quoted as Brighton. Indeed the 1851 census revealed Henry on holiday at the Clarence Hotel in Brighton with his mother, under her maiden name of Sarah Peake, whose place of birth was stated as Stafford. In the 1841 census, I found the mother and three boys living in Osnaburgh Street, St Pancras, with a certain Susan Price whom I could only assume was the late John's sister, John having disappeared off the scene presumably around 1831.

With official registering of births only starting in 1837, I then started looking through baptismal records, and found Alfred being baptised at St Marylebone Church on 11 January 1825, the son of John and Sarah Price of 29 Earl Street, John's occupation being described as 'Gentleman'. I also found Edmund's baptism recorded on 15 June 1827 at St Mary's Church, Bryanston Square, Marylebone (which had only opened in May 1825). Again, the parents are stated as John and Sarah Price, now of 16 Seymour Place, with John's profession stated as 'Tutor'.

I could find no record whatsoever of Henry's baptism either in Brighton or London. It seemed strange to baptise the younger two sons without baptising the oldest. Something made me look further through the baptismal records of St Mary's, Bryanston Square, and to my amazement I found all three boys being baptised there on 14 January 1829, revealing for the first time Henry's exact date of birth as 20 February 1823 (Alfred's being 24 December 1824 and Edmund's 20 May 1827). They are again stated as the sons of John and Sarah Price of 16 Seymour Place, John's profession now being stated as 'Esq'. This was really Henry's postponed baptism but, with Henry being nearly six-years-old and fully aware of the occasion, it seems he would only go ahead with it if his brothers were also taking part. If the clergy were aware that the younger two had already been baptised, they would have been happy to turn a blind eye.

I also searched high and low for the marriage of John and Sarah but with absolutely no success. Could this have been in Brighton or London or Stafford or anywhere else? This was made all the more time-consuming by the fact that 'John Price' was a very common name in the early 19th century and there seemed to be countless numbers of Johns and Sarahs getting married. Our couple seemed to come from a moneyed background which made the lack of a marriage record all the more inexplicable. It was in the promiscuous Regency period of London life but I tried not to become suspicious, despite finding a book in which the author refers to an up-market brothel in Seymour Place. A happy spin-off of this whole process was becoming acquainted with the social history of the time and realising the importance of putting such family history research in its correct historical context. This particularly applied to the examination of contemporary maps.

A further distraction from the scent was the fact that both Henry and Alfred subsequently referred to their father in their marriage certificates (1854 and 1858 respectively) as the late Charles Price, especially strange as Alfred goes on to refer to him as John Price on his mother's death certificate.

Indeed, there was another distraction. I still have a letter dated 10 October 1967 to my father from his cousin Alice Price who worked at St John's College, Cambridge. Somehow, she believed that Henry Price had been a student at Cambridge and, on consulting the records at Gonville and Caius College, found the following entry:

Price, Henry: son of late Charles Price, Esq., merchant of London. Born in Middx. (corrected to Sussex). Educated for two years by Rev. Mr Chapman, at Kilburn: and for two years by Rev. Mr Hutton, in

London. Admitted pensioner, June 8, 1842. Age 20.
B.A. 1846. Curate of Turville, Bucks., 1846; and of Aberpergwm, Glam., 1851-4.

Bearing in mind that our Henry married a Roman Catholic and was never to our knowledge an Anglican clergyman during the rest of his life, nor styled himself the Rev Henry Price, my father had written on this letter in pencil 'NOT our Henry Price!'. He was wrong, and how much do I regret that he cannot be reading this account now.

On numerous visits to London in the next few years, I tried to take things further. I determined many peripheral details but continued to get absolutely nowhere on any details of John Price. Nevertheless, I now realise that no crumb of information should be discarded, however apparently insignificant.

The youngest daughter of Alfred Price, Louisa Drummond Price (whom I can remember as a child as my very elderly, frail and slightly terrifying Great Aunt Louie), died in 1967 aged ninety-one when I was just fifteen, a veiled spinster in St John's Home, Oxford, a care home run by high Anglican nuns. I still have a letter she wrote to me in May 1965 enclosing a cheque for an unstated amount (my memory tells me £13) saying, 'It would have been left to you in my Will but you may have it now and draw interest on it'. She also left written records of what she knew, including details of her Uncle Henry, his family and where they were buried. I used these to locate the grave of him, his wife and infant daughter in the Roman Catholic cemetery at St Thomas of Canterbury in Fulham, only about a mile from where I lived between 2014 and 2018.

Still thinking about a merchant of London, I began to look at Livery Company records in the City. There were countless John

Prices being taken on as apprentices but none of them seemed to fit the bill. I thought I had found something in the records of the Haberdashers' Company, with a distinctly Welsh origin, Price being a Welsh surname, derived from ap-Rhys, ie son of Rhys, but this turned out to be yet another red herring. Another strange fact was that Alfred had eventually, after educating his large family in Edinburgh to the pleasure of Isabella, his Scottish wife, retired to Ross-on-Wye on the Welsh border for no explicable reason. They are buried in the idyllic country churchyard of Brampton Abbots outside the town, as my father had discovered. Perhaps he was returning to his origins? Not so, as it turns out, but perhaps that is what he wanted people to think.

I moved to Fulham from Orkney permanently in June 2014, more determined than ever to solve the mystery of John Price. I discovered how streets could be re-named, the present Broadley Street in Marylebone formerly being Earl Street, which I thought had been in the City, and very near Seymour Place. So, I then discarded the City and centred on Marylebone. All these streets were being built in the Regency period, being part of the Portman estates. Earl Street was built to house farm workers for the farm near Lords Cricket Ground. In examining the Land Tax Records, I found a John Price (or Pierce) between 1824 and 1829 in Earl Street, but in No 58 rather than No 29. Also, in the Land Tax records, a variously stated Susan Peak or Susan Peat or S Peat was resident at 16 Seymour Place. Who was this and could it be anything to do with the Susan Price I had found in the 1841 census residing in Osnaburgh Street? At No 22, I found the intriguingly named Madame Collett and later Madame C Lafertee – could this be the brothel mentioned in the recent book?

In the Guildhall Library, I found the Royal Blue Book, which describes itself as a 'Fashionable Directory containing the Town and Country Residences of the Nobility and Gentry'. One was published every year and you clearly had to pay for your own entry. For 16 Seymour Place, we find in 1830 'Mrs Peake' and then from 1831 to 1834 inclusive 'John Price', and this was another sign of money and status being in evidence. Just to confuse me even further, I found just around the corner at 23 Upper George Street variously in the Land tax records and the Royal Blue Book a 'Mrs Price' between 1828 and 1837 – as it turns out, yet another red herring.

I researched the family of Henry Price in as much detail as I could in the hope of picking up any crumb going. The family spent all its time in three different addresses close to each other around Drayton Gardens in Kensington. Nearby is the Roman Catholic Church of the Servite Brothers and one of Henry's sons became the first British priest there in 1874 – Father John Angelo Price. Henry died in 1897 leaving an estate valued at £13,052 (about £1m at today's money) all to his widow Margaret. She died in 1915, by which time the money had shrunk to £5,864. I checked that it had not gone to the Servites. Two other daughters became nuns. Another daughter died at the age of eight whilst the remaining two daughters lived as spinsters to great ages, dying in 1947 and 1955 respectively. The priest at St Thomas' helped me identify that they were in the same grave as their parents and child sister, but no one has put anything on the stone – perhaps a future project. A further son Frank remained single and died aged eighty in 1944 in Newbury (according to Great Aunt Louie). The very respectable houses in which the family lived in Kensington are still there (two out of three anyway) and I photographed them on one of my cycling expeditions.

Great Aunt Louie had said that Edmund was buried in Brompton Cemetery. I cycled there but only found a pile of wrecked tombstones amongst a late winter jungle of brambles and dead nettles. I obtained a copy of Edmund's Will and found that he had left an estate of £10,000 in 1873, £2,500 going to charities, £200 going to each of many Peake cousins (a very poor family of twenty-one children in Lichfield, being the issue from two marriages of Sarah's brother John), £160 to brother Henry, £100 to mother Sarah and the rest to brother Alfred who was also the executor. This seemed strange as Alfred was by then living in far off Ayrshire and Henry was down the street in Drayton Gardens.

On 25 February 2015, on my way back from Edinburgh, I stopped at the record office in Stafford and easily obtained the microfiche of the baptismal and burial records of St Mary's, Stafford. Clearly the Peakes were a prominent family in the parish, there being numerous Peake entries. I found the entry for Sarah and her brothers and sisters, as well as many others including a William Peake who died on 13 April 1811.

There were still a couple of local addresses I hadn't researched because I thought them to be insignificant. Firstly, there was Alfred's address in the 1851 census, 12 St Mary Abbott's Terrace, Kensington, where he lived with his maidservant of the time. By then, he would have been twenty-six. Also, there was 42 Edwardes Square, the address that both Henry and his bride Margaret Neenan gave as their address on their marriage certificate of 1854. I was interested to see that they had the same address, common in these days of co-habitation but certainly unusual for prudish Victorian London. He was thirty-one and she was eighteen, the daughter of an Irish 'farmer from Cork', almost certainly a market gardener from Fulham escaping the Irish potato famine. Could she have been his maidservant?

On 4 March 2015, I set off again on my bike and first found

42 Edwardes Square, a very respectable address in Kensington. The square had been built in 1819, a model of its time and the listed buildings being unaltered from the time they were built. Impressive. I then went looking for 12 St Mary Abbott's Terrace and found it only about 200 yards away on the other side of Kensington High Street – although the present houses are new and Alfred's residence clearly no longer exists. But these two addresses were close to each other. So what?

I thought I had exhausted research on Edmund, but on my way home on the bike it struck me that I had never looked him up in the census. What could that reveal that I didn't know already? But on the principal of not leaving a stone unturned, I fired up my computer on my return. I quickly found him in the 1851 census at (lo! and behold!) 47 Edwardes Square, very close to brother Alfred and even closer to No 42, where brother Henry was living three years later at the time of his marriage. I thought it would be interesting to see who was living at No 42 in 1851, so I scrolled up the page. This turned out to be a major 'Eureka' moment because who should be there but – Susannah Peake! This must be the same person as had been at 16 Seymour Place in the 1830s and presumably Sarah's sister, but not (as I had wrongly assumed from the 1841 census at Osnaburgh Street) John Price's sister. But why was she living so close to two of the Price boys? She must have died at some point and I soon discovered that this took place the next year in 1852, explaining Henry's freedom in 42 Edwardes Square at the date of his marriage in 1854.

Until 1858, all Wills were hand copied by the probate office and these copies are available on line. Susannah's Will (made on 11 February 1851) was easy to find. It revealed some vital information. She was late of Osnaburgh Street, Regent's Park, ie she was the Susan Price of the 1841 census, which is notorious for being full of errors, being the first national census. Sarah Peake was her cousin (not sister) and lived at 12 St Mary Abbott's Terrace, ie with her son Alfred and his maid, but away at census time with older son Henry having a break in Brighton, Henry's birthplace. Sarah, Alfred and Edmund each received £100 and Henry (the oldest brother, living with her at 42 Edwardes Square) was appointed the executor and received the rest, which presumably included the smart house. However, my accountant's mind told me that this would not account for all the money for Henry, Alfred and Edmund to live for their whole lives whilst earning nothing. This also perhaps explained why Edmund left most of his wealth to Alfred in 1873, as Henry had already had his share of the cake. But more importantly, as it eventually transpired, it revealed that Susannah was a fairly vital cog in the wheel and perhaps more vital than Sarah, despite the fact that Sarah was definitely the mother of the boys. Susannah was buried in her own grave in Kensal Green, the other large public cemetery in west London. I quickly determined from the 1851 census that she had been born in Stafford around 1785. In fact, the St Mary's, Stafford, baptismal records revealed that she was born on 14 January 1785, the daughter of William and Susannah Peake, William being the brother of Sarah's father, John Peake. This was presumably the William who died in Stafford on 13 April 1811.

But all this told me no more about the central problem – who was John Price, the father of Henry, Alfred and Edmund Price?

I had been sending all these details to my brother in Vancouver for recording on his computerised family records. Understandably, I was driving him crazy with a bombardment of uncollated information as I received it. The collation was only something that happened later. As an aside, he said he was back in touch with a very distant relation on our mother's Hollingdale side, who had researched the Hollingdales back to the late sixteenth century. I asked for her phone number and eventually we made contact on Thursday, 26 March 2015. At the time, my wife and I were driving south over the Borders on the way back from another Edinburgh trip.

The Hollingdale cousin's name was Jenny Turnbull and she then lived in Caerphilly in South Wales. We spoke for some time about the Hollingdales and she clearly was a very able genealogist, well acquainted with the workings of websites. So, before we said farewell, I thought I would tell her about my problems in tracing John Price. I gave her the bare bones of what I have described so far, mentioning the boys and Sarah and Susannah Peake. She said she needed 'an excuse not to do the ironing' and would look into the mystery for me.

Over the next three days, I received several messages from Jenny and in that time, she had managed to gather most of the details about the Price family that I had taken years to research. It was very impressive. She even found a further John and Sarah Price in the 1841 census living in Wyndham Place, just around the corner from Seymour Place. But she met the usual brick walls about John (or perhaps Charles) Price.

On the evening of Sunday 29 March 2015 (Palm Sunday), after a long day at church for my wife, who is a minister in the Church of Scotland, we decided to stop off on the way home at a cinema in the King's Road, Chelsea. Half way through the film, I felt in my pocket an email coming in on my smartphone. Curiosity got the better of me and I glanced to see from whom it came. It was from Jenny; the strap line was 'Source of Price Money' and this is what it said:

How about this ....

Was fiddling and looked up Susannah Peake. The first thing that came up was the Will of Charles Day which I thought a bit odd but ...

Charles Day 1783 – 1836 was a boot black manufacturer who made 'the kind of fortune that would easily place him alongside today's richest rock stars'. Charles Day's wife was Rebecca Peake who seems to have been the sister of Susannah Peake.
Attached transcript of the Will where he left an ANNUAL income of £300 to his wife's sister Susannah Peake and ANNUAL income of £100 to Sarah Peake daughter of John and Sarah Peake late of Stafford. According to a convertor that my husband Hugh found for me £100 in 1840 would be £8800 today.
Go to Susannah Peake all searches on Ancestry, which takes you to the transcription which will take you to Robert Ward who put this in his tree against Charles Day, at the bottom of Charles Day's page is the link to the Will.

Is this where the money came from??

Hoping
Jenny xxx

Marvellous as the film was, it was hard to concentrate on the rest of it. Afterwards, we cycled home in pouring rain with no waterproofs. On reaching home, drenched, my wife discovered she had lost her mobile phone. I was desperate to get online, but that had to wait. We went out again into the soaking London night in the vain hope of finding her phone that had probably fallen out of her bag on the way home. She walked back along the route whilst I took the car to the cinema. It wasn't there but my phone rang and it was my wife – she had found her phone in the gutter on the embankment. This was the first of what turned out to be several miracles that happened through the ensuing night.

Having met up with her, getting home and drying off, I finally sat down with the laptop at 11.30pm. I was sure I had already searched Susannah Peake online, and when I did, nothing much came up. But knowing something was there, I searched much further down the list than normal and eventually spotted 'Notes on the Will of Charles Day'. I went into it and found a summary of the Will done by a Robert Ward. There, highlighted by Jenny, were the names of Susannah and Sarah Peake, receiving their annuities. But why, and who was Charles Day?

I decided to google Charles Day and found the following entry on Wikipedia:

Charles Day (1782/3–25 October 1836) was a British industrialist who was co-founder and then sole proprietor of the Day and Martin boot blacking company, founded around 1801 in partnership with Benjamin Martin (c1774-1834).

It is said that the 'Real Japan Blacking' /'Black Diamond' formula was originally obtained in return for a favour from a soldier in Doncaster by Benjamin Martin's brother-in-law (or his father in another version). Benjamin Martin took the formula to London where he worked as a hairdresser with Charles Day's father. Martin and the Days then began manufacturing and selling the product. Business grew rapidly and by the end of 1805 Day and Martin had acquired new premises at 97 High Holborn. Day bought out Martin for £10,000 in 1808. Some versions of the story suggest Charles Day was also initially a hairdresser, but in 1835 the company stated he had only ever been in the blacking business. The Day and Martin company is an early illustration of the power of

advertising and marketing. It is reported they promoted the product by hiring large numbers of men wearing suits to ask for it in shops around London. The company also features in company law because they had to take legal action against numerous copiers and counterfeiters. One of these, after Day's death, was his own nephew, William Charles Day.
Charles Day married Rebecca Peake at Stafford St. Mary's on 6 September 1806. They had one daughter, Letitia Caroline, (c1808-1877), known as Caroline, who when young was a sought after heiress until she eloped with Horatio Clagett (or Claggett), a well-known 'playboy' and serial bankrupt, in 1836.
Charles Day left a colossal fortune of between £350,000 and £450,000. His Will mentions his main residence as Harley House, Regent's Park. He also owned a country house at Edgware, remembered for its lodge in the shape of a boot blacking bottle. One bequest of £100,000 founded a charity for the blind. He also built alms houses at Edgware. His Will, with five codicils, one of them invalid made just before his death, was heavily contested for several years, incurring huge legal costs. His widow Rebecca lived on at Edgware with her daughter and son-in-law until her death in 1843.

After about twenty further minutes of scratching about and fumbling for more information as to how John Price fitted into all this, if at all, I went back to Robert Ward's notes on the Will and I spotted the following in minute print:

'Three natural sons', unnamed but mentioned in the fourth codicil, reported in newspapers to be illegitimate sons, revealed only as Charles Day was approaching the end of his life.

The penny suddenly dropped.
It was about 1am and my shriek of recognition certainly woke

my wife and probably some of the neighbours. The 'three natural sons' – it was too much of a coincidence – they had to be Henry, Alfred and Edmund Price! But how?

I let my imagination run riot and came up with what was, on the face of it, a fanciful and far-fetched thesis that anyone, coming afresh to the enigma of John Price, would think was ridiculous.

Charles Day's wife was Rebecca Peake (who has no more children after Caroline in 1808). Her younger sister was Susannah Peake and her cousin was Sarah Peake, the mother of the three boys. Sarah and Charles start an affair and their first child is conceived in 1822. She is sent off out of the way to Brighton for the birth (which is not recorded anywhere at the time). A second child appears to be on the way and is born on Boxing Day, 1824. He is Alfred, my great-grandfather. Sarah is housed in 29 Earl Street, Marylebone, newly built farm workers' houses for the Portman Estate. Charles wants the boy baptised so invents a father with a very popular and common name, John Price. A third child comes along and is also baptised as Edmund under the same guise - perhaps a Charles Day servant was told to stand in as the mythical John Price for the baptisms. Henry still hasn't been baptised so, just to cement the myth, Sarah and mythical John turn up at church on 14 January 1829 to baptise all three at once. Cousin Susannah, the sister-in-law of father Charles, is actually in 16 Seymour Place, the baptismal address, keeping an eye on them all at the request of Charles, who lives not far away in Harley House, Regents Park. The boys eventually discover their father was called Charles, so in their context, he had to be Charles Price (cf. Henry's Cambridge record and their marriage certificates). Sarah's eventual death certificate says widow of John Price (informed by Alfred, who by then realised that the names John and Charles could be interchangeable, his mother living with him in Edinburgh, far out of harm's way).

Then I found the fourth codicil to Charles Day's Will and it stated:

> *I Charles Day of Edgware and Harley House being of sound mind so desire that the three post obit bonds for £5,000 each which will be presented at my decease may be doubled that is made £10,000 each and that the same may be invested for the benefit of my three natural sons by my Executors as trustees according to their discretion and this shall be their authority as witness my mark (Charles Day)...*

So, Susannah had £300 per year (c £30,000 today) and Sarah had £100 per year (c £10,000 today), and the boys had in trust £10,000 (c £1,000,000 today) off which they would receive an annual income of maybe £400 per year (c £40,000 today). So, their financial security for the rest of their lives was revealed.

In today's money, Charles Day's estate was probably worth a staggering £45m.

I eventually crawled off to bed and could hardly sleep. Had we found the solution to the puzzle that had troubled me for fifty-five years and my father before me? This may sound over-dramatic, but it honestly describes my sentiments and emotions in the middle of that eventful night.

I googled Robert Ward and found that he had written a book entitled *Wealth and Notability – the Lockwood, Day and Metcalfe Families of Yorkshire and London*, only published as recently as August 2014, and found his email address. Nothing ventured, nothing gained, and expecting him not to reply to junk messages from cranks, I sent him my theory. He soon confirmed his agreement – he knew about the three Price boys but could never see how they fitted into the Charles Day story. My theory seemed to be the perfect fit. He had been examining Charles Day's Will as part of his research into his wife's family, she being a descendant of Charles Day's sister. He explained that the Will had been disputed and that Sarah was certainly mentioned in reports of the case. He pointed me towards the National Archives at Kew. He had never managed to go there as he lived near Huddersfield, but I was only a thirty-minute cycle ride away. He knew that many records of the case were housed there and he also told me about the disputed codicil involving Frederick Dufaur. He explained how the case had dragged on for several years and sent me some newspaper reports that had appeared over the period.

He said that he had speculated in his book that the Prices were Day's sons, but it needed someone like me working backwards to make the link. He had actually spotted Henry Price as a fund-holder in some of the censuses, but couldn't be sure he was the right one, so did not look any further. I explained to Robert the subsequent Price history and that my three children were the only descendants of Charles Day in their generation.

I also contacted Jenny with this news and she came back with an interesting postscript:

What is interesting and certainly spooky is that I found the link to the Day Will when aimlessly searching for information on Susannah Peake and it was first on the list thrown up by Ancestry. When I came to put Susannah on my tree it wasn't there and I had to go via Ward's tree to find it. And when I now check on a search not through the tree but from the home page, it's still not there!
What a fluke I saw it!!

On Tuesday 31 March 2015, I was on my bike again to search out all the Marylebone properties whose addresses I had identified.

I am sure the original houses of Seymour Place have been pulled down and the street re-numbered. From contemporary maps in which the houses are actually numbered, I knew exactly where No 16 would be. But it is now a very respectable twentieth-century flatted residence. I went on to Broadley Street (formerly Earl Street) and the site of what had been No 29 was now unsightly modern offices. However, on the other side of the street, the original Portman workers' houses still stand and I photographed them, assuming (safely, I think) that the former houses opposite would have been a mirror image. The day before, Jenny had identified 'John and Sarah Price' in Wyndham Place from the 1841 census. I found that short street leading directly away from St Mary's, Bryanston Square, around the corner from Seymour Place. All was coming to life, but even more excitement followed when I found Harley House, the town residence of Charles Day. Now it occupies the entire block to the east of the Royal Academy of Music (RAM) in Marylebone Road. The present property is Edwardian and consists of some of the most desirable flats in London. Recent residents include Sir Thomas Beecham, Dame Joan Collins and Sir Mick Jagger in their number. Our daughter Catriona was a postgraduate student at the RAM between 2010 and 2012 and had difficulty finding any accommodation within reasonable distance of the building. To think that, if things had worked out slightly differently, she could have had a 'really cool pad' right next door. I have since found a print of Day's house dating from the 1850s as it appeared in the Illustrated London News. After being let to the Duke of Brunswick, the house was subsequently occupied by the Queen of Oude on her expedition to the Victorian court attempting to regain her realm following the British Empire's occupation of India. Day would have owned the entire block. It is impossible to speculate what it might be worth now.

But the first job was clearly to study the Will of Charles Day and the best way to do this was to transcribe it into a readable and accessible format. With the Will being 7,500 words long, this took me the best part of a week. It was Holy Week and by Good Friday I felt I had been on some journey.

19. The bound 962-page document kept in The National Archives, Kew, entitled *Dufaur v. Croft and Others – Process. Bro.t in 25th Feb 1839. P.C.53'*

On Maundy Thursday, I went to The National Archives in Kew and was impressed by the kindness and efficiency of the place. Within ninety minutes of arriving, I had registered as a reader and I had the document of *Dufaur v Croft and others: 1839 – PC53* in front of me. I looked at it for three hours. It was no small file, but a bound book of nearly one thousand pages, all in copperplate handwriting but with no referencing such as page numbers, contents or index. All I could do was randomly dip in and hope to find something. Eventually I found some interesting testimony by Susannah Peake, who certainly seemed to be pivotal in the whole business. I resolved that the only way forward was to return with my digital camera and photograph the entire document. This I managed to do a week later. It was 962 pages long and the photographing took three hours. But I could then take it home and pore over the details at my leisure, magnifying the pages on my computer. However, with the lack of any referencing, it soon became clear that the only way to ensure that I would miss no important facts was to transcribe and punctuate the whole document. Although the writing was legible, the lack of any punctuation, sentences or paragraphs, as with most legal documents of that time, made it impossible to read. This took me over two years and amounted to 170,000 words, but proved absolutely invaluable. Basically, through the evidence of about thirty witnesses, the document described in great detail the last two months of Day's life.

In the flurry of Holy Week activity, two more interesting facts emerged. The legal challenges to Charles Day's Will became celebrated for their length and general emersion in the fog of Chancery, so much so that Dickens actually used the case as the justification of 'Jarndyce and Jarndyce' in *Bleak House*.

The other emerging fact was that Day had been buried at St Margaret's Church, Edgware, along with other family members and a drive out along the Edgware Road and Watling Street, now the A5, would have to be planned soon. The Day country residence was Edgware Place where he actually died in 1836. He had also built a row of almshouses there in 1828, revealing a very benevolent character that was about to become even more apparent. Edgware was a quiet country village of some 700 inhabitants in the 1830s. It is now a busy suburb at the end of the London Underground's Northern Line.

So, on Easter Monday, my wife and I headed off in the car to Edgware having no idea what we might, or might not, find. The church was soon located, in the north-east corner of the busy crossroads now at the centre of modern, suburban Edgware. It is a medieval building with the graveyard now open to the street and a story board almost on the pavement. We looked at the story board and couldn't fail to see immediately 'Day's Tomb – Here rest the family of Charles Day, the well-known local benefactor and co-founder of the firm Day and Martin, shoe polish manufacturers. Day built the striking stone, ashlar-faced Almshouses on Stonegrove in 1828'. And there it was, right in front of us, at the east end of the church building.

The grave was a sad sight – a sarcophagus-type tomb, surrounded by a broken-down railing, and overgrown with ivy and other vegetation. We set to work immediately, stripping off the ivy and revealing inscriptions on three stone panels on three sides of the tomb. The first occupant was Mrs Susannah Peake who died on 4 October 1822. She would have been the widow of William, who died in Stafford in 1811, and the mother of Rebecca whom Day had married in 1806. She was also the mother of Susannah Peake, the superintendent of Day's three 'natural' sons, Henry, Alfred and Edmund Price by her niece Sarah. Did she have any idea of what had been going on?

On the opposite side of the tomb, mostly covered in ivy, we found Charles' parents, Francis who died on 12 September 1823 and Susannah who died on 26 February 1828. As Robert Ward's book had revealed, Francis was from Yorkshire and had set up a very successful hairdressing / perfumery / wig-making business at 9 Tavistock Street, a stone's throw from what is now the Royal Opera House, Covent Garden, and where Day and Martin started their boot polish manufacturing business, Charles as an enthusiastic, entrepreneurial teenager. Susannah Day was probably from a Sussex farming family named Parsons, being Francis's second wife, the previous one being her deceased sister.

On the back of the tomb is Caroline Clagett who died on 2 April 1877. She was Charles and Rebecca's only child, born in 1807 just the year after they were married. Caroline married the playboy and bankrupt but splendidly named Horatio Clagett in 1832 to the great disapproval of her father. The couple had no children but, it seems, an exciting life, residing eventually at (pre-Beatle) 1 Abbey Road, St John's Wood. He died soon after her and is supposed to be buried in the same tomb, although his name has not been added in the considerable space left available – presumably there was no one left to add it.

But on the front of the tomb, there should have been a panel with Charles's and Rebecca's details - Rebecca subsequently died in 1843 - but it was missing, and as we learnt later, had been since at least 1989. It matters not – we know the details. It is now a project to restore the tomb and replace the missing plaque.

We were surprised to find the church open on Easter Monday and went inside. I purchased an excellent history of the building in which Day is mentioned. We found panels in the church featuring the names of some of the witnesses in Charles's Will case (William Foote and others). Then we noticed a lady working in the back room. I went and introduced myself as almost certainly the great-great-grandson of Charles Day and her jaw hit the floor! This was Hazel Aucken, the parish administrator, but also as she explained the Clerk to the Day and Atkinson Almshouse

Charity. Good fortune was continuing to smile on us.

We sat with Hazel in the church for some time, explaining the whole story. She was marvellously helpful and produced many useful pieces of information, such as the Dickensian reference in *The Pickwick Papers*, where Day and Martin's polish is mentioned in Chapter X. She also gave me a copy of *Copies of the Deeds &c. Establishing the Almshouse Charity of Charles Day, Esq. at Edgware. 1842.* and suggested we visited the almshouses after lunch – no persuasion needed there.

Most interestingly for me, Hazel showed me a good, framed, black-and-white photograph of the painted portrait of Charles Day. I had seen a copy of this on the internet and in Robert's book, but on speaking to him, he had no idea of the whereabouts of the original. Neither had Hazel, so she suggested we took the photo out of its frame to see if there were any details inside. Sure enough, a notice inside revealed 'No date or artist's signature. Portrait held by The Clothworkers' Company, London'. Clearly a visit there had to be arranged – I had only been in the building three weeks earlier at the Annual Lunch of the Association of Accounting Technicians (AAT) of which I was President in 2010-11.

Over the road, in full view of the Day Tomb, and on her special recommendation, we took Hazel for a memorable Afghan lunch, before heading on to the Day Almshouses. Modesty had prevented Hazel telling us that the whole complex had undergone a total renovation and extension in 2003 to bring it up to modern standards. She had masterminded this with the very considerable fundraising required. For this, in 2004 HRH The Prince of Wales had visited the buildings to present The Almshouse Association's 'Patron's Award for an outstanding almshouse development on The Almhouses founded by Charles Day'. To cap a great visit to

Edgware, Hazel obtained access to one of the houses and introduced me as a direct descendant of Charles Day. Ridiculously, I felt the startled but very charming occupant was treating me like royalty!

By this time, I had completed the transcription of the Will and was able to analyse it in detail. My accountancy training came in useful. When planning Wills, the first thing to establish is how much the testator is actually worth so that he knows how much he can leave. Although Charles Day was fabulously wealthy, this basic point seems to have been overlooked. I had seen reference to the fact that his estate was worth between £350,000 and £450,000 although I have found no evidence to show from where this figure came. However, even if we use the upper figure (the figure on the probate certificate is the lower figure), the estate would have been hard pressed to meet its commitments without relying on the continued profitability of 'Day and Martin'.

Basically, Charles Day left a total of £194,923 in legacies to sixty-six different individuals or charities. If Dickens' estimate of £70,000 for legal costs is accepted, plus some more as the case was not finished when he wrote about it, it only leaves a residue of approximately £150,000. And this is not allowing for any legacy duty or what would now be called Inheritance Tax. However, Day also bequeathed annuities, which are annual payments of income from the residue of the estate, to thirty-eight people totalling £8,080 per year. The payments would have ceased on the death of each annuitant and therefore the annual commitment would have reduced in time. However, with Sarah Peake and Caroline Clagett both living on until 1877, this would suggest that the administration of the estate would have carried on at least until then, with associated administration costs. This would also suggest that the estate's commitments could only be met fully if the estate continued to enjoy the profits of Day and Martin. Subsequent research would clarify this point.

Charles Day went completely blind in 1816. One of the legacies in the Will was for £100,000 with which the executors were to establish a new charity entitled 'The Blind Man's Friend', to provide small subsistence grants for the blind poor. As such, the administration of this charity was entirely detached from the estate. It appears that this administration continued into the twentieth-century, but in 1909 it was transferred to The Clothworkers' Company in the City. The Clothworkers are renowned for administering many welfare charities and were happy to take on 'The Blind Man's Friend'. They ran other charities for the blind and only recently have they amalgamated all the funds together. As such, all the assets of the charity were passed over to The Clothworkers in 1909, including the splendid oil portrait of Charles Day referred to above and several documents that were instrumental in the establishment of the charity. Consequently, I telephoned the Company's archivist and arranged an appointment to see her on 23 April 2015.

She was interested in my story and was extremely helpful. Firstly, she showed me the portrait, one of countless paintings owned by the Company. It hangs in the Court's Lunch Room and on being confronted with it, I suppose I have to admit to having one of those rather emotional *'Who Do You Think You Are?'* moments. This really was the culmination of a very long quest by me, and my father before me. Here was my great-great-grandfather looking down on me, albeit in his blindness, and the painter had portrayed a clearly warm and benevolent personality with whom I was proud to be identified. And at last, after 179 years since his death, the discriminatory stigmas of illegitimacy under which the family had laboured for generations, had been swept away.

Amazingly, I am sure I had been in this room before, during my time with the AAT. We had had several Council meetings at Clothworkers' Hall, including my last in 2013, and have used the room in which the portrait hangs. Little did I ever realise that 'John Price', my great-great-grandfather, was looking down on me whilst I was presiding over a Council meeting. Quite an extraordinary experience!

The portrait has been repaired over the years and is in fine condition. In 1993, an expert considered that the portrait was 'Biedermeier', ie German, Austrian or Danish but at least from continental Europe, in a plain, severe style which flourished in the prosperous middle-class homes of continental Europe between 1815 and 1848. But it was almost certainly painted in London, given that Charles's blindness would have prevented him from travelling any further afield than his country house in Edgware and certainly not abroad (as subsequent research has confirmed). And thereby hangs a paradox which has yet to be solved, as there is no evidence of portraits such as this by German or Danish artists working in Britain. Continental painters did not come over to seek work in England where portraiture was thriving.

The portrait may have been painted to mark Day's thirtieth birthday in 1814, or perhaps to commemorate a high point in his impressive career.

The archivist then showed me various other documents that the Company hold including a contemporary copy of the Will and one of the original probate copies of the Will bearing original signatures. Also, there were several legal documents that actually listed all the beneficiaries of the Will by name, which the actual Will fails to do. This has helped greatly in subsequent research.

Another intriguing statement in the Will reveals Charles Day as a very rare beast – an early-nineteenth-century feminist! A paragraph in the Will is as follows:

> *And with respect to such legacies and annuities as are hereinbefore by me given to females, it is my positive, express will and meaning that the same shall not be in any wise or in any manner or upon any account or pretence whatsoever subject or liable to the power, control, intermeddling debts, engagements or encumbrances of any husband or husbands to whom they or any of them respectively are, is or shall or may at any time or times be married but shall at all times be and remain as a provision for them for their respective sole and separate use and benefit and shall for that purpose be paid into their respective proper hands or to such person or persons (other than their husbands) as they respectively by writing...*

This was probably as a result of experiences with his son-in-law, but is nevertheless admirable.

From the *Croft v. Day* document, I am left in no doubt that Henry, Alfred and Edmund Price were the 'natural' sons of Charles Day and that their father was very involved in every aspect of their upbringing. As Susannah Peake testifies, he was a very proud and emotionally involved father. Some pages almost read as though they were from a Dickensian novel and form a commentary on the contemporary attitudes to illegitimacy and the secrecy that it demanded. The sisters Rebecca and Susannah clearly did not get on and avoided each other. Susannah comes across as a determined character who earned the respect of Charles Day, whereas his wife Rebecca is described on several occasions as weak, timid and deaf.

What comes over to me generally in reading the document is that the only person who knew of Charles and Sarah's secret union, other than perhaps one or two trusted servants, was their redoubtable cousin, sister-in-law, confidante and friend, Susannah Peake. Rebecca and the rest of the family clearly knew nothing. And whilst Charles was alive, the boys probably looked upon him as their incredibly kind, generous and Blind Uncle Charles, who came to see them frequently. They believed that their father, John Price, had died when they were too young to remember him. Henry might have been old enough to suspect something, but would have been sworn to secrecy by Susannah and Sarah if he had let on. However, they discovered the real facts at the time of the court case, courtesy of Dufaur, and then would have been sworn to secrecy for the rest of their lives. They were being given enough money to live quiet but comfortable lives out of the public eye and no one need know. Consequently, when two of them married, they did so 'below their station' and I very much doubt if either wife ever knew that their husbands were illegitimate. Certainly, none of their eighteen children knew and the shame would have been shocking and unbearable if they had found out. To me, this explains why that generation were in turn quiet and shy people, only four of the eighteen ever marrying. The exception was my grandfather who married twice – he must have been the one to benefit from the injection of Scottish blood, and Glasgow blood at that.

However, as I came to the end of the document, a new aspect began to strike me. The appeal case of *'Dufaur v Croft and others'* seemed to cover not one but two issues. Not only did it cover the main dispute of whether Day agreed to Dufaur being an executor when his state of mind was past making any such decision as a result of his fatal illness, but it also covered the issue of whether Day had fathered illegitimately three 'natural' sons being Henry, Alfred and Edmund Price. This suggests to me (and at one point it is strongly implied in the text) that Dufaur was using blackmail. If the family would accept him as an executor, he would not proceed with the appeal, and he was assured of an income for decades to come. If they did not, he would proceed, thus exposing in public the existence of the three illegitimate sons and all the shame that would go with such exposure. The family decided to call Dufaur's bluff and managed to keep the cover going until Robert Ward, Jenny Turnbull and Neil Price come along 179 years later.

What the document never establishes is who was the boys' mother. It clearly states that Susannah was their superintendent and that Sarah was their guardian, but Susannah actually gives no answer to the direct question concerning the identity of the mother. Sarah is not even required to testify.

However, coming to this whole story from the other side, so to speak, and with the benefit of modern technology, I have taken DNA tests and have linked up with distant living cousins, from as far afield as New Zealand and Oregon, on both the Day and Peake sides of the family. I do have the evidence that Sarah was the mother, and therefore this bleak mystery is solved.

Appendix One
The responses of Susannah Peake in PC53

Prerogative

13 February 1837

Croft against Day and Others
Bowdler   R Townsend   Orme   Addams

On the Allegation given by Addams dated 27 December 1836

Susannah Peake of No 4 Osnaburgh Street, Regent's Park, in the County of Middlesex, Spinster, aged 51 years, a witness produced on her oath says:

First
To the first Article:

I was acquainted with Mr Day, the deceased in this Cause, upwards of 30 years.
His widow is my sister.
I have known the articulate Henry Price, Alfred Price and Edmund Price from their births.
The said Henry Price was born in February 1823, the said Alfred Price was born in December 1824 and the said Edmund Price was born in May 1827.

20. Part of the evidence given by Susannah Peake in PC53, describing the baptism of the three Price boys.

They were placed from their births under my superintendence by Mr Day and he always, from their births, recognized and acknowledged them as his natural children.

At first, they resided with me in Seymour Place, Bryanstone Square. Afterwards they resided with me in Wyndham Place, Bryanstone Square, and then they resided with me in Osnaburgh Street, Regent's Park, where they are now resident with me.

They were all baptised together in January 1829 in the church of St Mary, Bryanstone Square, which was their then district church and they were so baptised by the aforesaid names of Henry, Alfred and Edmund and as the sons of John and Sarah Price.

It was for family reasons, and to keep from public view Mr Day's relation to them, that the three children passed by and were baptised in the name of Price but he still continued to recognize them as his natural children as they advanced in life.

Mr Day augmented the allowance which he at first made to me for their maintenance, clothing and education.

It was in the year 1831 that Mr Day increased such allowance and he increased it to £400 a year which he paid me regularly by quarterly payments and continued to pay me until the time of his death.

In August 1835, I removed from Wyndham Place to Osnaburgh Street at Mr Day's request in order that the children might be nearer to Harley House, his residence, and to their school at the London University.

It was Mr Day's choice that the children should receive their education there.

Mr Day frequently visited the children in Seymour Place and Wyndham Place.

He continued to do so until about two years before his decease when he became lame.

He lost the use of his limbs entirely about that time and could not walk.

As long as he was able to walk, he came to see the children.

After he became unable to walk, he used to send for me frequently to his house to enquire after their [welfare] and his enquiries after them were expressed with the utmost regard and affection and he showed on all occasions the anxiety of a father for their welfare.

Second

In the second Article:

I was aware of Mr Day's intention to make a provision for the aforesaid children before he instructed Mr Barbrook to prepare the Bonds which he afterwards executed in my presence for that purpose.

He had spoken to me on that subject previously but without saying to what extent or in what way he should provide for them.

It was whilst I was resident in Seymour Place that the Bonds were executed.

I was present when he instructed Mr Barbrook to prepare three Bonds of £5000 each in favour of the said children.

I was also present when Mr Day executed those three Bonds in Seymour Place and Mr Barbrook attested the execution of all three Bonds.

Mr Barbrook was one of the Chief Clerks employed by Mr Day in his Blacking Manufactory in Holborn.

He, Mr Barbrook, is as I believe now in an insane state.

I have seen him since Mr Day's death and he was then in that state.

I attested the execution of two of the Bonds and a relation of mine attested the execution of the third.

After the execution of them, they were deposited by Mr Day with me.

They have been in my custody ever since and they are in my custody now.

And I will produce them at the hearing of the Cause if required to do so.

Those Bonds are in the penal sum of £10,000 each conditioned for the payment by Mr Day's heirs, executors or administrators or any person or persons on his or their behalf of the full sum of £5,000 to each of them, the aforesaid Henry Price, Alfred Price and Edmund Price, their executors, administrators or assigns respectively within six calendar months after his decease with interest for the same at the rate of five percent per annum until paid.

It was on 26 October 1832 that the said three Bonds were so executed by Mr Day.

Third

To the third Article and the exhibits therein pleaded and referred to marked 1, 2 and 3 respectively:

Mr Williams, my solicitor, copied one of the aforesaid Bonds in my presence, and he afterwards bought [sic] three copies of them which he examined with the original Bonds in my presence. And I likewise, the three paper writings produced to me by the examiner to be, and contain, true and faithful copies of the said three Bonds of which I have deposed and which are now in my custody.

The contents of these three exhibits now produced to me are true. All things were had and done as therein contained, and Henry Price, Alfred Price and Edmund Price mentioned in them are the three natural children of Mr Day of whom I have deposed.

Fourth
To the fourth Article:

At the time of giving instructions for the aforesaid Bonds, Mr Day stated that his reason for at once making a provision for the three children was that from his infirmity (he was quite blind) he might meet with some accident in crossing the road.

He alluded to the accident by which Mr Huskisson met his death and the possibility of being himself cut off suddenly and stated that as his inducement to make a provision at once for the children, but he at the same time distinctly said that he meant to do something more for them by and by 'by my Will or in some other way', he said.

And he frequently afterwards spoke in the same way to me concerning the three children and his intention to do something more for them than he had done by the Bonds.

He has said so often to me and frequently in the presence of a relation of mine, Sarah Peake, my cousin.

Fifth
To the fifth Article:

In August last, Mr Day proposed to me to go to Margate to join the children there.

They were all three there during the vacation time for the benefit of change of air.

They had been sent there by him.

Mr Day had appointed to meet me at Harley House on the twenty-ninth of the month.

And I was to have gone and stayed a day or two with him at Edgware, when we were to talk over and make arrangements about the children.

But he was taken ill on that day and instead of coming himself, he sent his carriage for me.

I went to him at Edgware on that day and stayed there until the following evening.

During that time, we talked over his arrangements and plans for the children.

He spoke of them with his usual affection and regard and when I mentioned that one of them had met with an accident and hurt his arm, he showed great anxiety for his recovery and desired that he should have the best medical advice.

The accident was not a very serious one, but Mr Day was very anxious about the child.

Mr Day being still unwell at the time, I proposed to defer my journey to Margate but he would not listen to it.

He would have me go there at once and see that the child had the best advice.

I went to Margate shortly afterwards. On the 1 September I went.

Seventh
To the seventh Article:

On 13 September last, I received a letter from Mr Weston, my brother in law, who had the management of the Blacking Manufactory, informing me of Mr Day's wish that I should immediately return with the children from Margate and of Mr Day's wish to see me, by one of the principle clerks in the manufactory.

Tenth
To the 10th Article:

In consequence of the note I received from Mr Weston on 13 September last, I returned home immediately with the children Henry and Alfred.
Edmund I had sent home a day or two before, he not being very well. I thought it better.
On 15 September, I went to Edgware to see Mr Day and I remained with him for several hours during that period.
I was several times alone with him and then he took the opportunity of enquiring after the children, and he did so very tenderly and affectionately.
I had much conversation with him about the children and he informed me that he had made a Codicil and done what he had promised me he would, that he had doubled the sum he had given to them before and that it would yield £1,200 a year, that he could put me in the way of making more of it, but that it would be intricate and troublesome to me.
He was very ill at the time and was speaking to me of the plans he wished me to follow when he was dead.
He said that he wished me to move into a larger house, such a house as he used to live in himself in Euston Square, and to bringing the children up according to their expectations.
And I, wishing to know what his desires were respecting them, asked him whether he would wish them to remain at the London University.
He said 'Yes' if I were satisfied, but that when they were sixteen, he should like them to be placed with a clergyman for two years. That was the effect of what passed between me and Mr Day concerning the children.

He told me that Mr Foote had made the Codicil for the children and that by the Codicil, he had doubled what he had given them before.

I am quite certain that, at this time during the whole time I was with him, Mr Day was of sound mind, memory and understanding.

He talked rationally and sensibly in every respect and, I am certain, well knew and understood what he said and did and what was said and done in his presence and hearing and was fully capable of the conduct and management of himself and his concerns.

I was with him from about 12 to about 4 or 5 o'clock.

Several times we were alone and something [sic] Mr Day was in the room, and the servants came in occasionally to assist him.

And in every respect Mr Day appeared to be perfectly sensible. He was very ill indeed.

Susannah Peake

The same witness examined on interrogatories administered on the part of William Croft.

First
I believe that Mr Barbrook, who prepared the Bonds of which I have deposed, is in confinement as a lunatic.

I cannot say how long he has been so.

I was present at the execution of the Bonds.

Second
I am not aware that any person excepting myself, my cousin Sarah Peake, Mr Barbrooke and Mr Day knew that he had

executed the Bonds enquired after, before 10 September last, unless it was the gentleman to whom Mr Barbrook applied for the form of the Bonds, Mr Antonine Dufaur, I believe.

Several of Mr Day's friends knew of the children before that day. Mr Duncan and Mr Goddard knew of them and Mr Carter might know of them, as he was in the habit of coming backward and forward to the house.

I do not know how many persons Mr Day made it known to on 10 September that he had the children and that he had executed the Bonds.

Third

There were reasons of a very peculiar nature which made Mr Day anxious to conceal the fact that he had the children and also the fact of that he had executed the Bonds.

His anxiety for the concealment of those facts might have been apparently less when I saw him on 15 September, than previously. But still he was so anxious about the concealment that if there was a difference, it was scarcely perceptible.

He was particularly cautious to ascertain that there was not any other person in the room before he alluded to them.

Fourth

Mr Day spoke of his intention to increase the provision made by the Bonds on the very day they were executed.

I believe that his intention to increase that provision was not made known to any person but myself and Sarah Peake, my cousin, previous to 10 September last.

The reason he assigned for intending to increase the provision was that he did not consider it sufficient according to his means.

He did not say how he should increase it except in a general manner – by Will or in some way.

Fifth
I saw Mr Day on 29 and 30 August last, on no other days between 26 August and 15 September.
I do not know what fits he had during that period.
When I saw him on 15 September, he appeared very much altered and enfeebled but his memory or mental capacity were not at all affected on that day that I observed.
I saw him once a week after 15 September and towards the last he appeared wandering in his conversation, so that his memory and mental faculties did not appear to me wholly unimpaired.
He was rational at times.
It was only now and then that he seemed to wander.

Sixth
I am first cousin to Sarah Peake, the party in the Cause, and Mrs Day is my sister.
I visited Mr Day frequently during the last two years of his life.
He took an opportunity when Mrs Day and the family were out of the way of making an appointment for me to call upon him.
It might be once a week or once a fortnight as it suited his convenience.
Before then, he used to call at my residence to see the children.

Seventh
When I visited Mr Day, I did not see Mrs Day or her daughter Mrs Clagett.
There were family disagreements which prevented our meeting.

Eighth
(The witness refused to answer this question.)

Susannah Peake

Repeated and acknowledged
before Dr Danbury, Surr.
in the presence of

E W Wadeson,
Examiner

[Author's Note: With respect to Eighth above, the question that was asked was:
'Who, as you know or believe, is the mother of the said children?']

Appendix Two
The Will and Codicils of Charles Day

This is the last Will and Testament of me *Charles Day* of Harley House, Regent's Park, in the County of Middlesex, Esquire. First I desire that the place of my burial be chosen by my dear wife Rebecca Day and that the funeral arrangements be under her direction and control if she shall survive me but otherwise at the discretion of my executors.

I direct that all my just debts, funeral expenses and the costs and charges of proving this my Will be paid and satisfied with all convenient speed after my decease and I charge all my real estate with the payment thereof in exoneration of such part of my personal Estate as may by any Codicil or Codicils be given for charitable purposes.

I appoint my friends William Underwood of Vere Street, draper, William Croft of Upper Gower Street, Esquire, and Pinder Simpson of Old Burlington Street, Gentleman, *Executors* of this my Will. And I give to each of them £500 sterling for mourning and for their trouble in carrying out and fulfilling the trusts of this my Will.

I give and bequeath to my said dear wife all the furniture, pictures, plate, linen, china, wine, horses, carriages, stock and stores of what description soever which may be in or about my Residence at Edgware at the time of my decease to and for her own absolute use and benefit and it is my Will that she my said dear wife be allowed the free use and occupation of my said house at Edgware together with the garden, pleasure ground, outbuildings and land thereunto belonging for and during the term of her natural life without paying any rent for the same, she keeping the premises in good order and repair and paying all expenses, tithes, taxes, rates and all other outgoings whatsoever during the time she continues to use and occupy the same.

I give and bequeath to my daughter Caroline, the wife of Horatio Claggert, Esquire, all the furniture, pictures, plate, linen, china, wine, horses, carriages, stock and stores of what description soever which may be in or about my Residence in the New Road called 'Harley House' at the time of my decease to and for her own sole and separate use and benefit independently of the debts, control and engagements of her husband and for which her receipt alone shall be a sufficient discharge and it is my will that she my said daughter be allowed the free use and occupation of my said house and premises in the New Road for and during the term of her natural life without paying any rent for the same, she keeping the premises in good order and repair and paying all ground rents, tithes, taxes, rates and all other outgoings whatsoever during the time she continues to use and occupy the same.

I also give and bequeath to my said dear wife all the paraphernalia and the ornaments of her person.

I give and bequeath unto each of my nephews and nieces, the sons and daughters of my sisters and of my late brother William Day who shall be living at my decease the sum of £1,000 sterling to become vested in and become paid to such of them who have attained the age of twenty-one years at my decease immediately on my decease and to become vested in and paid to such of them as shall be under that age at my decease when and as they respectively shall attain that age but without any interest in the meantime.

I give and bequeath £500 sterling to James Osborne now in my employ as Clerk.

I give and bequeath £500 sterling to Joseph Davis also now in my employ as Clerk.

I give and bequeath to each of the following persons to whom annuities are by this my Will given, a legacy equal to one half year's annuity and I desire the legacies to such several annuitants to be paid as soon as convenient after my decease.

I give and bequeath the following annuities or yearly sums of money to the several persons hereinafter named during the respective periods hereinafter mentioned, that is to say:

1. One annuity or yearly sum of £2,000 to my said dear wife Rebecca Day for and during the term of her natural life in lieu bar and satisfaction of all dower Freebench thirds and Widows part at Common Law or by Custom

2. One annuity or yearly sum of £3,000 to my said daughter Caroline for and during the term of her natural life

3. One annuity or yearly sum of £300 to my sister Mary Dey, the wife of William Claughton Dey, now or late of Doncaster in the County of York for and during the term of her natural life.

4. One annuity or yearly sum of £300 to my sister Susannah Lockwood, the wife of Joseph Lockwood of Doncaster aforesaid for and during the term of her natural life.

5. One annuity or yearly sum of £300 to my wife's sister Susannah Peake, Spinster, for and during the term of her natural life.

6. One annuity or yearly sum of £200 to my sister Elizabeth Poole of Brighton in the County of Sussex, Widow, for and during the term of her natural life.

7. One annuity or yearly sum of £200 unto Robert Barbrook of Holborn now in my employ as Clerk for and during the term of his natural life.

8. One annuity or yearly sum of £100 to Sarah Peake, daughter of John and Sarah Peake, late of Stafford, Spinster, for and during the term of her natural life.

9. One annuity or yearly sum of £100 to Harriett Day of the King's Road, Chelsea, Widow, for and during the term of her natural life.

10. One annuity or yearly sum of £50 to Elizabeth Bourne, wife of William Bourne of Gainsborough, in the County of Lincoln for and during the term of her natural life.

11. One annuity or yearly sum of £50 to Mary Anne Skegg, late of York House, Waltham Green, Spinster, for and during the term of her natural life.

12. One annuity or yearly sum of £20 to each of the sons and daughters of my mother's brothers and sisters excepting Samuel Virgo now or late of Brighton as may be alive at my decease for and during the terms of their respective natural lives.

13. One annuity or yearly sum of £20 to Thomas Brown Hunt now in my service as butler for and during the term of his natural life.

14. One annuity or yearly sum of £20 to William Sims now in my employ as gardener at Edgware for and during the term of his natural life.

15. One annuity or yearly sum of £20 to Frances Barton now in my employ as servant to my wife for and during the term of her natural life.

16. One annuity or yearly sum of £20 to Elizabeth Walker now in my employ as cook for and during the term of her natural life and

17. One annuity or yearly sum of £20 to Elizabeth Horton also now in my employ as housemaid for and during the term of her natural life.

And I do hereby direct that the said several and respective annuities shall be paid by four equal quarterly payments on 25 March, 24 June, 29 September and 25 December in every year and that the first payment thereof respectively shall be made on such of the said days as shall first happen after my decease.

I give and bequeath the sum of £2,000 sterling apiece to such of my nephews and nieces, the sons and daughters of my said sisters and my late brother, William Day, as may be living at the decease of my said dear wife to become vested in and be paid to such of them as shall have attained the age of twenty-one years at the decease of my said dear wife immediately on her decease and to become vested in and be paid to such of them as shall be under that age at the decease of my said wife when and if they shall respectively attain that age but without any interest in the meantime.

And I declare it to be my express will and meaning and do direct that all and every the aforesaid legacies and annuities respectively as well as any legacies (except legacies to charities) and annuities which may hereafter be given by any Codicil or Codicils shall be paid and payable to the said several and respective legatees and annuitants free and clear from the legacy duties payable to Government in respect thereof.

And that all such legacies shall be paid by my Executors out of and from my real Estates or the monies to arise by sale thereof and such part of my personal estate as shall not by any Codicil or Codicils hereto or given for charitable purposes.

And with respect to such legacies and annuities as are hereinbefore by me given to females, it is my positive, express will and meaning that the same shall not be in any wise or in any manner or upon any account or pretence whatsoever subject or liable to the power, control, intermeddling debts, engagements or encumbrances of any husband or husbands to whom they or any of them respectively are, is or shall or may at any time or times be married but shall at all times be and remain as a provision for them for their respective sole and separate use and benefit and shall for that purpose be paid into their respective proper hands or to such person or persons (other than their husbands) as they respectively by writing under their respective proper hands notwithstanding any coverture shall from time to time after the same shall have become due and payable but not by way of a charge or anticipation direct or appoint to receive the same and for which their receipts signed with their respective proper hands or the receipts of such persons as they shall respectively from time to time in manner aforesaid direct or appoint to receive the same shall notwithstanding any Coverture be good and in sufficient discharges.

And I hereby authorise and empower my said Executors to set apart and appropriate such part of my personal estate (not given by any Codicil or Codicils for charitable purposes), or of the monies to arise by the sale of my freehold, copyhold and leasehold estates hereinafter mentioned as they may think proper, to answer the payment of all or any of the said several annuities.

And I direct that as the said several annuities shall respectively cease and determine the monies, funds and securities if any so respectively set apart for the payment thereof shall sink into and form part of my residuary personal Estate and be applied and disposed of accordingly.

And until such appropriation shall be made, the said annuities shall be paid out of my general personal estate and the monies arising by sale aforesaid or the interest thereof and the rents and profits of such my freehold, copyhold and leasehold estates as shall from time to time remain unsold but that the same freehold, copyhold and leasehold estates and the respective sales thereof and the respective purchases thereof shall be and be considered as absolutely discharged from the payments of all the said annuities and every part thereof respectively.

I give and devise all my freehold, copyhold and leasehold estates whatsoever and wheresoever, except such as are or maybe vested in me as a trustee or by way of security, and all my estate and interest therein and all my stocks, funds, securities, monies, goods, chattels and personal estate and effects whatsoever and wheresoever not hereinbefore by me disposed of subject nevertheless as aforesaid, together with my stock in trade and the capital employed in business and the debts owing to me in trade or business, carts, horses, implements and utensils of any kind, and the Goodwill of my Trade and Business, unto and to the use of the said William Underwood, William Croft and Pinder Simpson, their heirs, executors, administrators and assigns according to the nature and quality thereof respectively upon trust that they the said William Underwood, William Croft and Pinder Simpson and the survivor of them and the heirs, executors, administrators and assigns of such survivor do and shall at such time or times as they or he shall think proper make sale and absolutely dispose of my said freehold, copyhold and leasehold estates and such parts of my personal estate as shall be valuable either by public auction or private contract and such lot or lots as they or he shall think proper (with full power and authority to buy in the same or any part thereof at any auction or resell the same without being accountable or answerable for any loss by any such resale) and remit and get in and receive such parts of my personal estate as shall not be valuable but with full power to retain any annuities, stocks or funds and also any determinable annuities belonging or secured to me at my decease and also to retain any part of my said freehold, copyhold and leasehold estates without selling the same for such term or terms of years, period or periods as they or he may think proper without being answerable for any loss occasioned thereby or being accountable for so doing or being compellable to sell the same.

And also that they the said William Underwood, William Croft and Pinder Simpson (their heirs, executors, administrators and assigns and the survivors and survivor of them and the heirs, executors, administrators and assigns of such survivor), do and shall at such time or times as he or they shall think proper and in the way that to them or him shall seem the most advantageous, sell and dispose of the Goodwill of my said Trade or Business for such price in ready money or on Credit or by way of Annuity for any term or terms of years as they or he may think fit and reasonable having the precise mode of disposing of my said business and premises entirely to the discretion of my said trustees or trustee for the time being do and shall lay out and invest all the monies to arise and be received from such sales as aforesaid and to be collected, got in and received as aforesaid in their or his names or name in or upon real or government securities or in some or one of the public stocks or funds and do and shall stand possessed thereof as well as of any annuity or annuities for which the Goodwill of my said Trade or Business shall be sold upon trust to pay, assign and transfer the same unto, between and amongst all and every the children of my said daughter Caroline Claggert (if there shall be more than one) in equal parts and proportions share and share alike.

And if there shall be but one such child then the whole to one such child, the portion or portions of such child or children to be paid, assigned and transferred to him, her or them respectively at his or her age or their respective ages of 21 years.

And upon further trust that my said trustees or trustee for the time being do and shall during the minority of any such child or children of my said daughter, pay, apply and dispose of any portion of the dividends, interest or annual proceeds of the said trust monies, funds and securities or such part or parts and do much thereof as they or he in their or his discretion shall think fit for and towards the maintenance, education, clothing and bringing up of all and every such child or children of her my said daughter until his, her or their share or shares of and in the same trust monies, funds and securities shall become payable, assignable and transferrable and in proportion to their respective shares and interest or presumptive or expectant shares and interest therein without any reference to the ability or inability of the parents or parent of such child or children to maintain and educate such child or children and shall and do accumulate the residue with the part or share of the fund from which such accumulation shall have proceeded and the same shall go therewith and as an addition thereto according to this my Will.

But nevertheless my Will and meaning is that it shall and may be lawful to and for my said trustees or trustee for the time being to pay, apply and dispose of all or any part or parts of the accumulations belonging or presumptively belonging to such child or children respectively in increase if his, her or their maintenance, education and bringing up in the next or any other succeeding year or years if they, my said trustees or trustee, shall so think proper provided always and my will is that it shall and may be lawful to and for my said trustees or trustee to transfer, apply and dispose of any part of the said trust monies, funds and securities unto or for the benefit of all and every or any of the children of my said daughter not exceeding the sum of £1,000 of lawful money for any one child as part of his, her or their portion or portions for the placing out in the world or providing employments for or otherwise preferring or advancing such child or children respectively in marriage or otherwise notwithstanding his, her or their portions or portion shall not then have become payable, assignable or transferrable or a vested interest or vested interests under or by virtue of this my Will.

Provided also and my will further is that if any such child or children of my said daughter shall depart this life before he, she or they shall attain his or her age or their respective ages of twenty-one years, then the part or share in part or shares of him, her or them so dying of and in the said trust monies, funds and securities so much thereof as may not have been sooner advanced as aforesaid shall go and accrue to the survivors and survivor or others or other of such children and shall be divided between and amongst them all (if more than one) in equal parts and proportions share and share alike and the same shall be considered as a vested interest or vested interests and shall be paid, assigned and transferred at such ages, days and times as his, hers or their original portion or portions shall become vested and payable, assignable and transferrable and in case of the death of any other or others of the said children before such accruing part or share or parts or shares shall become vested and payable, assignable and transferrable as aforesaid.

Then every such accruing or surviving part or share shall again be subject and liable to such further right chance contingency or condition of accruer of survivorship to and amongst the survivors and survivor or others or other of the said children as hereinbefore is declared touching his, her or their portion or portions.

Provided further that, if there shall be no child of my said daughter or there being such child or children and all of them shall happen to die under the age of twenty-one years, then and in such case, my will is and I direct that my own trustees (and the survivor of them and the executors and administrators of such survivor) shall and do stand possessed of the said trust monies, funds and securities and promises (or so much thereof as shall not have been advanced as aforesaid and the accumulations if any arising therefrom) In trust for all such of the persons mentioned in this my Will as annuitants and being my relations as shall be living at the decease and such failure of children of my said daughter as aforesaid in equal parts and proportions share and share alike to take per Capita and not *per stirpes.*

Provided always and I do hereby declare my will to be that if at my decease there shall be no child of my said daughter living or there being any such child or children then living or born afterwards all such children shall die without having attained a vested interest or vested interests in the said trust monies, funds and securities then and in such case and during such period or periods not exceeding twenty-one years from my decease as there shall no child living of my said daughter, my said trustee or trustees for the time being shall accumulate all the surplus income arising from such trust monies, funds and securities and which shall not be wanted for some or all of the purposes aforesaid and add the same to the fund from which such accumulations upon such and the same trusts as the funds from whence such accumulations shall have proceeded shall from time to time be subject.

And (from and after the expiration of the said term of twenty-one years during the then residue of the life of my said daughter or such part thereof during which there shall be no child living of my said daughter) do and shall pay such surplus amount and the amount arising from such accumulations as aforesaid to my said daughter for her own sole and separate use and benefit in such and the same manner in all respects as the annuity of £3,000 hereinbefore given to her for her life is hereinbefore made payable.

And I do hereby direct that the rents, issues and profits of my said freehold, copyhold and leasehold estates and the dividends, interest and annual proceeds of my residuary personal estate or such parts thereof as shall from time to time remain unsold or outstanding until the same shall be sold and got in shall be paid, applied and disposed of in such and the same manner as the dividends, interest and annual proceeds of the monies arising by sale thereof and to be collected and received therefrom and of the stocks, funds and securities in or upon which the same are hereinbefore directed to be invested would be payable and applicable in case the same were actually sold, collected and got in and the monies arising therefrom were invested as aforesaid.

And I do also declare and direct that the receipt and receipts of my said trustees and the survivors and survivor of them and the heirs, executors and administrators of such survivor for any money to be paid to them or him under and by virtue of this my Will or the trusts thereof shall be a good and sufficient discharge and good and sufficient discharges to all and every person and persons whomsoever for and to whom such receipt and receipts shall be given and to his, her and their respective heirs, executors and administrators for so much money as in and by such receipt and receipts shall be acknowledged or expressed to be or to have been received and such person or persons shall not afterwards be obliged to see to the application nor be answerable or accountable for any loss, misapplication or non-application of such money or any part thereof and it is also my will and meaning that my said trustees or trustee for the time being may make such insurances on my said real and personal estate or any part thereof and on any life or lives wherein I have or may have any annuity or annuities payable or depending as they or he may think proper and that it shall be lawful for them or him to compound for any debts owing to me at my decease and to liquidate all unsettled accounts in such manner as they or he may think proper and to do all other acts whatsoever relative to my said estates and affairs which they or he may think necessary or advisable for or with a view to the due execution of this my Will it being my intention that they my said trustees and executors shall be at liberty to act as I can or could do (if living) in any and every circumstance being satisfied that they ought to have the fullest powers and indemnity that I can give them on all occasions.

And I do hereby authorise and empower my said trustees and trustee for the time being from time to time as often as they or he shall think proper to alter and change the securities and funds on which all or any of the trust monies aforesaid shall be placed out and invested and any securities and funds belonging to me at my decease and from time to time as often as they shall think fit again to place out the monies arising from such alteration and change in or upon such funds and securities as aforesaid and so from time to time as often as they shall think proper.

And I do hereby declare it to be my will that in case the said William Underwood, William Croft and Pinder Simpson or any of them or any future trustee or trustees to be appointed as hereinafter is mentioned shall die or desire to be discharged of or from the trusts hereby in them reposed then and in every such case it shall and may be lawful to and for the surviving or acting or continuing trustees or trustee for the time being or the executors or administrators of the last surviving or continuing trustee for the time being at any time or times before the trusts aforesaid shall be fully executed, performed or discharged by any writing or writings under their or his hands or seals or hand and seal to nominate, substitute and appoint any other person or persons to be a trustee or trustees upon the trusts aforesaid and for that purpose the trustees or trustee for the time being or the representative of the last surviving or continuing trustee shall make, do and execute all proper acts, covenants, transfers, assignments and assurances in the Law so as legally and effectively to invest the said trust estates, monies, securities, funds and premises in such new or other trustee or trustees only or jointly with such continuing trustee or trustees as the case shall require upon the same trusts and for the same purposes as are hereinbefore declared of and concerning the same trust estates, monies, securities, funds and premises respectively and which shall be then subsisting undetermined and capable of taking effect and then and in such case all and every such new trustees and trustee shall and may in all things act and assist in the management and carrying on and execution of the same trusts to all intents, efforts, constructions and purposes whatsoever and shall have and be vested with such and the same powers and authorities as if he or they had been originally hereby nominated and appointed trustees or a trustee for the purposes aforesaid and my will further is and I do hereby expressly declare and direct that the said William Underwood, William Croft and Pinder Simpson and such trustees as may be appointed aforesaid and each and every of them, their and each of their heirs, executors and administrators shall be charged and chargeable only with and for so much of my estate and effects as they each and every of them shall respectively actually receive or shall come to his or their respective hands by virtue of or under this my Will and the trusts aforesaid and that no one or more of them shall be answerable or accountable for the others or other of them nor for the acts, receipts, neglects or defaults of the others or other of them (the joining in receipts for conformity merely notwithstanding) but each of them for his own acts, receipts, neglects and defaults only nor shall they any or other of them be answerable or accountable for any misconduct of any person or persons employed in the rounding up of my said Trade and Business nor for any bad debts, losses or casualties whatsoever arising or which may happen thereto nor for any Broker, Banker, Rider or other person or persons whomsoever with whom or with whose hands any part of my estate shall or may be deposited or lodged for safe custody or who shall or may be employed to act in my Affairs or Concerns or the Affairs and Concerns of my estate or otherwise in the execution of this my Will or any of the trusts thereof nor for the insufficiency or deficiency of any securities, stocks or funds in or upon which any part of my estate shall or may in pursuance of this my Will be placed out and invested nor for any other loss, misfortune or damage whatsoever which shall or may happen or come to my estate or any part thereof or in the execution of this my Will or any of the trusts thereof or in relation thereof except and unless the same shall happen by or through his or their respective will or neglect or default and also that they the said trustees and each and every of them and their and each and every of their heirs, executors and administrators shall and may by and out of my estate coming to their hands by virtue of this my Will and the trusts thereof retain and reimburse to and for himself and themselves respectively and also allow to his co-trustee and co-trustees all loss, costs, charges, damages and expenses whatsoever which he or she or any of them shall or may respectively suffer, sustain, expend, disburse, be at or put unto or which shall or may be to him, them or any of them occasioned for or on account or by reason or by means or in the execution of this my Will and the trusts thereof or otherwise howsoever relating thereto.

And I do hereby give and devise all such estates and hereditaments Term and Terms of years as is or are or shall be vested in me as a Trustee expressly or by implication or by way of mortgage or for securing any sum or sums of money or annuity or annuities whatsoever unto the said William Underwood, William Croft and Pinder Simpson, their heirs executors, administrators and assigns respectively for all my estate and interest therein as to such trust estates upon trust for the persons beneficially entitled thereto and as to the estates vested in me by way of mortgage or security to enable them the better to perform and carry into execution the trusts and purposes of this my Will.

And lastly I do hereby revoke, annul and make void all former and other Wills and testamentary dispositions by me made and do declare this to be my last Will and Testament.

In witness whereof I the said Charles Day, the Testator, have to this my last Will and Testament contained in ten sheets of paper all affixed together with my seal set, my hand and seal (that is to say) to first nine sheets thereof my hand and to this the tenth and last sheet my hand and seal this 1 May 1834 – *Charles Day* – Signed, Sealed, published and declared by the above named Charles Day, the Testator, as and for his last Will and Testament in the presence of us who in his presence at his request and in the presence of each other subscribe our names as witnesses hereto the whole thereof having on account of the Testator's loss of sight been carefully and audibly read over to him in our presence.

John Shaw, 81 Harley Street, Gentleman;
Joseph Jopling, 31 Somerset Street, Architect;
William Simpson, 9 Old Burlington Street, Gentleman.

This is a codicil to be added to and taken as part of the last Will and Testament of me *Charles Day* of Harley House, Regent's Park, in the County of Middlesex, Esquire, which Will bears even date herewith.

I direct that the legacies given by this my codicil and which may be given by any future codicil or codicils for charitable purposes shall be paid free of Legacy Duty out of such part of my personal estate as may by Law be given and bequeathed for charitable purposes and that the Legacy Duty payable in respect of all such legacies to charities shall be paid out of the same fund and that all such legacies for charitable purposes and the Legacy Duty for the same shall have a priority as to such part of my personal estate as last mentioned to all other legacies, annuities and bequests given by my Will or to be given by any codicil or codicils and also to the payment of all my debts which by my Will I have charged on the other parts of my personal estate and also on my real estates.

Whereas I have lately bargained, sold and conveyed a piece of land or ground at Edgware in the County of Middlesex with certain messuages or rooms therein erected unto and to the use of Nicholas Fiott, George Mutter, Richard Looseley and William Smith Tootell their heirs and assigns upon trust to permit the same to be occupied as an Almshouse or Almhouses by poor Men or Women to be nominated as therein mentioned and under certain regulations and with certain powers therein mentioned and with power from time to time to appoint new trustees thereof but I have not hitherto endowed the same and which conveyance is enrolled in Chancery or intended so to be.

Now in case I shall live until the said conveyance shall be effectual for the purposes therein mentioned, I do hereby direct that William Underwood, William Croft and Pinder Simpson the Executors named in my said will do and shall as soon as convenient after my decease purchase or transfer in or into the names of the said Nicholas Fiott, George Mutter, Richard Looseley and William Smith Tootell or of such other persons as shall be trustees of the said Almshouse or Almshouses at my decease such a sum of money partly in the three percent Consolidated and partly in the three percent Reduced Bank Annuities (and in equal proportions) as will on the dividends thereof produce the clear annual sum of £100.

And my will is that the trustee or trustees for the time being of the said Bank Annuities shall out of the dividends thereof in the first place pay and retain all costs, charges and expenses attending the execution of the trusts and powers of the before mentioned conveyance including the expense attending the appointment of new trustees and also of the trusts and powers hereby reposed in them and do and shall in the next place thereout keep the said Almshouse or Almshouses in repair and so and shall from time to time distribute and pay the residue of such dividends by weekly payments amongst the occupiers for the time being of the said Almshouse or Almshouses.

And I hereby direct that all trusts, powers and authorities contained in the said conveyance including the power of appointing new trustees shall be applicable so far as circumstances shall permit to the said Bank Annuities so directed to be purchased or transferred as aforesaid.

And until such purchase or transfer of such Bank Annuities shall have been made and until some one dividend on one of the sums of bank Annuities shall have become payable, I direct that my Executors shall pay four shillings a week to each of the said Almshouse or Almshouses and shall make the first of such weekly payments on the first Friday that shall happen after my decease.

And I give and bequeath unto the said William Underwood, William Croft and Pinder Simpson the sum of £100,000 upon trust with all convenient speed after my decease to lay out and invest the same in their names in the purchase of three percent consolidated or three percent reduced bank annuities or both and to stand possessed thereof upon the trusts and to and for the intents and purposes hereinafter mentioned that is to say upon trust by and out of the dividends thereof from time to time and at all times for ever to pay and discharge all costs, charges and expenses attending the execution of the trusts hereby in them reposed and the Salary and Allowances hereinafter directed to be paid and made to the Clerk and Treasurer of the Trustees for the time being and to apply the residue of such dividends in annual sums (not being less the £10 nor more than £20 for any one person) either half-yearly, quarterly or oftener to and amongst such number of poor Blind Men and Women as my trustees or trustee for the time being may deem to be objects of Charitable consideration and may nominate or appoint to receive the same.

And I direct that the Charitable Institution so to be established shall be styled 'The Blind Man's Friend' and I direct that the Nomination of such objects of the Charity and the removal of them from a participation in the benefits of the said Charity shall be left entirely to my trustees or trustee for the time being but in order to relieve my trustees as far as may be from trouble, I direct that they shall appoint some fit person from time to time (with power to remove him from time to time for any just cause) to be their Clerk and Treasurer.

And I request that John Simpson, the oldest son of the said

Pinder Simpson, may be the first Clerk and Treasurer and I desire that not less than £100 per annum be allowed to such Clerk and Treasurer for his Salary and that in case he shall allow the Business of the said Charity to be conducted at his house or office. I desire that a further sum of £200 be allowed to such Clerk and Treasurer as Compensation for the use of such house or office for the purpose aforesaid and for Coals, Candles, Stationary and other incidental expenses.

And I request that the trustees for the time being will meet three times or oftener every year at the House or Office of the Clerk and Treasurer to examine the accounts of the said Charity and to derive on Applications from Candidates for admittance to the Benefit of the said Charity and for other purposes.

And my will is that the power of appointing new trustees contained in my said Will and the clauses for their Indemnity and Reimbursement shall be applicable to them in their character of trustees of the said Charity to be called 'The Blind Man's Friend' in such and the same manner as if they were here repeated. But it is my express wish that every Warranty by the Oath or Resignation of a trustee of the said Charity may be filled up with as little delay as possible.

In witness whereof I have to this writing (which I hereby declare to be a codicil to my said Will) contained in three sheets of paper all affixed together with my seal set my hand and seal (that is to say) to the first two sheets hereof my hand and to this third and last sheet my hand seal this 1 May 1834 – *Charles Day* – Signed, sealed, published and declared by the above named Charles Day, the Testator, as and for a codicil to his last Will and Testament in the presence of us who in his presence at his request and in the presence of each other subscribe our names as witnesses hereto, the whole thereof, having on account of the Testator's loss of sight been carefully and audibly read over to him in our presence.

John Shaw, 81 Harley Street, Gentleman;
Joseph Jopling, 31 Somerset Street, Architect;
William Simpson, 9 Old Burlington Street, Gentleman.

This is a codicil to be taken as part of my last Will and Testament.

Whereas since the date and of execution of my Will I have purchased by auction the Manor Cottage and thirty acres of land with the appurtenances within the parish of Caterham in the county of Surrey, now I do hereby give, devise and bequeath the same and every part thereof onto the same persons upon the same trusts and for the same ends, intents and purposes as I mentioned and expressed with respect to my other estate at Caterham in my said Will.

In addition to the legacies given by my said Will, I give to each of my sisters and sisters-in-law (namely Mrs Day's sister and of the widow of my deceased brother William Day) £100 a year for their several lives.

Also, to each of the servants named or referred to by my said Will double the legacies to each of them thereby given in lieu and instead of such said legacies.

I confirm my said Will in all other respects and declare this to be a codicil thereto. In witness where of I have hereunto set my hand and seal 2 September 1836.

The mark of Charles Day
Harley House, Middlesex

Signed, sealed, published and declared by the said Testator, Charles Day, as and for a codicil to his Will in the presence of us.

William Lawrence, Surgeon, Whitehall Place
William Foote, Surgeon, Edgware
George Beaman, Surgeon, King St., Covent Garden

(Endorsed)

Codicil to the Will of Charles Day Esq of Harley House within the Parish of Marylebone, Middlesex.
Dated 2nd Sept 1836

This is a codicil to be added to and taken as part of the last Will and Testament of Charles Day of Harley House, Regent's Park, in the County of Middlesex, Esquire, which Will bears the date 1 May 1834.

I give the following annuities in addition to those given by my said Will and which I direct to be paid free of Legacy Duty in the same manner as I have directed with respect to the legacies given in my said Will (that is to say):

To each of the sons and daughters of my mother's brothers and sisters (excepting Samuel Virgo now or later Brighton) as may be alive at my decease one annuity or yearly sum of £20 for and during the terms of those respective natural lives.

In all other respects, I ratify and confirm my said Will.

In witness whereof I have to this writing which I hereby declare to be a codicil to my said Will set my hand and seal this 3 September 1836.

The mark of Charles Day

Signed, sealed, published and declared
by the above named Charles Day, the
Testator, as and for a Codicil to his last
Will and Testament in the presence of us
who in his presence at his request and in
the presence of each other subscribed
our names as witnesses hereof the whole
thereof having on account of the Testator's

loss of sight been carefully and audibly
read over to him in our presence.

Thos. Ans. Hewson, Surgeon, 6 Woburn Place, Russell Square
F Dufaur, Solicitor, 23 Queen Anne Street, Cavendish Square
John Shaw, Solicitor, 5 Berners Street

(No Endorsement)

I Charles Day of Edgware and Harley House being of sound mind so desire that the three *post obit* bonds for £5,000 each which will be presented at my decease may be doubled, that is made £10,000 each and that the same may be invested for the benefit of my three natural sons by my executors as trustees according to their discretion and this shall be their authority.

As Witness my X mark
Charles Day

Signed, sealed and delivered as my act and deed this 10th day of September 1836 in the presence of us and signed by us in the presence of each other.

William Foote, Surgeon, Edgware
Mary Day, Chelsea
Thomas Hunt, Servant to Charles Day Esq

(No Endorsement)

Sources, notes and references

From the outset, I carried out extensive research on my family using the websites Ancestry and FindMyPast. This was partially successful but begged many questions about the stories behind the people involved. I also conducted extensive research on the Internet, making special use of various Wikipedia articles and checking their references.

In order to gain more information on the Peake family from Stafford, I made several visits to the County Record Office and the William Salt Library in Stafford and examined numerous original documents including parish registers, newspapers, Wills and titles.

After making the major breakthrough on Ancestry concerning the Will of Charles Day, I was led to the work of Robert Ward and his book *Wealth and Notability – the Lockwood, Day and Metcalfe Families of Yorkshire and London* which he published in 2014, only a year before my discovery and containing a wealth of information about the Day family.

Discussions and very helpful meetings with Robert took me to the National Archives at Kew where I obtained the bulk of my material, which Robert had not been able to research. In particular, I found the document *Dufaur v Croft and Others – Process brought on 25 Feb 1839 – P.C. 53*. I also discovered a vast amount of extra information, being the Court of Chancery papers of the Day case covering the period from 1838 to 1879. These were randomly kept in numerous boxes, referenced but unresearched, and included the financial accounts of the Day Trust, as it became, and the business of Day and Martin. It would take more than a lifetime to research all these documents, but I have cherry-picked as much as possible given the limited time available.

Further sources included original documents in the archives of the Clothworkers' Company in the City of London, the London Metropolitan Archive, the Guildhall Library, the City of Westminster Libraries, the Kensington and Chelsea Library, the registers of the Roman Catholic Churches of St Thomas of Canterbury and the Servite Fathers in Fulham and the early Minute Books of 'Mr Day's Almshouses' and 'The Blind Man's Friend'.

I have combed through newspaper archives and have found much useful reporting on the Chancery case, on Day's litigation against counterfeiters and on the affairs of Day's colourful son-in-law Horatio Clagett.

Another useful source for the introduction to the Diary section of the book was a handwritten document, compiled by William Tootall of Edgware, entitled *A Brief Sketch of the Town of Edgware, Middlesex. In two Parts. Collected from various Writers, and continued, by A Resident . . . 1817* and kept in the Hendon Library (Barnet Libraries' Archives and Local Studies Centre).

I. Prologue

Although Storey, Tillotson and Easson state that Day's estate was 'over £100,000', this transpires to be a very considerable underestimate, the true figure being nearer £450,000, or £40-£50 million in 21st century values.

II. Life

Chapter 1

The parish records of the West Riding of Yorkshire have been well preserved revealing much useful information concerning baptisms, marriages and burials of the Day family. In addition, there are good records of Apprentices being engaged by Masters in various trades including joinery. Nostell Priory is now under the auspices of the National Trust who supply much useful information about the stately home. In the descriptions of hair-dressers' shops in eighteenth century Covent Garden and the possible connection with the Turners, a principle source was *The Extraordinary Life and Momentous Times of J. M. W. Turner* by Franny Moyle (Penguin Paperback, 2017). The main source of the story describing how Martin obtained the blacking recipe is the article 'Shining Characters' which appeared first in *Bell's Life in London* on 13 November 1836, soon after Charles Day's death, and was repeated in many publications thereafter, as far afield as *The Colonial Times*, Hobart, Tasmania on Tuesday 19 May 1846.

Chapter 2

Sources continue to be all the usual ones associated with family history research, in particular the *Westminster, London, England, Church of England Marriages and Banns, 1754-1935*, the *UK, Register of Duties Paid for Apprentices' Indentures, 1710-1811* and the *1784 Trade Directory for Stone, Staffordshire*. In addition, there was the *Abstracts of Nottinghamshire Marriage Licences Vol II*, ed Blagg and Wadsworth 1935. Wills recorded by the Prerogative Court of Canterbury provided some useful information about Samuel Brookes. Finally, Alison Weir's *Britain's Royal Families – The Complete Genealogy* pp302-304 (pub. Vintage 2008) is an invaluable resource when dealing with all issue, legitimate or illegitimate, in the history of the Royal Family. John Weston's background in Day and Martin is given in an affidavit he made to the PCC dated 7 December 1838 which I found in the National Archives.

Chapter 3

Newspaper reports were important sources for this chapter. Another key source for the original intellectual property case was *Landmark Cases in Intellectual Property Law* (Jose Bellido, ed), Ch 4: Lionel Bentley – Day v. Day, Day and Martin (1816). Bentley's article gives a very detailed account of the case. I was also given fascinating information on Lord Eldon by James McNeill KC who referred me to Twiss, H. (1844) *The public and private life of Lord Eldon*, vol III, p. 361-363, London, John Murray.

Chapter 4

In the search for a country estate, Caterham featured strongly but, with the convenience of Edgware, the latter won the contest. Nevertheless, Caterham was seen by Pinder Simpson as a good investment and Charles Day bought many properties there through the 1820s. This is described in detail in a later chapter. The description of Edgware Place was found in a document in the National Archives. All of Day's assets had to be inventoried by the Court of Chancery for the administration of the estate. All trace of Edgware Place has gone and the area now forms part of suburban Edgware. The last remaining building was the Blacking Bottle Lodge which survived into the twentieth-century, for which there is photographic evidence.

Chapter 5

The main sources were from the County Records Office in Stafford. I found the titles of The Goat Inn which revealed much about the early Peakes. The parish and other records of Staffordshire are some of the best kept historically in the UK and have been very revealing. I also consulted newspaper records in the William Salt Library. Other useful sources were *The Inns and Alehouses of Stafford – Through the South Gate* by John Connor (Matador, 2013) and the *Stafford Street Series* produced privately by local historian Roy Lewis. In fact, I visited Roy Lewis at his Stafford home and he proved to be a mine of useful information. In addition, I had helpful correspondence with Jacob Simon of the National Portrait Gallery and Jayne Shrimpton concerning the portrait of Charles Day, the latter giving a useful date estimate based on the clothes worn. The fact that Day built Harley House himself and the costs and dating of the project were obtained from *London Grand Junction Railway Bill: Minutes of Evidence taken before the Lords Committees*, p271.

Chapter 6

Information on the Portman Estate was gleaned from various internet articles. The Land Tax records were the source of discovering 'John Price' living in Earl Street. Research in the Guildhall Library revealed original copies of The Royal Blue Book and details of the Peakes/Prices living at 16 Seymour Place. On a visit to the City of Westminster Library, an 1831 census of Marylebone was found showing the family at 16 Seymour Place. The various baptisms of the Price boys were found in the registers and daybooks of St Marylebone Church and St Mary's Church, Bryanston Square. The burial of John Price on 29 November 1831 was found in the register of St George's, Hanover Square. The details of the founding of the Almshouse Charity and the first residents are printed in the *Deed establishing the Almshouse Charity of Charles Day Esq at Edgware* of which I have been given an original copy.

Chapter 7

The history of the Clagett family was obtained from *The Bowies and Their Kindred – A Genealogical and Biographical History* – Walter Worthington Bowie (Cromwell Bros. 1899), pp 392-421, being a very detailed account of the early settling families of Maryland. On Horatio's colourful life before his marriage, I relied on *The Satirist (or The Censor of the Times)*: 1 May 1831 and Robert Ward's excellent book (ibid.) Lucia Elizabeth Vestris (*née* Elizabetta Lucia Bartolozzi; 3 March 1797 – 8 August 1856), an English actress and a contralto opera singer, appearing in works by, among others, Mozart and Rossini, is described in *John Orlando Parry: The Poster Man*. Much of the background of the Dufaurs was taken from newspaper extracts and evidence given by Day's relations as stated in *Croft v Day and Others, PC53*. Again, Alison Weir's book (ibid.) was the source about the issue of the brothers George IV and William IV.

Chapter 8

Much of the material in this chapter is taken from the document in the National Archives *Dufaur v Croft and Others – Process P.C.53*, including the previous versions of Charles Day's Will that preceded the final 1834 version. The archives of University College School (UCS), which relocated to Hampstead in 1907, showed the Price boys as early pupils. The school started as a junior department of the London University, later University College. A similar process was taking place at King's College, London, which founded its own Kings College School (KCS) in 1829, relocating to Wimbledon in 1897. Coincidentally, one of Alfred Price's sons (my grandfather) was to become the Vice-Master of KCS in the twentieth-century, my father, my brother and I going on to be pupils there. Further material was gathered from various internet articles.

III. Death
The diary of William Foote

All of the material for this section has been taken from the document in the National Archives *Dufaur v Croft and Others – Process*

P.C.53. The diary itself does not exist. It is merely a device for telling the story of the last two months of Charles Day's life as portrayed in the above document. The document contains, in fairly turgid, mid-nineteenth-century form, the evidence of thirty witnesses presented to the Prerogative Court of Canterbury (PCC) in written form over the period from November 1836 (just after Day's death on 26 October 1836) to the judgement pronounced on 29 June 1838. These witnesses are listed as *Dramatis Personae*. The judgement was duly appealed by Frederick Dufaur to the Privy Council. The document itself is this actual appeal, but presenting all the evidence that was given to the PCC.

William Foote certainly did exist as commemorated on the plaque still to be seen in the St Margaret's Church, Edgware. He was one of the witnesses giving evidence to the PCC. His son, the Rev John Andrews Foote and the writer of the diary's preface, also existed and is recorded in the 1901 census as a retired clergyman living with his sister at 25 Blomfield Road, London, W9. The interesting background to the Foote family was obtained from various genealogical and other internet websites.

The diary's Introduction relies heavily on material gained from Tootell: *A Brief Sketch of the Town of Edgware, Middlesex. In two Parts. Collected from various Writers, and continued, by A Resident . . . 1817* as already mentioned. This was never published but remains in handwritten form and kept in Hendon Library (ibid.).

Dufaur v Croft and Others – Process P.C.53 also contains all of the dictation that was taken down by various witnesses as instructed to do so at the time by Charles Day. Much of this is completely unintelligible but merely demonstrates the deterioration of Day's mental state over the two-month period.

IV. Aftermath

Chapter 1

Details of the post mortem are given by George Beaman in his evidence to the Prerogative Court of Canterbury. The other details of the events leading up to the funeral and the start of the PCC case are taken from John Simpson's evidence to the PCC. The burial of Charles Day's remains is recorded in the Edgware parish registers. Newspaper articles of the court proceedings have also been quoted.

Chapter 2

The early history of the Dufaur family and Frederick Dufaur's descendants is taken from various sources including John's Notable Australians 1906 (describing Frederick Dufaur's son, Eccleston Dufaur), 'Le Grand dictionnaire historique…', Moreri and Goujet (1732) and various internet articles. Details of Frederick Dufaur's legal training were taken from the *Articles of Clerkship* in the National Archives (CP5/169). Details of Charles Dickens's residence at Furnival's are referred to in *Mr and Mrs Charles Dickens Entertain at Home,* (Helen Cox, Pergamon, 1970) and David Parker: 'Dickens, the Inns of Court and the Inns of Chancery', *The Literary London Journal* (March 2010). Otherwise all sources in this chapter are newspaper and internet articles.

Chapter 3

Susannah Peake's affidavit and Williams' subsequent statement of facts are in the National Archives (C124/368). The details of Henry Price's Cambridge career are taken from *Biographical History of Gonville and Caius College 1349-1897*, p259 (CUP Archive). Turville in Buckinghamshire was to become famous 150 years later as the location used for the BBC comedy series *The Vicar of Dibley*. The paintings and drawings stated are part of the collection still retained within the Price family.

Chapter 4

The details of the Robert Barbrook legacy are given in C124/371 at the National Archives. The initial minutes of the almshouse charity are given in *Mr Day's Almshouses: Trustees Minute Book* now held at the London Metropolitan Archive. The initial minutes of 'The Blind Man's Friend' charity are given in *'The Blind Man's Friend' Minute Book April 1842 to July 1899* kept by the Worshipful Company of Clothworkers archive at Clothworkers' Hall in the City of London. Samuel Scott's appointment and duties are described in *The Law Journal Report for the year 1840* at p287. John Weston's affidavit is also in the National Archives at C32/74 with his death being recorded in the accounts book at J32/74. The Trust Accounts for the year ended 15 May 1854 are at C124/341. There are numerous boxes of unresearched papers in the National Archives, some of the references being C124/348, C32/74, C124/368, C124/371, C124/374, C124/341, C124/369, C101/4923/5449/5716,

C30/925. There is no knowing at this stage what information these might reveal. They do not seem to be in any logical order and an army of researchers would be required to unearth the secrets contained in these boxes.

Chapter 5

All of the information in this chapter was gained from various documents discovered in the National Archives, as mentioned above.

Chapter 6

Rebecca Day's death notice appeared in various newspapers on 2 December 1843, the day after the notice of the petition relating to her son-in-law's debts. Concerning the newspaper report that Caroline Day would have been receiving £25,000 per year (roughly £2.5m in today's money), there is no evidence that this was ever the case. Previous versions of Charles Day's Will are all included in the court papers PC53 and there is no reference whatsoever of the daughter's annuity ever being intended to be £25,000. The Abbey Road household is clearly described in the 1861 and 1871 censuses with the resident staff and their duties. Horatio Clagett's certification that he was of 'unsound mind' can be found in the National Archives at C211/45. All the other information in this chapter has been gleaned from newspaper articles.

James Weston Clayton is an interesting character who could probably be the subject of another book. His origins are an unsolved mystery. There is no doubt that he was John Weston's grandson, born in 1831. His baptism is clearly recorded in the St James, Westminster, parish records, being the son of James and Sarah Clayton. But there is also no doubt that his father was James, son of John, Weston. So, from where did the name Clayton come? After he purchased Day and Martin, he went on to accumulate considerable wealth, owning several ships built on the Clyde in Glasgow. His descendant Charles Atkinson has been a source of much information. By an extraordinary coincidence, during our discussions, it transpired that Charles was also a descendent of Charles Day's youngest sister Susannah, who married Joseph Lockwood.

Chapter 7

The John Forster reference to the case of Gridley can be found in *The Life of Charles Dickens:* John Forster, Volume the Second, Book Seventh, Ch 1. The copy of the Challinor pamphlet bearing Dickens's inscription is now held in the William Salt Library, Stafford (ref 170/97). For a detailed description of The Swan in Stafford, see *'The Inns and Alehouses of Stafford, Part 1'* p48 et seq: John Connor (Matador). 'A Plated Article' appeared in *Household Words* on 24 April 1852. Dickens's visit to Stafford on 2 and 3 April 1852 was reported in *The Staffordshire Advertiser* on 10 April 1852. The actual Cook v. Finney case is linked to Gridley by E T Jacques in his article 'Dickens and the Court of Chancery', *The Dickensian*, 13 January 1917, p16. Original documents are in the National Archives at C14/204/C59. The letters between Dickens and Wills can be found in *'The Letters of Charles Dickens'*, Vol 7, 1853-55 (The Pilgrim Edition), pp128-129: Ed. Storey,

Tillotson and Easson. The idea of the brick being a symbol of transformation came about from a discussion I had with Dr Julian Crowe of St Andrews University.

V. Epilogue
The Unmasking of John (or Charles) Price

The contemporary book that reveals there was a brothel in Seymour Place is *The Secret History of Georgian London:* Dan Cruikshank, Random House, 2009. I had a fascinating correspondence with Jacob Simon of the National Portrait Gallery in London about the Charles Day portrait. This confirmed who the artist was not, and that the likely painter was of the continental Biedermeier school. This merely leaves another puzzle to be solved.

Bibliography

Primary Reading

Barber, Peter, *LONDON – A History in Maps*, London, London Topographical Society / The British Library, 2012

Connor, John, *The Inns and Alehouses of Stafford, Through the South Gate*, Leicestershire, Matador, 2013

Corr, Gerard M, *Servites in London*, Newbury, The Servite Fathers, 1952

Cruickshank, Dan, *The Secret History of Georgian London*, London, Random House, 2009

ed. Fookes, Gwyneth, *Village Histories, 2. Caterham*, Caterham, The Bourne Society, 1997

Lewis, Roy, *Images of England – Around Stafford*, Stroud, The History Press, 2008

Lewis, Roy, *Stafford Past – An Illustrated History*, Chichester, Phillimore, 1997

Moyle, Franny, *The Extraordinary Life and Momentous Times of J.M.W. Turner*, London, Viking, 2016

Robinson, Jane, *In The Family Way*, London, Viking, 2015

Sanders, Andrew, *Charles Dickens's London*, London, Robert Hale, 2010

Sanders, Andrew, *Charles Dickens – Resurrectionist*, London, MacMillan, 1982

Skærved, Peter Sheppard with Janet Snowman and Frances Palmer, *John Orlando Parry: The Poster Man*, Royal Academy of Music, 2007

Summerson, John, *Georgian London*, New Haven and London, Yale University Press, 2003

Taylor, Pamela and Corden, Joanna, *Barnet, Edgware, Hadley and Totteridge – A Pictorial History*, Chichester, Phillimore, 1994

Tomalin, Claire, *Charles Dickens – A Life*, London, Viking, 2011

Ward, Robert, *Wealth and Notability – the Lockwood, Day and Metcalfe Families of Yorkshire and London*, Self-published, lulu.com, 2014

Weir, Alison, *Britain's Royal Families – The Complete Genealogy*, London, Vintage, 2008

Wilson, A N, *The Mystery of Charles Dickens*, London, Atlantic Books, 2020

Inspirational Reading

Atkinson, Richard, *Mr Atkinson's Rum Contract*, London, 4th Estate, 2020

Burnet, Graeme Macrae, *His Bloody Project*, Glasgow, Contraband, 2015

Chesterton, Fiona, *Secrets Never To Be Told*, Canterbury, The Conrad Press, 2021

Cumming, Laura, *On Chapel Sands*, London, Vintage, 2019

De Waal, Edmund, *The Hare with Amber Eyes*, London, Vintage, 2011

Freedland, Jonathan, *Jacob's Gift*, London, Hamish Hamilton, 2005

Jarvis, Stephen, *Death and Mr Pickwick*, London, Jonathan Cape, 2014

MacKenzie, Duncan, *Cappuccino and Porridge*, Stornoway, Acair, 2020

Peake, Clare, *Under a Canvas Sky*, London, Constable, 2011

Robb, Farifteh, *In the Shadow of the Shahs*, Oxford, Lion Hudson, 2020

Smith, Chris, *The Last Cambridge Spy*, Cheltenham, The History Press, 2019

Summerscale, Kate, *Mrs Robinson's Disgrace*, London, Bloomsbury, 2012

Ward, Christopher, *And the Band Played On...*, London, Hodder and Stoughton, 2011

Acknowledgements

This book has been eight years in the making, beginning (as described in the Epilogue) with the events of Palm Sunday 2015. The help and support that I have received on this journey from so many people has been huge. I am anxious to thank and acknowledge all of them but fearful that I may omit some given the expanse of time. If that is the case, I offer my apologies before I begin.

Firstly, I have to mention the truly amazing Jenny Turnbull. From the moment she advised me to research 'The Will of Charles Day', the floodgates opened, and she has followed events and continued to help avidly ever since. Without her fluke discovery, this story would never have been revealed.

This led me on to Robert Ward in Yorkshire, whose wife Joanna I now believe to be my fourth cousin, twice removed. He has since been constantly encouraging and helpful, pointing me in the direction of the National Archives and what turned out to be a vast amount of information on Charles Day and the legal implications of his Will case.

The staff at the National Archives (whose names are sadly unknown) were extremely helpful. Within ninety minutes of crossing the threshold, the key document PC53 was sitting on a table before me. Their kindness on all my subsequent visits was so gratifying. To this I should also add the staff at the Staffordshire Record Office and the William Salt Library, as well as the Guildhall Library in the City of London, the City of

Westminster Libraries, the Kensington Central Library and the London Metropolitan Archives. Hannah Dunmow and Jessica Collins, the archivists at Clothworkers' Hall, were kind in giving me access to all their relevant records as well as allowing me to see again the portrait of Charles Day. My thanks to them for giving me the excellent digital photograph of the portrait. In addition, I had valuable support from the staff at The Charles Dickens Museum, 48 Doughty Street, London, in identifying the letters that revealed Dickens's interest in the Day Will case.

Family research has been helped along by new-found and distant Peake cousins Pat Sanders (who provided the photograph of Sarah Peake 'Price', my great-great-grandmother) and Pauline Holbrook (whose doctor husband George also gave me some useful thoughts on the cheerful subject of syphilis and its transmission).

Edgware contacts and help were started by Hazel Aucken with her invaluable knowledge of Charles Day's almshouses. I soon found myself a trustee of 'The Day's and Atkinson's Almshouse Charity' and my fellow trustees and our staff have been endlessly encouraging. In particular, Lachie Munro has helped with smartening up the Day Tomb in readiness for full restoration. Local historian John O'Connell at Edgware Music has been the source of much historical background information.

Being a complete novice on Dickens and nineteenth-century literature, an early discussion with Prof Andrew Sanders gave me confidence to pursue my thoughts on the connections between Charles Day's story and the plot of *Bleak House*.

I made a fortuitous early connection with Leslie Katz (formerly a judge in the Federal Court of Australia and now retired in Winnipeg, Canada) and his paper, *Bleak House in Australian Reasons for Judgment* (2015). His most helpful guiding in the complexities of legal practice and terminology, especially that of the mid-nineteenth century, was invaluable during my transcription of PC53. For the chapter on intellectual property, I am indebted to my good friend James McNeill KC for his added insights on the topic and Lord Eldon in particular. Additionally, I had a helpful correspondence with Prof Lionel Bently who is an authority on the subject.

For the chapter on Caterham, it was wonderful to meet Dorothy Tutt of The Bourne Society whose knowledge of the area is encyclopaedic. Ray Howgego was also a great help.

Early encouragement in the project was received from Howie Firth of the Orkney Science Festival and from Hugh Pym. Howie invited me to give a talk on my detective work on Charles Day which, he kindly maintained, demonstrated good scientific research methods. I have now given the talk ten times, up and down the country, and have had tremendous assistance with readings and slide presentations from Desmond and Val Watson.

Many friends and family have been kind enough to look over my scripts since the writing process started in 2018. These include Patricia Clark, Gill Cloke, Barbara Crawford, Lara Feigel, the late Sheila MacLeod, Pam Martin, Peter Martin, Ian Price and Val Watson. Their insights, constructive criticisms and recommendations have been so useful. Andrew Lownie's advice on presenting a book proposal shone light on a task with which I was completely unfamiliar, and authors Richard Atkinson, Graeme Macrae Burnet, Fiona Chesterton, Penrose Halson, Stephen Jarvis, Duncan MacKenzie, Clare Peake, Jane Robinson and Christopher Ward have encouraged me to pursue the goal of a published book.

There are many others who have kindly offered assistance. They will know how and include Jo Van Kool, Andrew Milne-Skinner,

Prof Sally Mapstone, Rona Black, Charles Atkinson, Annabelle Holland, Prof Geoffrey Parker, Julian Crowe, James Holmes, Frith Robb and Faith Lawrence.

I cannot be too grateful to James Essinger and The Conrad Press for accepting me into their publishing family. What they offer to unknown, first-time writers cannot be overstated. Also my special thanks go to my superb and patient designer Charlotte Mouncey of Bookstyle.

I am indebted to my daughter-in-law Fiona Price for applying her wonderful calligraphic skills in drafting the family trees.

Finally, my sincerest thanks go to my three children, Catriona, Julia and Marcus (Charles Day's only descendants in their generation) for realistically keeping my feet on the ground, but principally to Andrea, my long-suffering wife, who somehow has summoned up a genuine interest in this whole matter. At first, she even helped with the transcriptions, typing my dictation of the text, as her typing skills were vastly superior to mine. However, after a while, she understandably suggested an alternative – voice recognition software – resulting in a quickening of the pace and restoration of family unity almost immediately. But she has always been there to help and encourage lovingly and to put up with my long periods of isolation at the computer. I am so fortunate.

NEIL PRICE
Edinburgh, August 2023